Shifting Contexts

One way in which different orders of knowledge are brought together is through the transformation of context. This book is concerned with contexts of a particular kind. Claims to know 'more' or see 'further' or to be able to encompass local facts by a global perspective take on a special meaning in the world-view of societies, such as those of the west, that imagine they are part of a life that is itself global in scale.

Shifting Contexts offers an original critique of current western thinking: it does not take it for granted that 'global' and 'local' indicate orders of magnitude or scales of importance. Rather, it addresses the techniques by which people shift the contexts of their knowledge and thus endow phenomena with local or global significance. This is an unusual and original collection of essays by seven leading social anthropologists, in the company of two specialists in research policy.

This book examines a range of contexts in which people (including anthropologists) make different orders of knowledge for themselves as a prelude to questioning assumptions about the 'size' of knowledge implied in the contrast between global and local perspectives.

Shifting Contexts will appeal to anthropologists and all those working in areas such as the philosophy of social science, cultural studies and comparative sociology.

Marilyn Strathern is Professor of Social Anthropology at Cambridge University.

ASA Decennial Conference Series
The Uses of Knowledge: Global and Local Relations
Series editor: Marilyn Strathern

Other titles in this series include:

Shifting Contexts

Transformations in Anthropological
Knowledge

Edited by Marilyn Strathern

London and New York

First published 1995
by Routledge
11 New Fetter Lane, London EC4P 4EE

Simultaneously published in the USA and Canada
by Routledge
29 West 35th Street, New York, NY 10001

© 1995 Association of Social Anthropologists, selection and editorial
matter; individual chapters, the contributors

Typeset in Times by LaserScript, Mitcham, Surrey
Printed and bound in Great Britain by
Biddles Ltd, Guildford and King's Lynn

British Library Cataloguing in Publication Data
A catalogue record for this book is available from the British Library

Library of Congress Cataloguing in Publication Data
A catalogue record for this book has been requested

ISBN 0–415–10794–6 (hbk)
ISBN 0–415–10795–4 (pbk)

Anthropologists have been criticised for their preoccupation
with 'very small and remote cultures'
(comment quoted in James 1988: 151).

If they were 'very big and near', what difference would
that make?

Contents

Figures

Contributors

Mary Bouquet gained her PhD in Social Anthropology from the University of Cambridge. She has subsequently held research and teaching posts at the universities of Exeter, Lisbon and Amsterdam. She has also been involved in the making of two exhibitions: one at the Portuguese National Museum of Ethnology (*Melanesian Artefacts, Postmodernist Reflections*, and the other at the Dutch National Museum of Natural History (*Man-ape, Ape-man*).

Angela P. Cheater is Professor of Sociology and Social Anthropology at the University of Waikato, New Zealand, having formerly held a personal chair at the University of Zimbabwe. She is the author of several books on rural development and industrial anthropology in Zimbabwe, and of *Social Anthropology: An Alternative Introduction*. Her widely varied interests include cultural management and cultural policy.

Mary Douglas, formerly of University College London, is now retired. An anthropologist with Africanist experience and interests, she is particularly interested in methodology in the social sciences, how to avoid an ethnocentric basis for social thought, the politicisation of nature, rival representations of danger, and rival theories of psyche and justice. Current research concerns pollution ideas, with special reference to the priestly books of the Bible. A lifetime of major publications includes *Purity and Danger* (1966), *Natural Symbols* (1970), *How Institutions Think* (1986), *Risk and Blame* (1992) and *In the Wilderness: the Doctrine of Defilement in the Book of Numbers* (1993).

Simon Harrison is reader in Social Anthropology at the University of Ulster. He gained his PhD degree at the Australian National University, and has carried out ethnographic fieldwork in the Sepik region of Papua New Guinea. His publications include *Stealing People's Names: History and Politics in a Sepik River Cosmology* (1990) and *The Mask of War: Violence, Ritual and the Self in Melanesia* (1993).

Stephen Hill is Professor and Director of the Centre for Research Policy, University of Wollongong, a 'Special Centre' funded by the Australian Research

Council. Previously Professor of Sociology at the same university, Stephen Hill is trained also in physical chemistry and business administration. His continuing research interest for three decades has concerned the relations between science, technology, society and culture, from which he has published eight books and over 250 other publications. He has worked in the UK, USA, throughout Asia and in Australia, and is currently Chairman of STEPAN, the UNESCO Science and Technology Policy Asian Network, and of APEC's (Asia Pacific Economic Co-operation forum) industrial technology and human resource development programme.

Tim Ingold is Professor of Social Anthropology at the University of Manchester. He has carried out fieldwork among the Skolt Saami of northeastern Finland and among northern Finnish farmers, and has written extensively on comparative questions of hunting and pastoralism in the circumpolar north (*Hunters, Pastoralists and Ranchers*, 1980), on evolutionary theory (*Evolution and Social Life*, 1986) and on human ecology (*The Appropriation of Nature*, 1986). From 1990 to 1992 he was editor of *Man* (the Journal of the Royal Anthropological Institute), and he is also the editor of the *Companion Encyclopedia of Anthropology* (1994). His current research interests are in the anthropology of technology and issues of environmental perception.

Marilyn Strathern is William Wyse Professor of Social Anthropology at the University of Cambridge. Her interests are divided between Melanesian (*Women in Between*, 1972) and British (*Kinship at the Core*, 1981) ethnography. *The Gender of the Gift* (1988) is a critique of anthropological theories of society and gender relations as they have been applied to Melanesia, while *After Nature: English Kinship in the Late Twentieth Century* (1992) comments on the cultural revolution at home. A monograph on comparative method is called *Partial Connections* (1991). Her most recent publication is the co-authored *Technologies of Procreation* (1993).

Tim Turpin is Associate Professor and Principal Research Fellow at the Centre for Research Policy, University of Wollongong. His main academic interests cover the general areas of cultural theory, institutional change and the communication of knowledge and culture. Since he has been at the Centre for Research Policy he has carried out fieldwork on research cultures at universities, research institutions and research and development enterprises in Australia and China. His most recent publications have been concerned with cultural change and organisational boundaries.

Richard Werbner is Professor of African Anthropology and Director of the International Centre for Contemporary Cultural Research at the University of Manchester. Author of *Tears of the Dead* (1991) and *Ritual Passage, Sacred Journey* (1989), he has carried out extensive fieldwork, since 1960, among Kalanga and Tswapong of the Zimbabwe–Botswana borderlands.

Series editor's preface

This book is one of five to have been produced from the Fourth Decennial Conference of the Association of Social Anthropologists of the Commonwealth held at St Catherine's College, Oxford, in July 1993. Sections were organised by Richard Fardon, Wendy James, Daniel Miller and Henrietta Moore, each of whom has edited their proceedings. In addition Wendy James acted as Oxford Co-ordinator, and it is principally due to her untiring efforts that the conference took place at all. As Convenor, I take the opportunity of acknowledging our debt to her, and of registering gratitude to Priscilla Frost for her organisational assistance and to Jonathan Webber for acting as conference Treasurer.

The Institute of Social and Cultural Anthropology at Oxford gave material as well as moral support. The following bodies are to be thanked for their generous financial assistance: the Wenner–Gren Foundation for Anthropological Research, the British Council, the Oxford University Hulme Trust Fund, the Royal Anthropological Institute and the Association of Social Anthropologists itself.

To suppose anthropological analysis can shift between global and local perspectives may well imply that the two coexist as broader and narrower horizons or contexts of knowledge. Indeed, the relationship seems familiar from the ethnographic record: in cosmologies that set a transcendent or encompassing realm against the details of everyday life; or in systems of value that aggrandise this feature while trivialising that; or in shifts between what pertains to the general or the particular, the collective or the individual. And if knowledge consists in the awareness of context shift, then such scaling may well seem routine. However, this book does not take scale for granted. It examines certain contexts in which people (including anthropologists) make different orders of knowledge for themselves as a prelude to questioning assumptions about the 'size' of knowledge implied in the contrast between global and local perspectives.

Marilyn Strathern
University of Cambridge

Foreword

Shifting contexts

> Objects of reference are at once more particular and more general than the
> expressions used to designate them.
>
> (Sahlins 1985: 148)

'The importance of culture': the phrase is used as a heading to the final section of
a document published in 1993 in Britain by the Committee of Vice-Chancellors
and Principals. The reference is to a 'P (performance) Factor', with respect to the
overall theme of the document, 'Promoting people: a strategic framework for the
management and development of staff in UK universities', and the culture in
question is 'university culture'. In introducing changes, the document states, 'it
is vital to take account of organisational values and culture'. Elsewhere, it
promotes change in culture itself. A group was sent to study staff management in
other universities in the Netherlands and the United States; the USA turned out to
be the states of Maryland and Virginia. The report came to the conclusion that pay
structures 'should reflect cultures and be adapted or transformed to match new
cultures'. The group also studied two public sector initiatives and three commercial organisations, and was particularly impressed by British Petroleum.
What impressed them was that 'one of the world's biggest commercial organisations' recognised the need to communicate directly with all its employees in an
effort to harness their commitment. In particular the group considered a programme
called OPEN BP designed 'to bring about a culture change'. The programme had
four elements (open thinking, personal impact, empowering and networking),
and contrasted a new 'open culture' against what was called an 'old culture'.

1993 was the year Unipart, the huge UK car parts group, launched what it
called a 'company university' in Oxford. *The Times Higher Education Supplement* (7 January 1994) reported that Unipart U, with its faculties each headed by
a dean or senior manager, is intended to help train employees in Japanese-style
production processes, a deliberate anglicisation of Japanese ways of working.
'This is not a Japanese solution. This is our British answer to how we make
Japanese techniques our own', said its part-time principal; 'It is a tool of culture
change.' The visitor may expect to feel something of a culture shock, comments
the reporter, 'and that is just what Unipart wants you to feel'.

No doubt its usage in these two instances has come from anthropology via the mangement studies in which it lodged in the 1970s and 1980s, but the 'culture' invoked thus is not confined to corporate or organisational culture. On the contrary, there is something here of very general note for late twentieth-century social anthropology. Culture has become a global phenomenon. By that I mean that a Euro-American perception of the role of culture in human affairs can be summoned in almost any context, at almost any level of human interaction, a ubiquity seemingly underscored by the fact that it refers to what is taken as a universal condition of human interaction.

It follows that it is not necessary to know about the functioning of the British university system, about what exactly Unipart produces, nor indeed about how these bodies propose to implement cultural change, in order to respond to the appeal to culture. Once articulated, culture appears self-evident, a synthesis of what is already known about the contextualisation of human affairs. It offers the flexibility of a concept simultaneously normative and comparative. Culture, in other words, is being used with just that range of connotations with which anthropologists have invested it in their writings. The concept points to differences between systems of value, to the link between practice and ethos, to the need to change habits if one is to change the way people think. Culture is seen as a means of empowerment, whether for staff or management. This is where Unipart's culture shock tactics come in; as the Unipart principal put it, 'We're not really worried about giving out tickets [certificates]. We're more worried about seeing the effect in the workplace.' According to the CVCP document, culture offers the possibility of making explicit the effects of an organisational ethos which will result in a particular kind of pay structure for university staff.

The bathos is intended. I use the CVCP example to observe that culture is also being contextualised in ways that anthropologists may find novel. While they might well recognise the fact that particular organisational practices (such as the administration of a pay structure) are embedded in a very specific matrix of values, they might not have thought that cultural models could be so readily borrowed from elsewhere (such as the state of Virginia), as though there were some world-wide consensus about the appropriateness of values, nor thought that the CVCP should be so impressed by the scale of British Petroleum and the significance of its attribute as one of the world's biggest commercial organisations. Note that the study group seems to have confined itself to the texts that BP put out, although they did do a site visit elsewhere. What is arresting about the Unipart experiment is less the idea of a company university, or of borrowing industrial management techniques from competitors, than the articulateness with which culture is given a role as an agent for change. The immediate culture shock experience for the visitor lay, as the *Higher Education* reporter saw it, in an artifact located in the foyer of Unipart House: a video screen set into a translucent floor and projecting a flicker of fast-moving images skywards.

When the organisers of the Fourth Decennial Conference of the Association of Social Anthropologists of the Commonwealth planned the programme for Oxford, they did not know that its rubric, 'The Uses of Knowledge: Global and Local Relations', could be applied so near to 'home'. By that I mean the anthropologist's home in the university system. Not all anthropologists work in universities, but they invariably start there, and it would be surprising if the new traffickings in university culture did not affect their production of knowledge. In any case, as we have just seen, the traffickings themselves put universities into other contexts. These traffickings are certainly apposite to the theme of the conference. The conference was concerned with the changing contexts of anthropological inquiry; what is brought home, as in fresh implementations of the concept of culture, is part of the larger 'world' anthropology now inhabits.

There are two common perceptions of this world at large: an increasing homogenisation of social and cultural forms seems to be accompanied by a proliferation of claims to specific authenticities and identities. In terms of the scales by which anthropologists customarily approach their materials, they seem to witness both global spread and local fractioning. It is of course a convention in social anthropology to take knowledge practices in the plural, and the discipline has a long investment in the study of different modes of apprehension. Traditionally, however, bringing together separate orders of knowledge has been accomplished through concepts such as 'level' and 'context', 'structure' and 'event', or through the conventions of comparative analysis. Such solutions have in turn rested on the further middle-range constructs of 'culture' and 'society' which served as reference points for evaluating the significance of diversity and homogeneity. These middle-range constructs no longer seem sufficient in the face of transformations attributed to world movements, cultural creolisation, international consumerism, proliferating nationalisms and so forth. The reason for singling out culture is that it is a prime example of a concept that appears subject to transformations of this kind. Indeed it would be hard to resist the conclusion that it is itself a major contributor to these common perceptions.

The CVCP document is suggestive in this respect. It points to one reason why 'culture' ceases to work as a middle-range construct. The question is not just of its inadequacy in dealing with new collective forms: its current ubiquity has at once aggrandised it and trivialised it out of all proportion. To have culture everywhere on hand in this way does indeed bring home to anthropology the very phenomenon that the conference was seeking to address. The uses to which anthropological knowledge can be put are, as always, already recontextualised.

Shifting contexts should be of intense interest to a twentieth-century anthropology which has taken the contextualisation of knowledge as one of its epistemological foundations. If, as participants in a modernist enterprise, anthropologists were once intent on making explicit the contextualising effects of everything they made contextual ('cultural'), their enterprise is recontextualised by, so to speak, the self-promotion of 'culture', by cultures. The concept of 'society' has had a very different fate. At times in the past the two have worked together as a pair.

It would be a fascinating exercise to track contemporary disparities in anthropological usage through the five volumes produced from the conference.

This first volume is a commentary on practices in the making of anthropological knowledge, including the fate of culture in this regard. The book takes as its basis the two addresses (Cheater, Douglas) and three papers (Harrison, Ingold and Werbner) with which the conference opened. In this sense it may be read as an introduction to the four volumes that follow. But it is also written in hindsight, after the conference took place, and has taken one paper from an associate section (Bouquet, from Nigel Rapport's section on 'The idea of the global: motive and motif') and one (Hill and Turpin) from another venue – another conference, another discipline – altogether. Here the book stands on its own as an exploration of how anthropologists might bring separate knowledges together and how in the process they put their concepts to work.

I began with a university instance not simply to underscore a principal vocation of academic anthropology but to draw attention to an effect of cultural promotion. To imagine universities as having cultures makes evident the specific nature of the institutional bases from which much anthropological work is done. After all, this volume would not have been possible without the props, the compendium of resources to be found in university institutions: libraries with old or forgotten books that enable one to revitalise ideas laid down years ago; research materials initially collected by those who travelled to 'the field' and then worked into texts; items transported from an original (peripheral) place to new (central) places for the purpose of exhibition; the conventions of literary composition that enable scholars to compose and recompose their data; the word processors and CD-ROMs of communications technology. These are resources specific to metropolitan institutions. Culturally speaking, we may refer to them as Euro-American; in economic terms, they belong to the well-endowed. At the end of the conference there was an eloquent plea from Kwame Arhin, Director of the Institute of African Studies in Legon, Ghana, that we should not forget the material disparity between the kinds of conditions under which academic anthropology is produced in Britain or Australia (say), and the experience of sustaining academic life in some other parts of the Commonwealth. This is a comparison which metropolitan anthropologists would do well to keep at the front of their minds.

What is true of the way anthropologists set about describing the world is also true of the conditions of description. Indeed it is a truism that theories or models, and especially models that purport to speak to universal conditions, are produced out of specific circumstances. How the universal is apprehended may even be taken as a veritable index of the parochial. Anthropology has long used for its own heuristic purposes (investigating the local distinctiveness of people's conceptions of themselves) those constructs about person or society that people often offer as the most general or global statement they can make about the human condition. Indeed, when the fieldworker is told something is 'natural', the chances are he or she will take it as an artificial construct. If anthropologists are newly aware of their institutional location, then, those whose books get published or whose words are otherwise transmitted remain in a very partial situation: they are producing their knowledge, however general they would wish to make it, out of specifics.

Conscious of the lack of resources under which academics in many countries have to labour, I wish none the less to point to one that affects the otherwise well-funded. Indeed it is a condition of their continuing funding. The subject is under something of a taboo, not surprisingly, endlessly talked about everywhere except in print. Yet it is crucial to what counts as knowledge production, and could be the single most significant factor in persuading metropolitan scholars of the utility of information technologies. I refer to time.

Several of the chapters in this book were written under a pressure of circumstances which afford 'no time' to think. And that we can lay at the feet of, among other things, 'the importance of culture': its promotion is what counts. Universities must promote values, habits and ways of doing things that must in turn be made increasingly explicit. It takes time to do so, although in a context where time is generally registered not as a virtue but as a cost. The culture of performance – having to perform culture – is one epitome of instrumental rationality. A specific form of ambition that once moved some colleagues but left others untouched is now institutionalised as management, however flexibly and empoweringly it is presented. Modernity might call itself postmodern, but that is only to lighten the unbearable weight of paperwork. Like other academics, university anthropologists are required to give accounts of themselves as 'members' of their institutions, to stipulate how they 'feel' about their opportunities, to identify their 'effectiveness' as employees, and to endorse 'teamwork' because commerce endorses it, so that their studies may be understood not as study but as performance. For this explicitness has a displacing effect. The issue becomes what can be witnessed: not reflection but production; not thought but output.

In these pages we shall still find scholarship. The contributors focus on the detail and complexity of their materials, aim to extract from what is to hand some general understanding of being in the world, and in agreeing to contribute voice the value of collective (collective, not team) enterprise. And their word processors continue to yield bibliographies. I only break the taboo in talking about the conditions of production in order to underline the recontextualising effect of new practices. Academic anthropologists are as much caught up in cultural change as anyone. What was once a necessity to analysis (thought, reflection) is now regarded as a luxury; the temporal duration and lapsed moments of an unfolding project must be compressed; the means to synthesis (writing as composition) and to communication (publication) have become ends in themselves. Does it or does it not help to see these little local pressures as part of a global phenomenon?

The chapters in this book deal with diverse processes of recontextualisation. In a (cultural) context where pointing to culture change is not the retrospective description that follows reflection on people's changing circumstances but becomes an institutional programme, policy even, in order to effect further change, all shifts can come to seem like cultural shifts. When they evoke comparisons, no cultures are seemingly too remote for borrowing from; when they evoke values as desirable, then the new displaces the old under the normative desirability of what is new. But we could also say that such shifting is simply a condition of all knowledge. Is the call to culture mimicking what we always understand or routinely accomplish in making knowledge? If so, it captures only a part of a diverse set of human processes. There are different modes of shifting for a start.

Euro-Americans might define knowledge as the *transformation* of already existing awareness. It is the outcome of practising the facility to turn one kind of perception into another, and thus to effect and perceive transformative process at the same time. Anthropologists routinely recontextualise their subject matter thus – move deliberately from one intellectual framework to another: from evolution to function, from structure to process, from representation to evocation. In fact, they may hope in doing so to capture differences between the cultural milieux they are aware they inhabit. This kind of shifting is instrumental to the perception of new significances.

It comes as something of a shock, then, to read Stephen Hill's and Tim Turpin's account (Chapter 7) of the systematic transformation of parts of the academy into a market. On the face of it, intellectual (paradigm) shifts within are one thing; academic (institutional) shifts propelled from outside would seem another. Their principal case might be Australian, but the phenomenon is world-wide, the entrepreneurial scientist as much a Chinese as a North American figure. Yet to see the issue as an argument between academic purity and threatening market forces misses the point: cultural change is located, as they argue, within. University discourse that promotes unifiable knowledge and research relevance predisposes the academy to the market.

But there is a more fundamental predisposition, which lies in that very suppleness that encourages frame-switching in intellectual terms. Academically produced knowledge makes a specialism of such intellect, creates an expertise out of finding new frames, out of transforming itself through discovery, invention and redescription, out of new conceptual epochs. (One never wants to be accused of nostalgia, of course, but 'looking back' to scholarship is also looking back to a former epoch.) The very expertise that academics (Euro-American ones at least) most defend against the market, making knowledge, makes not just transformation but *displacement* part of its own internal processes. One recognises the effect of being over-taken.

Consider transformation again, in the facility to switch frames not across epochs but across scales. It is equally possible to change what is seen / known by focusing on detail as by enlarging one's scope. Miniaturisation and magnification both appear transformative; such transformation keeps the knowledge that each moment has so to speak emerged from the other. This knowledge in turn conserves scale, that is, the difference between what applies under narrowly defined conditions (focused) and what applies under general (enlarged) ones, as in the contrast between specific and universal phenomena. It is thus out of the most concrete and localised details imaginable – campsites and the layout of settlements – that Tim Ingold (Chapter 3) derives a general and abstract statement about how to think of the condition of being human. For he finds in the details of dwellings a material exemplification of a postulate initially made on the grounds of evidence from elsewhere, that it is because they dwell that people think. The shift between thinking about the kind of camp made by Mbuti people of the Ituri forest in Zaire to a model of the environment of human development is an example of the kind of shift anthropologists could imagine as taking place between orders of the same phenomena, that is, at different points along a single scale. The separate orders do not demarcate different 'cultures' except in so far as each domain of knowledge summons its own vocabulary and insights, and they do not stand in relation to one another as new and old, for either may be transformed into the other.

In the course of his argument, however, Ingold does introduce a switch he would have us regard as directed and irreversible, between two epistemological frames, the model of building and the model of dwelling. For although he substantiates his 'dwelling perspective' through reference to the scholar Jakob von Uexküll whose insights might otherwise have remained lost, once this dwelling perspective is articulated it is impossible to recover the naïvety of the other. Whether or not one follows Ingold in his shift, the building perspective is irrevocably recontextualised and thus displaced by this challenge to it. It is revealed not as a universal assumption but as a specific paradigm. (By the same token, Ingold makes thoroughly evident the provisional status of the perspective he puts forward himself.) This displacement creates a contrast between epochs. The new may also appear on a different scale from the old, that is, it introduces a new spectrum of values by which to locate phenomena. The knowledge the new model organises, how the world becomes a meaningful environment for people, is newly comprehensive in its implications. An avowedly specific way of making knowledge (the dwelling versus building perspective) is thus made to yield understanding of highly general applicability. Indeed its scope becomes the broadest imaginable: the way one understands 'being in the world'. Here it has some similarity to the shift men from the Middle Sepik in Papua New Guinea make between two modes of sociality.

Manambu men (Chapter 4) would have themselves move between two existential frames, between two modes of experiencing their relations with others. The possibility of so shifting constitutes a fundamental condition of their existence; each mode affords a particular and specific state of being. On the one hand, relations between 'men' are also relations between spirits, relational worlds in parallel. On the other hand, men creates the circumstances under which the parallelism does or does not apply. They may, as it were, act as 'men' or as men.

Although we might say that Manambu men put themselves into different cultural states – summon a different ethos, mobilise different values, fashion different sets of material apparatus – each state exists only as a precipitate of the other. The result is neither displacement nor transformation, alone; rather, men demonstrate the capacity to *alternate* between modes of existence. This comes about as a result of deliberate ritualising and de-ritualising effort. Spirits either are (in war) or are not (in peace) made present. Conversely other people's spirits (rituals, powers) offer a challenge to one's own knowledge. As a consequence, the grounds on which the identity of persons is knowable alter between the two modes; as a spirit a Manambu 'man' does not 'see' the enemy facing him in battle or the woman whom he is about to ambush as a man sees a neighbour from the next village or his brother's wife.

It is salutary to frame whatever claims anthropologists might make for their paradigm shifts, and indeed for their knowledge at large, by reference to the diverse ways in which people (including them) shift the contexts of perception and thus make knowledge for themselves. From an anthropological, Euro-American view, Manambu men are undertaking a journey as radical as Ingold's in altering the way phenomena are classified in order to alter perceptions of the world. But whereas Ingold wishes to make the ways of knowing explicit, Manambu men seemingly wish to be explicit about the power that their identifications yield and thus how they will act in the world. In turn, the cannibal marauders which Manambu men become when the spirits take them to battle are different in character from the ancestors who dwell in Lupondo's family (Chapter 5). Asocial and amoral, the Sepik spirits urge men to violations they would never commit in their human habitation. They (the spirits) thus point to discontinuous forms of the same relations, and discontinuities are expected; hence they (the men) put the outrageous advent of Australians and Japanese down to the machinations of their neighbours. The Kalangan problem was, by contrast, that of continuity.

Richard Werbner's multiple account of Zimbabwean terror raises the question of continuities between events external and internal to the family. Forgotten atrocities subsequently brought to light led to self-chastisement: how to deal with events that must be assimilated to one's own past. The same question applies at home. This is a world of potentially *encompassing* morality, where the family locates itself within an environment of community or chiefdom, and their attendant ancestors, within a widening circle of relations where conflict at any location can be interpreted as conflict at any other. Relations encompass relations, with the effect that acts of domestic violence seem no different in moral kind from national outrages, of which they could almost be a part. Werbner first talked to Lupondo's family on the eve of its splitting apart: destructive capacities were seen as the work of human beings not as spirits but as themselves. What is true of other spheres of action is also true of the past; it is not to be forgotten. And the present is certainly no alternative to the past. In grasping the dovetailing of phenomena that are near and far at the same time, Werbner draws on the concepts of local and global.

By local he means what takes place in a relatively closed fashion, affairs that may dominate and consume the individual but with restricted moral outcome.

Such affairs become global, as he points out, when the narratives of individual persons are publicised, made the subject of commissions of inquiry, or generally come to stand for circumstances that affect other people. Global includes the organisational reach of the state, the promotion of terrorism and heroism, and what Werbner would identify as the makings of civic culture, that is, where individual persons bear the burden of being members of particular populations. For Lupondo's family there was a principal issue that could be summoned at any point: accountability. In this sense the reach, or magnitude, of affairs is irrelevant.

Angela Cheater's essay (Chapter 6) could be read as problematising accountability. Global information technology personalised viewers' perceptions of the Gulf war. Yet what kind of shift was this? She dwells on a distinction between information, which involves an act of communication between persons, and knowledge, which becomes understanding one created for oneself. If anthropologists' diffident representation of such situations raises questions about their professional credibility, she also suggests that collective anthropological knowledge may no longer be possible under the regime that offers information on a customised basis. But the anthropologist can comment that this personalised 'knowledge' is at the same time being depersonalised at the point of production: the new sensory realities appear without authorship. The 'dehumanising' move to which Cheater refers entails an *elimination*. With the elimination of the author goes the elimination of certain transformative and other possibilities contained in switching perspectives (as between author and reader or personal and collective representations). From Hill's and Turpin's perspective, a market for customised and personalised knowledge drops actors back into view, but at the expense of the collective and traditional value of communicative action and accountability.

Cheater contrasts those metropolitan institutions resourced to take advantage of information technology with those that are not. The contrast creates the possibility of cultures alien to one another by virtue of their mutual invisibility. What her account brings out is the way in which the claims of IT and its presentation as a world-covering tracery of networks is taken as the global phenomenon it claims to be, despite the fact that it is not universal, and indeed requires highly local installation and attention. What is global about it? It is as global as the networks of commerce which afford the simultaneous availability of the same products at multiple outlets. It also compresses, she observes, the time-frames of decision-making. Durations, lapses and intervals cease to be visible in the purveying of knowledge.

Cheater's future world has no need for perspective, nor for exchange of viewpoints: technology can create the screenie as both consumer and producer. The same seems true of Hill's and Turpin's present one: colonisation by the market can relocate the actor within its enterprises. By contrast the *Pithecanthropus* centennial exhibition that Mary Bouquet helped to mount (Chapter 2) is orchestrated round shifts of perspective. Hers is a deliberate attempt to create multiple views through multiplying the sense of authorship. Indeed, we might say the aim is to make paradigm shifts accountable (attributable). Each room affords a particular context as each item of knowledge is given its pedigree or genealogy. But at the same time as individual items of knowledge are given their pedigrees and thus related to a specified past, the pasts do not so to speak add up in the form of a continuous sequence. Rather, the constellation of objects assembled in the exhibition points to dispersed and diverse origins. They are *juxtaposed* by virtue of the context created by the exhibition.

The museological transformation does not involve alternating between modes of social action (Manambu), nor wishing to persuade the reader of the value of one model over another (Ingold), nor eliminating authorship in favour of personalised information (Cheater). Rather Bouquet's is an enterprise much more akin to the collection of evidence with which Kalanga have had to deal, where items from the past simultaneously speak to and are intrusive in the present. But whereas the Zimbabwean dead were untimely exhumed, here *Pithecanthropus* is deliberately given presence in a late twentieth-century museum in order to evoke a history and prehistory one would not otherwise trace. The items might be dated then but they exist now. The question of responsibility that Bouquet posed was the kind of anthropological connection to be drawn between these different times, between the different persons involved (in some but not all cases nameable) and how continuity might be made culturally persuasive.

Mary Douglas (Chapter 1), for her part, deliberately jumps over the connections other Bible scholars have made in order to suggest a specific reading for a Hebrew conceptualisation of a violated past. She pursues the question of accountability by posing the readings as two interpretations. The effect of taking one or other view has many antecedents in the scholarship of competing interpretations, where shifts between epistemological frames appear reversible. But the two interpretations she describes have different consequences for the propriety of interpretation itself. This leads to another articulation of responsibility; Douglas questions the propriety of digging up things people might prefer to leave buried, things best forgotten. Finally, her rereading attends not only to the appropriate context in which we might understand how one interpretation could become another, but to the *disuse* into which artifacts fall. Disuse may be desirable; it can also lead to future error. She refers for instance to the rhetorical form of the pastoral in which primitive simplicity is a contrived effect of urban stylistic convention. One has to understand the cultivated and literary basis of this mode in order to understand the apparent 'pastoral' setting of the narrative. Without this learning, misunderstanding abounds.

But if some artifacts endure, evidence of past technologies that demand attention by their presence, as the Bible has endured, others become lost altogether, and Douglas notes some of the since neglected procedures by which anthropologists once made things known to themselves. More generally we might add the corollary that the perception of knowledge as gain must inevitably proceed hand in hand with the perception of knowledge as loss. This is not simply a matter of memory; such loss begins with the form that knowledge takes, with the fact that it is always conveyed through artifacts which are always reductions or, after Lévi-Strauss, miniaturisations. For artifacts – including literary forms and ethnographic techniques – are always less than the awareness with which they are used. They are always specific. As a consequence, when people are aware of shifting from one context to another, the use they make of some forms of knowledge anticipates the uselessness of others.

If people routinely shift the basis of their awareness of the world, and know this as 'knowledge', the process involves encompassing and focusing moves that, as Euro-Americans would say, create orders, scales and levels. But before we take differences of scale for granted, we might note a corollary of such shifts. Alternative existential states, problems in tracing continuities, an interest in origins: these shifts are embedded in practices that seek connections or transform one entity into another or make translations 'between' disparate or incommensurate phenomena. But how are phenomena rendered incommensurate in the first place? It follows that if different knowledge practices produce different forms of incommensurability, then their foundational or transcendent concepts (their instruments) will also have different work to do. Culture was one such instrument in traditional anthropology: the context of contexts. The concept of cultural difference, for instance, simultaneously created incommensurables (the differences) and a comparative frame for making them commensurate (as examples of culture). Culture thus worked as a potentially totalising context that rendered everything as evidence of itself. We may even say it was global in this scope. Chapter 8 returns to the question of certain local appropriations of it; these have, to put it shortly, out-contextualised the anthropologist. By the same token, anthropology's culture comes to seem not so different from everyone else's.

This introductory comment has focused on knowledge for one very good reason. The issues that the conference addressed really are very near to home as far as the discipline is concerned. In what anthropologists might experience as an appropriation of the concept of culture, I shall argue that they have lost a heuristic, that is, one way of creating knowledge though endorsing/transcending incommensurables. Yet in the very act of referring to culture as 'global', whether with old connotations or new ones, I summon one of the discourses that are its dislocation and relocation.

M. S.

REFERENCES

James, W. (1988) *The Listening Ebony: Moral Knowledge, Religion and Power among the Udek of Sudan*, Oxford: Clarendon Press.

Sahlins, M. (1976) *Culture and Practical Reason*, Chicago: University of Chicago Press.

1   Forgotten knowledge

Mary Douglas

I chose forgetting as my topic because it is uppermost in my mind during my current research on the Bible. It is relevant to the subject of this volume because any shift from local to global or back again involves reorganising the stock of knowledge. Forgetting includes different kinds of selective remembering, mis-remembering and disremembering and it is quite different from ignorance. Sacred books will always be a good *locus* for the topic since any sacred book is bound to exemplify selective remembering, with meanings added and meanings dropped even while the words remain unchanged. Jewish interpretations of the Bible would have changed in the great vicissitudes of their own history. It would be too much to expect that there should have been been no selection of emphasis. What interests me here is a particular reading of the Bible which presented it in a timeless present, and essentially denuded it of any historical context.

FORGETTING

The Bible is a book giving the history of the Creator's dealings with His own people, from the beginning of the world, through their journey from Canaan to Egypt, and then their perilous journey all the way back. It is always assumed to be in a historical genre. Yet, no; in the reading of the first century onwards the history (as well as much else) was disregarded and the timeless aspects of the message made prominent. This is what Jacob Neusner has said about Mishnah, the authoritative explanation of the laws. The question he raises is central to a view of global and local knowledge: 'What do we learn from people from the things they say and cease to say?' (1977: 180). In the same article he points out that Mishnah itself is presented as 'a document wholly exempt from historical circumstances'. This allegedly ahistorical bias is a remarkable insight of Neusner, who has thought a lot about the relation of a text to the history of its making as well as to the explicit treatment of history in the text – and wholly convincing. It helps to explain the selective reading of Leviticus and Numbers that persists to this day. The question is why peoples sometimes eschew the historical dimension of their own history.

There they were, Judaeans in a colonial dependency, first of Babylon, then of

Persia, then of Rome. Their ancient texts are believed to have been given their final form in a process of redaction which began in the Babylonian Exile and was completed around the fifth century BCE. There is scope for scholarly disagreement about when exactly the canon was fixed, perhaps later. The period I am interested in lies between the two destructions of the temple, one by Nebuchadnezzar in 586 when he carried off the noble families and the learned men of Jerusalem to Babylon, and the other by the Romans in 70. The editing of the Pentateuch would have been completed early within this period, and I am assuming that some coherent sense was attributed by the redactors to the work of their hands; in the period immediately following it was reread and closely studied by the rabbis. The major shift of readings which poses the subject of my research concerns the priestly work, and particularly the doctrines of defilement and purification.

A very widespread, traditional, reading of the priestly work places it in contrast to the messages of the prophets. Peter Ackroyd has voiced the 'strong suspicion that the main trend of Protestant scholarship has been to write of the Chronicles (very often along with the priestly writers) as priestly, concerned with the cult, and therefore at a lower level than the prophetic, the religion of the word' (1991: 291). The cult itself is presented as dealing with mere materials of worship. The way they are summarised even suggests that the priests substituted the prophets' and psalmists' themes of divine love and divine justice with an alternative doctrine of divine abhorrence of ritual impurity. But an anthropological reading (Douglas 1993a) of the priestly books finds unison in the priestly and prophetic voices and suggests that the priests were as concerned as any of the prophets, Isaiah, Jeremiah, Ezekiel, Amos and Hosea, with teaching the Lord's demands for justice and mercy. On this account I have to challenge the accepted readings of Leviticus and Numbers on several fronts.

The social anthropologist is always bound to look for the community for which a text is issued, the relevant 'speech community', or the arena for claims and counterclaims in which the text has been introduced. This involves attempting to know some history. If the final editing of the Bible can be attributed to the second temple period, the priestly editors appear as universalising theologians teaching a brand of liberation theology. This is the trend of their writing and doctrines, and not the narrow ritualistic message presented in many traditional readings. In this light, their intellectualist, metaphorical and highly philosophical codification of purity laws are found to discriminate against no social class, nor against outsiders or strangers. Their liberal doctrines would make sense if they were trying to resist populist pressures to downgrade immigrants and foreign workers. In context, the theological programme of the priestly editors appears as an effort to combat popular xenophobia and governmental exclusionary pressures.

This may sound like a mild and quite congenial amendment to the conventional reading. But it is just here that problems with forgotten knowledge cluster thickly. It may be offensive to suggest that someone forgot the reading that was current when the book was edited. In this case there are two gaps in memory to discuss: one, when the priests reread the old religion of the prophets, or alternatively, another one, when the rabbis reread the priests. This is why I want to point out, before I publish my version, that everyone recognizes that any document has its own history as it goes through multiple stages of interpretation, and that forgettings and misreadings are normal.

Usually there is an obvious material reason for forgetting. In this case the records were lost when the Romans destroyed the second temple. But the material reason is hardly enough. There is also a political reason. Neusner (1976) has eloquently argued that the calamity of the second destruction of the temple was too traumatic for the Pentateuch to be read as it had been before. The new leaders of the religious community, the rabbis, could not bear to recall the ancient promises which the Pentateuch celebrated. The story of the Lord's dealings with his people over time, the faith that he would be with them always, that he was merciful and would never abandon them, was now contradicted. To recall those ancient prophecies, unfulfilled, was too painful. The rabbinical movement developed a new interpretive mode. What is important to my theme is his argument that the rabbinical way of reading the Book eschewed history.

This should interest those anthropologists who think that everyone has a right to have a history (see Fabian 1983). A gap in historical knowledge, even a large one, may sometimes be preferred; knowledge lost may be knowledge well lost. It is not necessarily good, whatever Freud taught in a clinical context, to recall the past. It is not wrong to forget, it is not necessarily sad to forget, and we should not, cannot, strive strenuously to remember everything we ever knew.

In saying this I am not meaning to challenge the conservationist efforts of the Ancient Monuments Commission and British Heritage or the whole profession and work of archaeologists. It must be important to preserve things of the past and to seek to know past ideas that have been lost. I am addressing a much narrrower question about fast receding events on the mid-term frontier of memory. Short-term forgetting is generally funny. Granny's forgetting where she put her glasses makes her a figure of fun. In MIT the absent-minded genius, Norbert Wiener, was stopped in the corridor by a student with an elementary maths problem. After helpfully explaining the formula, the inventor of cybernetics asks (note the narrative present tense) if the student would mind helping him:

'I can't remember which way I was walking down the corridor just now.
Can you?'
'Yes Professor, you were coming from that direction.'
'Oh, thank you very much, that means that I haven't had lunch yet.'

The shorter the term in which recall has been lost, the funnier, but middle-term forgetting can be regarded as reprehensible and long-term forgetting is a classic cause of rebuke. An effective oratorical trick puts an audience in the wrong by listing what it has forgotten – the virtues of the murdered Caesar, past glorious campaigns, or the sorrows of the widows. The narrower question I want to address is about the comfortable convenience of forgetting quite recent knowledge. My intention is not to blame for forgetting, but rather the opposite, to lift the burden of reproach.

CHANGING THE GROUND RULES

First remember that knowledge is always being forgotten. It is its nature. Presumably there are no anthropologists who subscribe to creation *ex nihilo*, but if there were, we could warn them that it is inherently difficult to prove and generally a block to further inquiry. I side with the philosophers who hold that creating one thing means using the elements of something else. Whenever new knowledge appears, something old will have been rejected. Knowledge does not float in the air; it has practical and social bases. The dissolution of empires entails the collapse of structures of knowledge. When an organisation disintegrates, the forms of knowledge that have been called forth by the effort to organise disintegrate too. The process is sad for some, joyful for others.

We are currently witnessing several such dissolutions and can testify to the sense of liberation and excitement in the ensuing period of disorder. We have first-hand experience of the increased fragmentation, and of new co-ordination. In the slow picking up of pieces, the reconstruction process is noticeably selective. It is salutary for my generation to observe that the making of a new way of life comes with self-justificatory postures. We hear old forms of knowledge being rated not just useless, but morally bad. We note the straining to formulate a superior morality, and the attack on the old order. Some weep, others rejoice. In that context the papers presented at the ASA Decennial conference are interesting. How different is their tone from the earlier Decennial conferences. There is a feeling of confidence, openness and enthusiasm. At the same time, there is the generous sharing of the anguish of victims, anger on behalf of the oppressed, shouldering of important political concerns, and, with all this, I observe less anxiety of the purely academic sort. Looking back, I can see that there is something to celebrate over and above having survived another ten years.

Archaeology had an old and respected place in the ranks of academic life, which anthropology and ethnology shared in the nineteenth century. But social anthropology was a new kind of study, establishing its identity by repudiating its immediate ancestry and the straining towards academic acceptability. The founders of social anthropology in their elitist colleges had to mix with historians and classicists: as students we heard Evans-Pritchard boasting of how many languages he could speak: why ever did he bother to keep listing them? Meyer Fortes would warn us against lapsing into 'the higher journalism', which was a risk anyone studying a modern society had to fear (Goody 1991). We never learnt what the lower journalism would have been.

For the unwary, the path of scholarship was strewn with pitfalls. It was not done to write nostalgic, idealising ethnography of the semi-fictional wind-whispering-in-the-palm-trees kind. Self-advertisement was reproved, an ethnographic text was not the place for personal reflections and the author should not let his own image intrude in an ethnographic photograph. We knew better than to indulge philosophical or historical speculations. At appointment committees we would hear this or another worthy candidate rejected as not a 'true scholar' or 'not a real anthropologist' – it would be hard to say which insult stung most. Now those conformist cares seem to be behind us. We do whatever we think is important. A new generation of anthropologists should try to understand the cultural context of what they read. Those professional standards were not invented by the social anthropologists. They had long been established as requirements for being taken seriously in any scholarly writing: classics, Bible studies, history. And the anthropologists who sought to conform were honouring continental demands on proper academic behaviour.

ASA 1993 makes me think of a family which used to feel socially insecure and finally discovers that it is established in the neighbourhood. When I said this, a distinguished anthropologist involved in the early decades of the ASA protested against the implication of social anxiety: 'We were not keeping up appearances, we were keeping up standards in the normal way.' Yes, true, and I should not be ungrateful. I remember what those standards involved: criteria of valid reporting, canons of relevance, tests of competence, discovering how to recognise learning gaps and political lobbying. The two main lessons were how to be systematic in research, and how to avoid questions to which there was no conceivable answer. It was an attempt to control in the interests of academic probity unscholarly tendencies referred to as mystification, subjectivism, idealism, and gobbledygook. It was as elitist and restrictive as any grammar school, yes, indeed, but a good training in logical discourse, for all that.

If the metaphor of social class jars, try the cultural theory model (Thompson and Wildavsky 1990): first, the 1950s were the hierarchical period of the ASA in which priestly personages performed the solemn rituals. With a codified set of concepts and strictly defined vocabulary they marshalled the ceremonies, selected neophytes, marginalised or excluded deviants, hierarchised research topics. Through the 1960s 'Big Men' emerged, no corporate schools of thought, but brilliant leaders who made the new rules, Leach, Geertz, Marshall Sahlins, Lévi-Strauss. Anthropology started to be rethought (Leach 1961) but by the end of the decade the world seemed to be running away. Hierarchical control and codification were finished, sectarianism loomed. For the last twenty years the mood has become more and more evangelical and political. Political alignments are overt, and though there are more messages of toleration and love they tend to be delivered in tones of deepening anger and contempt. The cultural cycle entailed plenty of forgetting and other changes too.

Anthropology keeps changing its ground rules and requirements for research and training. One of the advantages of training in University College in the 1930s was that some basic Egyptology used to be thought essential: the prime controversy was about the claim that all the arts came from Egypt. Whether the people being studied remembered their Egyptian affiliation or not made no difference: implicitly it was a theory of fossilised memories. Something that the people had long ago forgotten about themselves could be the clue to why they now do what they do.

Knowing how to play string games was once held proper preparation for fieldwork. Evans-Pritchard published an illustrated article on 'Zande string figures' in 1972 using the terminology of Dawkins, Rivers and Haddon, whose previous important works on the subject he cites. This interest was not merely a field-worker's ploy to gain the friendship of the children. String games were supposed to help tracing the geographic diffusion of cultures; they might even be an abstract key to forgotten knowlege.

Other ideas about fieldwork training have also changed. Daryll Forde reproached me for not having mapped the slash-and-burn fields made by the Lele so as to be able to assess the crop output per acre compared with the Bushong. He would not accept my plea that those so-called fields were too hilly and irregular for me to measure. Any well-trained fieldworker, he maintained sternly, would know how to make a survey with a chain or a bicycle and pedometer. Now film, tape and camera are essential . . . and so on. Knowledge and techniques of acquiring it change in line with technology and with changes in the inquisitive-ness of investigators, and this in turn changes along with their fundamental assumptions about why they are undertaking their work. Torday took an artist to the Congo for recording what he saw, and the artist depicted beautiful young women reclining in postures that would have done honour to Madame Récamier (Torday and Joyce 1910). Some were (for the sake of displaying their tattoo marks) portrayed otherwise naked (1910: plate X), both posture and undress quite disapproved by local custom. There goes another change, the increased attention to the susceptibilities of the people being studied.

MEMORY HOLES

In the early part of the century the notion of primitiveness dominated the subject and posed the central problem. The unlettered state of a primitive culture was regarded as due to failure either to attain or to hold fast to the arts of civilisation. On this view the cultures of the peoples then dubbed primitives would be like fossilised remains of early humanity. Such an assumption itself directed research to the question of how these relics had got left behind, and entailed a close link between anthropology and archaeology. The opposite view was that these people had descended to the magic and polytheism level from some original higher common starting point. In either case the focus on upward or downward cultural mobility has become distasteful. None the less, if we go back to English anthropology before the foundation of the ASA, we find in the work of A. C. Haddon and W. H. R. Rivers an unselfconscious, politically serious and wide-ranging interest such as I am saluting in the present state of the art. They also had theories about forgetting.

In an early paper on 'The disappearance of the useful arts', Rivers (1912) speculated on how canoes, pottery and the use of the bow and arrow had disappeared from certain parts of Oceania. This anthropologist, in spite of his bias towards psychology and physiology, proposed a sociological explanation for the loss of skills. He noted that technical knowledge was often the preserve of specialists, and he feared that over-specialising would put the survival of useful crafts at risk: if for any reason the specialist group declined in numbers, so would the transmission of the skills be endangered. Though he was hostile to the work of the Durkheim school, Rivers' explanation of collective forgetting is very close to that of Maurice Halbwachs who taught that history is carried in the minds of individual people: a hole in the population would make a hole in the collective memory. This in itself was original at a time when it was the fashion to attribute the guardianship of chiefly genealogical knowledge to individual specialists. Halbwachs (1925) shared Rivers' more sociological view: he saw chunks of collective memory falling into oblivion if a memory-bearing sector were to be weakened by migration or to die out. Though they would have disclaimed any such alliance, their view would only need a little adaptation to suit a Marxist view of the social influences on knowledge.

That peoples were dying out was a major concern for Rivers. He was concerned that the peoples living in the archipelago of Melanesia suffered fatally from lack of interest in life due to western expansion and trade destroying their old traditions. This weakness he put above the list of local customs then held to be damaging to demographic survival, such as infanticide or killing off widows. Rivers (1922) considered lack of cultural autonomy to be the main cause of population decline. In his view this was the worst deprivation, with disastrous effects on the psyche and on health. If he had an explicit psychological theory of memory it would have connected national forgetting with an unfavourable demographic situation, and the latter with the traumas and hopelessness of living under a foreign colonial regime. In effect, we can draw out of Rivers' writing two implicit theories about lost knowledge – first, a demographic theory of memory holes resulting from shifts of population, and second, a psychological explanation based on emotional trauma. Since both shifts of population such as exile and national disaster such as military defeat (memory holes and trauma) have been advanced to explain how the Bible was reinterpreted ahistorically, we have come back to my main theme.

If it is true that most arts get lost and most knowledge is forgotten, it will easily be agreed that any ancient document will have received a brand new interpretation at every great historical change, and also agreed that little daily shifts of meaning will always erode the cutting edge of its first statements. This is acceptable hypothetically, but tell it to anyone who is committed to a given interpretation, and you will find it is unacceptable in practice. For many pieces of knowledge there is an investment in asserting antiquity. In such a case, to hint there has been a change in the way the text has been read over millennia is taken as a gratuitous attack. That the Bible tends to be read as timeless and outside of human history makes the anthropologist's task here delicate.

READING THE BIBLE

Though they are different, some problems about misremembering and dis-remembering apply with the same force to knowing, ignorance and ignoring. I would like to know how to treat the Bible's repeated assertion that the Canaanites sacrificed their children to Molech. In the absence of convincing evidence of child sacrifice, I would expect the assertion to be part of the definition of the 'other' that defines the self by contrast. The idea would be that the God of Israel likes children and does not want to hurt them, unlike the god of Canaan who wants them dead. I would expect this belief to receive the same kind of careful scepticism that anthropologists give to assertions about cannibal eating of enemies or the idea extant in Africa that whites eat black children (Douglas, awaiting publication).

Then there is the Bible's treatment of its own history. Is it an historical archive? Was the Pentateuch really composed at a time before kings? Or did its final editing, coming after the end of the monarchy, wipe out the mention of kings from its constitutive documents? Deliberately? Or unintentionally? What were the dates? Questions of this kind are already treated with immense sophistication by Bible scholars and the anthropologist is well advised to take what is handed out by them as to dating.

Bible scholars expect anthropologists to know about the kinship and symbolic systems of the earliest times and consequently the misty period of the Bronze Age is thought the most fit for anthropological comment. Since the Bible's redaction is the work of an historic, urban civilisation this makes intervention in the research more difficult. Biblical scholars are as well aware as anthropologists of the danger of selective imposition of models. For example, George Mendenhall (1973) sardonically calls the common view of early Israel as a community of nomadic herders the 'Bedouin mirage'. This puts the anthropologist on her mettle. One could plausibly suggest the equivalent notion that it was the priestly editors of the Pentateuch who first fancied the Bedouin model. Thus anthropologists' 1940s presentation of Nuer society in the paradigm of early Roman law, or of the Papua New Guinea Highlands in the 1960s according to African lineage models, would be paralleled by the Bible presenting Moses and Aaron in a pastoral setting.

Let me describe briefly two themes which constitute a new anthropological approach to the history of Bible interpretation. One is about the biblical notion of defilement and purity and the other is about the literary evidence. In other religions ideas of defilement have a practical use in keeping social classes and gender categories apart and in sustaining the social structure. On close examination the purity code of Leviticus could not be used in this way, even for keeping strangers out of the cult, and still less for full members of the society. So what was a philosophical disquisition on defilement for? Much follows on the realisation that biblical impurity is not like ritual impurity in other religions. It next appears that 'atonement' would translate much better, in accordance with its

Hebrew root, as mend, cover, put right (as mending something broken or torn, putting right an injustice, covering a loan, anointing a wound, or covering a hole or rift). *Kippur* in Hebrew is to cover or mend, not to wipe clean. When I presume to say it would translate better as 'cover', I am relying on the illustrations, given at great length in the book itself, of broken or torn skins and other defective coverings that need atonement to be done for them (see Douglas 1993b).

Between two possible interpretations, atoning as cleansing or atoning as repairing, how can the choice be made? The word translated as cleansing sets it in the discourse of impurity, and is congenial to the anticlerical idea of the priesthood as having a peculiar agenda of its own, different in emphasis from that of the prophets. Traditionally purity and correct performance of ritual would have been the priests' prime teaching, while the prophets were preaching justice and compassion. My claim is that the priests did not embrace a different religious programme from that of the prophets. If defilement has to be read not as stain to be wiped off the surface but as a deep rift in the cosmos, then the priests who defined atonement would have been addressing and deploring the very same breaches as the prophets: the unrighteousness and infidelities of Israel and Samaria. If biblical defilement does not mean stain or dirt in the familiar ritual sense, it would originally have stood for the broken covenant, and / or for the rift between the northern kingdom and Judah, and / or for breach of the commands of the Lord. This is the substance of the misreading and its causes would be the same as eliminated the history of the people of Israel and the quarrel between the two kingdoms of Israel and Judah from the reading of the priestly books.

The boldest part of the anthropological claim is that the choice between the two translations of the word atonement is not free: Leviticus tells how it is to be read. The literary form indicates how the choice is to be made between possible interpretations. Examining the Book of Numbers in the light of Jacobson's work on poetic and grammatical structures, certain rhetorical features in the priestly books become apparent. The style is highly structured: contrary to commentaries, the many repetitions mark structure, and the structure marks the meaning, so that many otherwise likely readings can confidently be ruled out (Douglas 1993c). The question about forgetting now expands into a question of forgetting a literary convention. How did the later generation not know how to read a text presented according to archaic literary practice (Douglas 1994b)?

After great political upheavals old literary forms often seem too contrived, perhaps too elaborate and artificial. The poetic structures of the priestly work depend on long rhetorical periods in a complex balance of similars or contraries, a genre called parallelism. When first assembled, Leviticus and Numbers must have been recognized as a literature of incomparable elegance and artistic control. The literary accomplishment has evidently been overlooked in subsequent inter-pretations. One only has to see how puzzled are commentators to this day by repetitions which are used to highlight rhetorical structure. If unsuspecting readers are led by the pastoral setting to look for primitive simplicity they might not recognize the highly contrived effects. Without knowing that the pastoral is the product of an urban civilization in which the artifical conventions of the city are contrasted with rustic simplicy and directness, uneducated readers could well be misled as to the meanings of the text. This might not be a question of forgetting, but a simple learning gap. By the fifth century BCE literary parallelism had begun to be superseded by the fashion for metric verse, depending on shorter concordances and quicker phonetic matching. Without saying more about the obsolescence of literary forms, we can add its effect to the other explanations for the forgetting of how the books should be read.

One more remains. Without diminishing the strength of Neusner's argument from trauma, there is a complementary historical reason for the rabbis not being happy with the old interpretations of the holy book. The long-standing political and cultic rivalry between Judah and Samaria had become more bitter at the time when the rabbis picked up the threads of the religion after the second destruction of the temple. As Neusner wrote, there was too much anguish and doubt in recalling the bright hopes inspired by the prophecies:

> history – the world-shattering events of the day – was kept at a distance from the centre of life. The system of sustaining life shaped essentially within an ahistorical view of reality went forward in its own path, above history. . . .
>
> (1987: 73)

However, he draws the distinction between the sages and the people at large. Evidently the ahistorical vision was very contrived and specialised:

> A view of being in which people were seen to be moving toward some point in time – the fulfilment and the end of history as it was known – clearly shaped the consciousness of Israel after 70, just as it had in the decades before 70. So if to the sages of our legal system, history and the end of history were essentially beside the point, the construction of a world of cyclical eternities was the purpose and centre, and the conduct of humble things like eating and drinking was the paramount and decisive focus of the sacred, others saw things differently. For those who hoped and therefore fought, Israel's life had other meanings entirely.
>
> (1987: 76)

Add also that now in the first century it was impossible for everyone to grieve in the same way as the prophets used to grieve over the loss of the northern kingdom.

The sixth- and fifth-century prophets had prayed and preached for peace between the sons of Jacob. Once Samaria had emerged as a powerful enemy, richer, more populous, more in favour with the Roman colonial power than was Judah, the once dear project of unification became politically unacceptable. In the end, the unforgivable thing was not her military and political threat so much as that Samaria had built a temple which bid fair to rival that of Jerusalem. This would provide a strong reason for why the priestly message of prophecies fulfilled would stand as a contradiction, and why their praise of unity would have rung hollow to ears committed to hearing a different political message. When the old books no longer spoke to political reality, not only did they receive a reading that separated their teaching from the prophets, but prophecy itself went into abeyance (Barton 1986). This is the basis of my attempt to find a reading of the priestly books that would be closer to how they were edited, the reading that held good before all these things happened.

HISTORICAL CONSCIOUSNESS

Arguing from changes in the distribution of power is standard anthropological practice, following Malinowski's saying oft reiterated that myths are constructed for social contexts to which they supply a charter (Tonkin 1992). And myths are reconstructed for equivalent modern purposes too (Herzfeld 1986). Time past is remembered, privately or publicly, when it can be used in time present to control the future. Forgettings are the results of weak spots or holes in the memory-bearing constituencies. Weakly supported versions get crowded out and their version of history goes by the board. For a very large or complex constituency, the more uncomplicated version will draw the largest support. This time-honoured approach seems to do well for accounting for a major rereading of a sacred text such as I have described. The Bible case demonstrates also the theme that people do not necessarily want to have the old readings or the full details of their history.

After developing this thesis, I find it confounded by the notion of 'historical consciousness'. It has been said that the new generation of cultural anthropologists is more interested in 'the forms and content of indigenous historical consciousness' (Marcus and Fisher 1986: 78) than was an earlier generation of social anthropologists. This notion needs to be strongly contested, for it is another example of forgotten knowledge, but first it needs to be examined. It is argued that ethnographers who wrote in the colonial period in a single fictional 'ethnographic present' did so because they had an ahistorical bias, and this was because they were not interested in the consciousness of the people they were living with and studying. Two quite different criticisms of a previous generation of anthropologists are here: one the use of the ethnographic present, and the other, the alleged lack of interest in consciousness. I accept the former and the second I deny.

First, as to the use of the ethnographic present, of course everyone used it and, as Simon Sinclair has elegantly pointed out (1993), tense structure in narrative reporting is too subtle and sensitive a medium to be dubbed inherently ahistorical. But, as to consciousness, what on earth does 'historical consciousness' mean? Again, we have problems enough with the idea of individual consciousness, but what sense does it make to aggregate the consciousnesses of individuals? As younger anthropologists begin to study the implications they discover that no two persons present at an event can be relied on to give the same account of what happened (Borofsky 1987). So the idea of a shared historic consciousness becomes very suspect. Finally, if it is the content of historical consciousness that is to be honoured, how stable is it thought to be? Very unstable, I would have thought. History is always in process of being reconstructed: history text books follow a similar path of paradigm change as the text books of the history of science (Kuhn 1962) except that in the case of history they are revised to keep pace with political events (Fitzgerald 1970). If proof were needed that old work is dropped off the curriculum, the current anthropological writing that announces this as a fresh discovery appears without any remembrance that Halbwachs had said it very clearly already.

Anthropologists do forget, then, and they even forget the past of the bit of the subject that interests them most directly. Renato Rosaldo's (1980) account of the role of local landmarks for referencing Ilongot memories of their own past would have been richer if it had related to Halbwachs' earlier and theoretically stronger account of the unreliability of Christian memory of places in Palestine.

Earlier, when I referred to the criteria of right scholarship enforced in the anthropological writing of the 1950s, I mentioned that the standards were not native to Britain. This is the point at which to honour the intellectual influence of foreign scholars on the development of the subject. Speaking for my own experience of Oxford between 1947–51, I should say that what distinguished the teaching of the subject at that time was the strong interest in epistemology. What was called 'field methods' was in fact learning to question the conditions of knowing. This interest in the theory of knowledge marks the work of the members of the Rhodes–Livingstone Institute who followed Max Gluckman from Oxford to Manchester, as well as of the others connected with the Oxford Institute of Social Anthropology. Some names should make my point about the impact of continental philosophy: Louis Dumont, Srinivas and Franz Steiner were very significant scholars who shook our English naïvety by introducing us to branches of European, Buddhist and Hindu thought. Godfrey Lienhardt was trained first in the philosophically informed School of English in Cambridge dominated then by F. R. Leavis. Anyone writing about British anthropology in the 1950s who forgets the fieldwork that prepared *Divinity and Experience: the Religion of the Dinka* (Lienhardt 1961) might well mistake what was going on (Douglas 1994a).

In this context I recall Steiner's subtle passion for truth and objectivity (Steiner 1954a) and his concern to ground observation in sound methodology (Steiner 1954b, 1956, 1957). His own methodological principle was to turn the telescope the other way round: he required his students to imagine the subject of anthropological study looking through the glass at the investigator, in other words the creation of observational reciprocity.

To answer some of the rebuke administered to dead social anthropologists who set the tone for the 1950s, I return to Rivers' idea of memory holes caused by memory-bearing sectors of the population dying out or dispersing. Clearly the shape of the memory-bearing infrastructure changes with changes in the distribution of power and with each new intake of persons importing their own superstructural ideas into the inventories. This being well known, the feasible task for a researcher interested in consciousness would be to categorise the relations between levels, and to ask some elementary sorting questions about the types of memory-bearing units. This I maintain was an implicit objective of much of the social anthropology of the 1950s to 1960s, one which I have described in my brief study of Evans-Pritchard's work (Douglas 1980, 1986).

David Bakhurst has written a superb account (1990) of Soviet psychologists' studies of mind which is relevant to this theme. Vygotsky always insisted on the socially mediated character of consciousness. The priority which he gave to the semiotic side of the culture–nature divide earned him disgrace from the Bolshevisers of philosophy in 1931. The balance and richness of his theory was missed and it was even distorted by those who otherwise preserved the memory of his teaching. Bakhurst makes his own account of the controversy a self-referencing model for the power-distribution critique of public memory.

Partly in self defence Vygotsky's supporters found that the way that he drew the distinction between 'natural' and 'cultural' was flawed; he was shown by them as over-weighting the importance of the ideal side and under-weighting the material; they tried to rescue his political reputation by reversing his emphasis, placing the material over the idealist elements, with the result that even his devoted followers misread what he had said. Bakhurst uses V. S. Voloshinov's work to reformulate and refine the relation between the material (neurological) basis and the semiotic processes:

> Like Vygotsky, Voloshinov insists that the human mind cannot be treated as a natural phenomenon intelligible by appeal to natural laws. Mind is 'a socio-ideological fact and, as such, beyond the scope of physiological methods or the methods of any other of the natural sciences'
>
> (1990: 220)

Such Vygotskian thoughts abound in Voloshinov's writings. However, Voloshinov's position suggests a way to defend them not articulated by Vygotsky himself. For Voloshinov the relations between the contents of consciousness and the physical states of the thinking subject's body or brain is analogous to the relation between the meaning of a text and the physical form in which it is inscribed, or (to use a more dynamic model) between the content of a drama and the physical states of the medium (for example, television) in which it is presented.

The relation between the material electronic basis of the TV set and the semiotics of the narrative it displays, works well as an analogy for the relation between the neurological basis of memory and the content of what is remembered. It also does well as an analogy of the relation between the social institutions and the structure of archives and genealogical records. The political conflict expressed in terms of idealism versus materialism gave the Soviet psychologists just two levels, the physical vehicle and the semiotic freight it carried. There is no reason for us to stick with two: at each level a vehicle carries a variety of freights. Even on the TV screen there are the announcers and the news they give, and the news has been processed through the newsroom before it is presented. There are the disc jockeys and the music, and in the music there are the instruments, the vocalists, the composers, the teachers, the concert halls, and much more. Every conceivable medium has its own array of vehicular forms, its levels of greater physicality and greater ideality. There are endlessly different points in the production of experience. It is arbitrary to stop the subdivisioning at any one point, except if one level were easier to study accurately than another.

THE PAIN OF REMEMBERING

In this perspective the interest taken by the social anthropologists in the 1950s in consciousness arose from a sophisticated technical interest. At that time computer studies were in an early stage and questions about artificial intelligence would have seemed moonstruck. They were writing in the philosophy of history in the vein of Collingwood, and addressing then recognisable questions about how unwritten history is stabilised and given canonical status. Only a hasty and prejudiced reading would suppose that they were trying one-sidedly to portray foreign cultural realities without reference to their own. All the work that they did on time and memory, like that on filial and paternal relations, religion, homicide, suicide and witchcraft, was inherently reflexive: otherwise they would not have thought it worth doing. It was to understand our own history and our own mentality that comparisons were made between the kinds of infrastructure, the form of village or descent organisation and the number of generations for which present claims on the past were allowed to go back. Even the work on lineage segmentation that to another generation seems esoteric was a sustained attempt to observe the mechanism by which the past and future are encapsulated. Interest in the machinery of claims, transactions and future commitments complemented the research on genealogical charters. Rights of succession and religious claims based on descent were not being studied for their own sake like collections of masks or colonial curios, but as sources of discovery about how the guide-rails of consciousness work. Memory and forgetting were therefore of prime interest at that time.

Furthermore, it is worth noticing that the conversation of social anthropologists about remembering and forgetting tried to be exact. This was because of professional practice that I have explained above. This is why it was restricted to matters that could be described with precision, such as law, kinship and succession. Gluckman made a direct connection between Zulu ritual and the celebrations of the Manchester United football team, between English Common Law and Barotse jurisprudence (Gluckman 1962). The paradoxes he saw in Barotse legal theory, for example that their law was eternal despite changes they themselves made in it, helped him to interpret parallel paradoxes in our own case. In the same spirit consider Douglas Lewis's (1988) account of how rotating the descent group that ceremonially sings an Indonesian legend of creation allows the accumulated claims supported by one version to be regularly superseded: this is no arranging of exotic objects in a museum case. Rotation of information-carrying cohorts or straight intergenerational polarity are models of forgetting that could be brought to bear on the superseded claims of my own teachers, now dead.

When the 'Other' is found somewhere remote from my life, it is easier to interpret the other's cultural realities by a careful 'constructive negotiation involving at least two, and usually more, conscious, politically significant subjects'. This is the 'innocent' ethnography that James Clifford (1983: 133) desires to read when the 'Other' is near to home. Loud demands for innocence, like claims to honesty, make me feel uncomfortable. Certainly interpretation is always beset with problems, and it seems to be very difficult for this generation to pay attention to what the earlier social anthropologists' writing was about.

Reflections of this kind open the question of whether consciousness is such a simple idea. It is certainly dubious sense to write as if all peoples equally desired to have their own history intact (whatever that might mean). People may prefer to live in the present or to skip bits of their history. It is usually wise to leave bygones to be bygones. If doing without history is the path of forgiveness, it is also true that forgetting on one's own behalf is easier than forgetting injuries done to the dead. This partly explains the current passion for researching what collaborators did in Nazi-dominated Europe (Judt 1993). Recalling the recent civil war in Zimbabwe, and her family's sufferings at the hands of the guerrillas, a woman of the eastern Kalanga said: 'We really suffered. But God came and freed us. So now, though it is not forgotten, we act as if it was forgotten. But when you do think of it, you remember others of yours who are gone' (Werbner 1991: 167).

ACKNOWLEDGMENTS

I would like to acknowledge the help given by David Middleton whose book *Collective Remembering* (1990) has been a beacon in the field and who was kind enough to read and criticise this text. I also thank Josep Llobera for his reading and suggestions.

REFERENCES

Ackroyd, P. (1991) *The Chronicler in His Age*, Sheffield: Academic Press.
Bakhurst, D. (1990) 'Social memory in Soviet thought', in David Middleton and Derek Edwards (eds), *Collective Remembering*, London: Sage Publications.
Barton, J. (1986) *Oracles of God: Perceptions of Ancient Prophecy in Israel after the Exile*, London: Darton, Longman & Todd.
Borofsky, R. (1987) *Making History: Pukapukan and Anthropological Construction of Knowledge*, Cambridge: Cambridge University Press.
Clifford, J. (1983) 'On ethnographic authority', *Representations*, 1 (2): 118–45.
Douglas, M. (1980) *Edward Evans-Pritchard*, Brighton: Harvester Press.
—— (1986) 'Institutionalised public memory', in J. F. Short Jr (ed.), *The Social Fabric: Dimensions and Issues*, American Sociological Association Presidential Series, New York: Sage Publications.

—— (1993a) 'The forbidden animals in Leviticus', *Journal of Studies of the Old Testament*, 59: 3–31.

—— (1993b) 'Atonement in Leviticus', *Jewish Studies Quarterly*, 1: 109–30.

—— (1993c) 'Balaam's place in the Book of Numbers', *Man*, 28: 411–30.

—— (1994a) 'Godfrey Lienhardt', *Anthropology Today*, 10: 15–17.

—— (1994b) 'The Glorious Book of Numbers', *Jewish Studies Quarterly*, 1: 193–216.

—— 'Child sacrifice and cannibalism: Robertson Smith's attack on mythology', awaiting publication in W. Doniger (ed.), volume on Mythology.

Evans-Pritchard, E.E. (1972) 'Zande string figures', *Folklore*, 83: 225–39.

Fabian, J. (1983) *Time and the Other: How Anthropology Makes its Object*, New York: Columbia University Press.

Fitzgerald, F. (1970) *America Revised: History School Books in the 20th Century*, Boston: Little Brown.

Gluckman, M.G. (1962) *The Ideas in the Barotse Judicial Process*, New Haven, Conn.: Yale Law School.

Goody, J.R. (1991) Memorial, 'Meyer Fortes, 1906–1983', *Proceedings of the British Academy*, 80: 275–88.

Halbwachs, M. (1925) *Les Cadres Sociaux de la Mémoire*, New York: Harper & Row.

—— (1941) *La Topographie Légendaire des Evangiles en Terre Sainte, Etude du Mémoire Collective*, Paris: Presses Universitaires.

Herzfeld, M. (1986) *Ours Once More: Folklore, Ideology and the Making of Modern Greece*, New York: Pella.

Judt, T. (1993) 'The past is another country: myth and memory in postwar Europe', *Daedalus*, 83–117.

Kuhn, T. (1962) *The Structure of Scientific Revolutions*, Chicago: Chicago University Press.

Leach, E.R. (1961) *Rethinking Anthropology*, LSE Monographs, 22, London: Athlone Press.

Lewis, E.D. (1988) 'A quest for the source: the ontogenesis of the creation myth of the Ata Tana Ai', in J. Fox (ed.), *To Speak in Pairs: Essays on the Ritual Languages of Eastern Indonesia*, Cambridge: Cambridge University Press.

Lienhardt, R.G. (1961) *Divinity and Experience: the Religion of the Dinka*, Oxford: Clarendon Press.

Lloyd, G. (1987) *Revolutions of Wisdom*, Berkeley and Los Angeles: University of California.

Marcus, G. and Fisher, M.M.J. (1986) *Anthropology as Cultural Critique*, Chicago: University of Chicago Press.

Mendenhall, G.E. (1973) *The Tenth Generation: Origins of the Biblical Tradition*, Baltimore: Johns Hopkins University.

Middleton, D. and Edwards, D. (eds) (1990) *Collective Remembering*, London: Sage Publications.

Neusner, J. (1976) 'The teaching of the rabbis: approaches old and new', *Journal of Jewish Studies*, 27 (1): 23–35.

—— (1977) 'History and structure: the case of Mishnah', *Journal of the American Academy of Religion*, 45: 161–92.

—— (1987) *Self-fulfilling Prophecy: Exile and Return in the History of Judaism*, Boston: Beacon Press.

Rivers, W.H.R. (1912) 'The disappearance of the useful arts', *Festschrift Tillagnad Ed. Westermarck*, Helsinki: J. Simelii Arvingars Boktrycheviaktiebolag.

—— (ed.) (1922) *Essays on the Depopulation of Melanesia*, Cambridge: Cambridge University Press.

Rosaldo, R. (1980) *Ilongot Head-Hunting, 1883–1971: a Study in Society and History*, Stanford: Stanford University Press.

Sinclair, S. (1993) 'The present tense again', *JASO*, 24 (1): 33–48.

Steiner, F. (1954a) 'Chagga truth', *Africa*, 24: 64–9.

—— (1954b) 'Notes on comparative economics', *British Journal of Sociology*, 5: 118–29.

—— (1957) 'Towards a classification of labour', *Sociologus*, 7: 112–30.

—— (1967) *Taboo*, Harmondsworth: Penguin.

Thompson, M. and Wildavsky, A. (1990) *Cultural Theory*, Boulder: Westview Press.

Tonkin, E. (1992) *Narrating Our Pasts: The Social Construction of Oral History*, Cambridge: Cambridge University Press.

Torday, E. and Joyce, T.A. (1910) *Les Bushongo, Notes Ethnographiques sur les Peuples Communément appelés BaKuba*, Aquarelles par Norman Hardy, Brussels: Ministère des Colonies.

Voloshinov, V.N. (1929 (1986)) *Marxism and the Philosophy of Language*, trans. Ladislaw Matejka, I.R. Titunik, Boston: Harvard University Press.

Werbner, R. (1991) *Tears of the Dead: the Social Biography of an African Family*, Edinburgh: Edinburgh University Press.

2 Exhibiting knowledge
The trees of Dubois, Haeckel, Jesse and Rivers at the *Pithecanthropus* centennial exhibition

Mary Bouquet

Very old are the woods;
And the buds that break
Out of the brier's boughs,
When March winds wake,
So old with their beauty are –
Oh, no man knows
Through what wild centuries
Roves back the rose.
                    (Walter de la Mare)

(Reproduced by permission of the Literary Trustees of Walter de la Mare
and the Society of Authors as their representative)

The museum world has opened up as a field of anthropological investigation over the past ten years or so. This chapter will consider the anthropologist as exhibition maker, rather than analyst or even collector or documenter of objects. The focus is upon a new kind of anthropological brokerage: the mediation of specialist knowledge, usually dubbed 'science', between a restricted population of scientists and the general public, however this may be defined. If, as Macdonald (1993) has suggested, science museums now use *commissaires d'expositions*, what might an anthropologist bring to this position?

I will discuss, by way of illustration, aspects of my own observant participation in making the centennial exhibition of the type specimen of *Homo erectus* at the Dutch National Museum of Natural History. This fossil, comprising a molar, a skull-cap and a thighbone, was discovered by the Dutchman Eugène Dubois between 1890 and 1892 near Trinil on Java, and christened *Pithecanthropus erectus* by him in 1893. *Pithecanthropus* underwent the dislocation typical of the period: removal, together with about 12,000 Pleistocene faunal fossils from the same site, to become the Dubois Collection in Leiden.

The *Pithecanthropus* fossils, which Dubois identified as the missing link between mankind and a common ancestor with the apes, are now seen as the type specimen of the species *Homo erectus*. The name *Pithecanthropus erectus* means 'upright walking ape-man'. During the century that has elapsed since Dubois's discovery, the ape connection has receded further back in time through the additional human and Australopithecine fossil finds that have subsequently come to light. Dubois's *Pithecanthropus*, as *Homo erectus*, is now positioned somewhere between *Homo sapiens* and *Homo habilis*, the latter referred to by some as the first 'real man'. Man's apish forebears are now thought to be Australopithecines, who lived some three million years ago in sub-Saharan Africa. The Australopithecine (southern ape) discoveries have made the original ape-man seem so much more like one of us that Philip Tobias was moved to declare (in Leiden, June 1993) that *Homo erectus* is probably not a separate species at all, but just like *Homo sapiens*. However the *Homo erectus* problem is resolved, it was the very act of positioning fossils relative to one another that intrigued me when I was invited to conceptualise the centennial exhibition of this million-year-old fossil being held to commemorate its identification, in the seventeenth-century Pesthuis building. The fossil had never been on display to the general public until 1993. It usually lives in a safe, in a locked inner room of the museum depot.

Anthropologists have long been considered as cultural brokers. Translating esoteric science for the (Dutch) man in the street and, because this is a national museum, for an international audience, presupposed somewhat athletic brokerage on several dimensions. Not only the publics, but also the commissioners, sponsors, scientists, designers, educational department, PR men and other interested parties, all had to be able to live with the concept. The storyline could be original, then, but not too original. Having said this, Leiden must define itself (particularly since it is engaged in developing a new permanent exhibition due to open in 1997) in relation to its counterparts in Paris, London, Brussels, Frankfurt, Washington and the rest. This implies a very different kind of audience from the 'local' one: well-educated, cosmopolitan globe-trotters for whom current Dutch ideas about natural history displays for the Dutch public are of little relevance.

The story of human evolution has (in its most simplified form) global pretensions. It concerns the origins of the species *Homo sapiens*; it assumes the genealogical unity of mankind; indeed, it presupposes the ultimate kinship of all living forms on earth. One of the assumptions underlying this scientific story is that it is *human* in explanatory scope. Take, for example, this recent statement: 'All general accounts of the history of life are accounts which have been written by humans from the human standpoint, and this has caused us to possess a deeply coloured view of evolutionary history' (O'Hara 1992: 143). Cross-cultural accounts of human origins collected by social anthropologists suggest, however, an alternative perspective. Evolutionary theory is not simply *the* human account: it is rooted in a western scientific tradition, as much embedded in cultural practices and communities as, say, Trobriand myths of origin (cf. O'Hara 1992: 144; Latour 1987).

How could an anthropological perspective be used in putting *Pithecanthropus erectus* on display? The prospect of composing an exhibition for the general public around what the museum saw as three such unpromising items (compared, for example, with dinosaurs) was as much a theoretical as a practical challenge. Previous work on a forgotten collection of Melanesian artifacts in Portugal

(Bouquet and Freitas Branco 1988) had convinced me that ethnographic objects are constituted as much during life-histories led *out* of their original contexts as in them; and that these histories can be traced through texts and images which are themselves, of course, artifacts. The layers added to the 'same' object in different contexts can produce discrepant meanings: I have discussed elsewhere the case of Melanesian carved figures labelled as *Götze* (in Berlin) and *ídolos* (later, in Oporto), or the Sepik over-modelled skull that was a *Zierschädel* in Berlin and a *cránio melanésio embelezado com conchas de marisco*, in Oporto (Bouquet 1991, 1992). I argued that the times and places of an object's retrieval for display are also vitally constitutive of meaning. Would this argument apply for an object of science? Could the exhibition of such an object embody the way context forges meaning?

Let me briefly locate this project in relation to other forms of anthropological involvement in the museum world: it contrasts with the analysis of finished exhibits – such as Haraway's (1989) of the American Museum of Natural History; or Macdonald's (1994) participant observation of the making and reception of the exhibition *Food for Thought* at the Science Museum in London. My approach was closer to Vogel's involvement in and reflection upon the 'Art / Artifact' exhibition at the Center for African Art in New York in 1988. Indeed, I found her idea of placing *mijikenda* posts in a series of different settings, which altered their impact and meaning in each case, particularly inspiring (Vogel 1991).

The *Pithecanthropus* fossils seemed to me an excellent test case for examining how far an object of science, with a place in a specific sort of scientific discourse, could be recontextualised ethnographically, thereby producing unexpected aesthetic and pedagogical effects. *Pithecanthropus erectus* conventionally belongs to the story of human evolution: it is part of standard text-book material on the discoveries that have altered our perception of our relationship to the primate order, and place in nature. Any exhibition of this object demanded that that story be present as an explicit pedagogical objective. I was reminded of the way British kinship theorists of the first half of the twentieth century are (in condensed form) part of the standard fare of anthropology students. My observant participation in teaching that material in the context of 1980s Portugal (in Portuguese) had brought some surprisingly vivid ethnography implicit in the theory into the foreground (Bouquet 1993a). I was curious to see whether the same might be done in the Netherlands of the 1990s, when presenting the theory of human evolution for (Dutch general and international) public display. Could one conceive of the vestiges of a human forebear in evolutionary terms, and then disclose the specificity of those terms?

Several interlocking issues were addressed in making the exhibition. Could anthropological experience in writing ethnography be harnessed to the project of narration – using objects, images and texts – through space? Could such a composition be translated into design? Could the material objects available be orchestrated through a specific space to create an aesthetically as well as conceptually satisfying presentation? Would such an approach be pedagogically challenging, in the sense of setting human evolution in a fresh perspective?

COMPOSITION

I decided that it would be necessary, in compositional terms, both to tell the story of Dubois and his contribution to the science of palaeoanthropology, and to try to show the specificity of that story. The clue is, in fact, given by the history of the fossil itself. The physical removal of this (one of the first) human fossil from its findplace on Java to Europe clearly indicates where evolutionary theory developed. That very dislocation could be used to emphasise the local character of evolutionary ideas. Secondly, the sheer accumulation of human / Australopithecine fossils discovered since Dubois's debut with *Pithecanthropus* is ordinarily supposed to provide material evidence for the arithmetical growth of knowledge about human evolution. This knowledge is nowadays regarded as the kind of information that ought to be imparted to schoolchildren as part of a liberal education – something to which a scientific institution such as the National Museum of Natural History ought to contribute. Yet, there is inevitable simplification. As O'Hara has put it:

> When natural historians step back from the details of their research chronicles, back to textbooks, popular essays, museum exhibits, and the like – works in which they endeavour to give abbreviated views of the whole of evolutionary history – they are once again in a situation similar to that faced by authors of abbreviated human histories . . . [they] . . . must select, abridge, and simplify the results of primary research.
>
> (O'Hara 1992: 143)

What should or could be done with that process of simplification? The question is intriguing since it hints at precisely the way the sacred stories (of Dubois's find; of the other finds that somehow embody the great steps of human evolution) could be orchestrated in space. One could ask, thus, how simplification – in this case of the complexity of evolution – comes about, and pose this as a question about the relationship between western science and popular culture at the very beginning of the exhibition. How might this be done?

The space available for presentation was the large (*c.* 1500 m²) seventeenth-century Pesthuis building, square in form, with two large rooms on each side, and an Italianate pillared courtyard in the middle. Leaving aside the eighth room for restaurant and shop purposes, there were seven large rooms that could be used to present seven different phases of an argument. Each architectural division would be imbued with a specific character and atmosphere, pacing the narrative in a similar way to a textual composition. The circularity of the trajectory through the building also lent itself to developing a kind of argument through it. Let us briefly examine that sequence.

The exhibition began in The Movies, which posed a question about the persistence and even multiplication of popular images (such as Tarzan, King Kong and the Flintstones) which continue with *their* stories, at times even appropriating and sending up scientific discoveries. Nick Downes' cartoon of an astonished Australopithecine shaking hands with another and exclaiming, 'Not *the* Lucy?' is an apt illustration from his (still more aptly entitled) *Big Science* (Downes 1993). People remain oddly attached to older cultural stereotypes despite the growth of scientific knowledge about the evolution of man, and man's relationship with the apes. Why should that be so? What is the relationship between scientific and popular discourse on man and ape? The outer frame of the exhibition was thus an unexplained mixture of still (cartoons and slide sequences) and moving images (popular entertainment and scientific documentary) on the origins and consequences of man's special relationship with the apes.

The second division, The Library, introduced Dubois and various strands of nineteenth-century thought on man's place in nature, his relationship to the great apes, and Dubois's originality in searching for fossil evidence to prove (as he saw it) evolutionary theory. The third room, The Fossil Collection, displayed Dubois's finds: the three *Pithecanthropus* fossils, together with a selection of spectacular Pleistocene fauna fossils from the Dubois Collection.

The fourth section, The Island and the World, then recontextualised *Pithecanthropus erectus* among the many hominid fossil finds made during the century that has elapsed. The multiplication of human fossil finds has transformed the interpretation of Dubois's fossil from being the missing link to being a now extinct species of man – *Homo erectus*. The implicit schema whereby fossil finds are ordered (and presented) is the phylogeny that starts with the Australopithecines (three to four million years ago) and proceeds through *Homo habilis*, *Homo erectus*, Neanderthal Man, to *Homo sapiens*. The fifth division, The Forest, dwelt upon the nature of the phylogeny of man embodied in the previous section, as a way of demonstrating the cultural specificity of evolutionary theory. The phylogeny, as a simplification of ancestral connections, developed in a particular locality. Scientists drew inspiration from two versions of a cultural model: the genealogy (ancestry traced through historical time), and the Tree of Jesse (Christ's earthly ancestry traced through biblical chronology). This was the moment in the exhibition when anthropological perspective came into play. Three versions of genealogical notions of ancestry were juxtaposed with a fourth vision of ancestry which does not embody genealogical reckoning. I will discuss this section in greater detail below.

The sixth room was an Art Gallery containing two- and three-dimensional reconstructions of how prehistoric man may have looked, as imagined by artists collaborating with scientists over the past century. Variations in the appearance of *Pithecanthropus / Homo erectus* show the effects of genre as well as changing perceptions of the apishness of early man.

The final section, a kind of coda to the exhibition, was The Depot, filled with representatives of the entire primate order, the majority of which were set up by taxidermists at the Dutch National Museum of Natural History in the nineteenth century. The anthropomorphic postures given to the specimens underlines the continuing influence of images from seventeenth- and eighteenth-century natural history tracts upon the daily practices of scientific institutions. The visitor, *Homo sapiens*, was literally mirrored whilst inspecting the order to which he himself has been assigned.

A Dutch–English guide to the exhibition provided the curious with further material for reflection in the form of an illustrated souvenir (Bouquet 1993b).

AESTHETICS

The exhibition began in a tent-like construction leading into the darkened Movies. My own idea had been to step into The Movies as if through the black cloth used by photographers earlier this century. The exhibition designer, Isabelle Galy, argued (on the contrary) that the entrance should be light so that visitors could be provided with some general information about the exhibition and the first section, before being beset by images. The controversy surrounding the exhibition poster, which was also displayed in the tent, has been discussed elsewhere (Bouquet 1995). The Movies was supposed to be a Plato's cave of a place, with shadows flickering on the walls and a musical collage filling the air with excerpts from Mahler's Third, the Flintstones and Saint-Saëns' *Carnaval des Animaux*.

The Bible was placed next to Darwin's *On the Origin of Species*, in a small corridor between The Movies and The Library, with a reproduction of Rubens' and Breughel's *Adam and Eve in Paradise* as the backdrop. These were the two competing accounts of human origins and man's place in (or above) nature available by the mid-nineteenth century. Dubois's Library was formally arranged with his desk and books at the centre, ten selected volumes displayed in the surrounding pillars (church lecterns, which should have been used, were unobtainable), and ten clusters of objects evoking some aspect of each thinker's work, beneath their portraits. The fossil *Homo diluvii testis* thus evoked Cuvier, who unmasked it as being a giant salamander while on a visit to Teyler's Museum in Haarlem. A giraffe signalled Larmarck's presence, and his theory of evolution which preceded Charles Darwin. Passages from *On the Origin of Species* (1859) and *The Descent of Man* (1870), concerning the morphological similarity of the hand among different species and the kinship of different species, respectively, were made to materialise beneath portraits of Darwin as a young man and in old age, facing each other across the study. The very size of the Library, contrasted with the tiny corridor where the Bible was displayed, referred to Lyell's discovery of the enormity of geological time dwarfing the biblical chronology and paving the way for Darwin's theory. There were embryos to conjure up Haeckel's Law, skeletons to bring Huxley's Frontispiece to life, a microcephale beneath Vogt's portrait, four orders of prehistoric artifacts according to De Mortillet, reference to Schmerling's cave finds near Liège, and a nineteenth-century Bird of Paradise cabinet to summon Wallace into the room.

Between The Library and The Fossil Collection hung the cast-iron noticeboard from the Vreewijkstraat depot where *Pithecanthropus* and the rest of the Dubois Collection are usually stored. The noticeboard bears the inscription, *Verzameling van Indische Fossielen (Collectie Dubois). Niet toegankelijk voor het publiek*

(Collection of Indonesian Fossils (Dubois Collection). Not open to the public). The fossils were blatantly on display. *Pithecanthropus* itself was located at the far end of the room lined, like the levels of an excavation, with petrified antlers, stegodon's tusks, cows' horns and many other remarkable fossils. Visitors walked along a passarelle with fossils on each side of them to reach the bomb-and bullet-proofed vitrine containing the three relics which were the centrepoint of the exhibition. A ship-model of the type taken by Dubois and his wife to the East Indies, reproductions of Indonesian landscapes by the nineteenth-century Belgian Payen, and further information about Dubois's excavations on Sumatra and Java (and the Wadjak skull), were displayed at the beginning of the room. The manuscript with Dubois's change of mind (from *Anthropopithecus erectus* to *Pithecanthropus erectus* in 1893), endocranial casts in cigar boxes from his later work on the brain, and the decorations he received from the Dutch authorities were displayed at the far end. There were also photos of the three curators of the collection since 1940, when Dubois himself died and was buried in uncon-secrated ground at Venlo. These photos were displayed vertically as a sort of line of descent.

The Island and the World explained first, from a contemporary perspective, how mankind reached Java one million years ago, and presented casts of subse-quent human fossil finds from Java (The Island). Second, it gave an overview of human fossil discoveries throughout the world (China, Africa and Europe) during the twentieth century. Casts of these finds were arranged in large catacomb-like vitrines in phylogenetic order running from the Australopithecines, through *Homo habilis*, *Homo erectus*, to Neanderthal Man. Behind the casts stood reconstruc-tions of their likely appearance made by Museon in Den Haag. The outer wall of the catacombs was covered with Jay Matternes' line of running men (see Weaver 1985). A world map gave a painstaking overview of the sites where human fossils have been found.

The final figure in Jay Matternes' sequence, *Homo sapiens* was running into The Forest: a darkened room, hung with four enormous (6-metre-high) panels placed at regular intervals but tilted at various angles along the centre of the room. Each panel depicted a prototype, and was surrounded by further examples of its kind (see Figure 2.1). The first tree, immediately inside The Forest, was Haeckel's *Systematischer Stammbaum des Menschen* (1874). Historical and contemporary phylogenies from Darwin, Haeckel and Dubois to Stringer, Johansen and Leakey, exemplified the continuing importance of the phylogenetic diagram for presenting various interpretations of human evolution that can be taken in at a glance.

The second tree was Dubois's own family tree, going back to 1500, and incorporating his coat of arms: three trees, referring to the name Dubois – of the woods. We tend to think of 'the scientist' (the Dubois introduced in The Library) separately from 'the man'. The conventional way of pinning down the latter is by giving parental co-ordinates. Precisely that genealogical way of thinking per-meates the phylogeny. How separate are the two? Juxtaposing them forces the

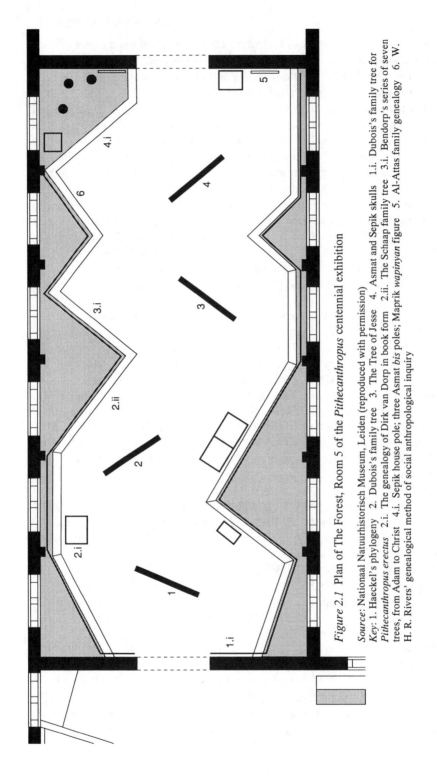

Figure 2.1 Plan of The Forest, Room 5 of the *Pithecanthropus* centennial exhibition

Source: Nationaal Natuurhistorisch Museum, Leiden (reproduced with permission)
Key: 1. Haeckel's phylogeny 2. Dubois's family tree 3. The Tree of Jesse 4. Asmat and Sepik skulls 1.i. Dubois's family tree for *Pithecanthropus erectus* 2.i. The genealogy of Dirk van Dorp in book form 2.ii. The Schaap family tree 3.i. Bendorp's series of seven trees, from Adam to Christ 4.i. Sepik house pole; three Asmat *bis* poles; Maprik *wapinyan* figure 5. Al-Attas family genealogy 6. W. H. R. Rivers' genealogical method of social anthropological inquiry

viewer to confront a problem that is usually hidden from view. A score of eighteenth- and nineteenth-century Dutch genealogies borrowed from the Centraal Bureau voor Genealogie in Den Haag underlined the aesthetic analogy. Most genealogies were two-dimensional, but there was also a seventeenth-century example in book form.

The third tree was a 1930s print of an eighteenth-century black and white Tree of Jesse, showing Christ's earthly ancestry going back to Adam. Additional eighteenth- and nineteenth-century engravings of the Tree of Jesse, and a pair of wooden carvings of kings thought to come from a Lower Rhine altarpiece embodying the Tree of Jesse (de Werd 1989), were on display in the vicinity. So, too, was a family Bible (an official translation dating from 1649), with the names of family members inscribed inside the cover in imitation of Genesis.

The concept for this room drew inspiration from the exhibition *Liens de Famille* held at the Musée National des Arts et Traditions Populaires in Paris in 1991 (see Segalen 1991). The two-dimensional kinship diagrams used to great effect, although much earlier on, in that exhibition left a lasting impression. There was much discussion in the museum about whether a room full of family trees could be aesthetically sustained, or would be boring. Galy's solution, which conjured with vertical and horizontal planes at dramatic angles, captured the prolific growth and the sense of depth of this forest of symbols. This was no mere designer's whim: the aesthetic disposition of the four prototypes was an essential part of the argument. Galy's addition of two carved pears and two carved apples on four of the posts supporting the panels, referred to the Dutch expression, 'Je kunt geen appels met peren vergelijken' (literally, 'You cannot compare apples and pears'). Aesthetically it *could* be done, despite the reservations some expressed about the intellectual project embodied in the display. The purely visual impact *was*, in one sense, the message: the three trees *can* be ranged alongside one another as iconographical artifacts.

Finally, the fourth hanging panel did not show a tree but rather housed four rows of Asmat and Sepik skulls staring back at the three versions of genealogical thinking – scientific, historical and biblical. Three Asmat *bis* poles, a Sepik house pole carved with crocodile skin, and a Marpik hanging figure were displayed in one of the corners beyond the skull-rack (see Figure 2.1) and were visible through the vitrines built into the panel to house the skulls. These large, three-dimensional objects were meant to evoke notions of ancestry, and the relationship between man and the animal world, quite different from those embodied in the various transformations of genealogical thinking so far presented in The Forest. Older *bis* poles are carved into the form of a soul canoe for transporting spirits to the other world. They may also show ancestral figures standing on one another's shoulders, and contain stylised symbols of, for example, the hornbill – one of the birds in which spirits of the recently dead are thought to reside (Konrad *et al.* 1981). The birds, animals and plants depicted in these Melanesian carvings were intended to bring the evolutionary identification with the primate order into perspective. Genealogies and the other associated artifacts are, of course, filled with natural symbols: Pama (1987: 136) indeed remarks that if all the animals that have ever appeared in heraldry had been catalogued in his chapter on natural heraldic figures, it would have resembled a natural history course! Yet this use of natural history is subordinated to the genealogical project: coats of arms, which incorporate natural and other symbols, are in fact condensed genealogies and can be read as such. The Melanesian artifacts were deployed in this specific context to constitute a contrast: to render comparable, in effect, that which could have been all too easily designated incomparable – namely the palaeoanthropological, historical and religious uses of the genealogy.

Genealogical plates from the Vienna Manuscript, genealogies from the Yemen, Sumatra and Sulawesi, indicated the importance of the genealogy elsewhere, especially in Muslim areas. A photograph of W. H. R. Rivers, however, made it clear that the genealogical method *qua* scientific method has a much more specific origin. Furthermore, anthropological knowledge of other kinship systems is mediated by a method that is explicitly genealogical. This method, which was summoned into The Forest by displaying Rivers' famous article open at the genealogy of Arthur or Kurka of Guadalcanal, brings the visitor full circle, showing the limits as well as the potential afforded by this anthropological perspective on the representation of human evolution. It was clearly time to switch perspectives again.

The over-modelled ancestral and enemy skulls displayed in the last part of The Forest provided a point of articulation with the next room, The Art Gallery. The aesthetic informing the Art Gallery in some ways developed from The Forest: the gathering together of objects usually shown next to their fossil inevitably fore-grounds different sorts of relationships from those which are the conventional focus. Dubois's full-figure reconstruction of *Pithecanthropus* for the 1900 Paris World Exhibition was deliberately reserved as the nucleus of The Art Gallery in this exhibition, rather than placing it (like a resurrection from the dead) next to the fossils in The Fossil Collection. Like Dubois's phylogeny for *Pithecanthropus*, the reconstruction is an historical artifact belonging to a different period that can be conceptualised along with different classes of objects – phylogenies and reconstructions – even though they were generated by the fossil. Or were they? One of the messages in The Library was that *Pithecanthropus* existed as an idea, a theoretical construct (Haeckel's) *before* there was a fossil! It was, in fact, the wish to find concrete proof of an idea that sent Dubois searching for evidence in the Dutch East Indies.

The Art Gallery differed aesthetically from The Forest in that no cross-cultural contrast was brought into play. Two- and three-dimensionality were not as conceptually important here as they had been to embody contrasting notions of ancestry in the previous room. The effect of the dozen or so different visions and versions of the ape-man, made at different moments during the twentieth century, assembled on pedestals and behind vitrines, was something like a cocktail party – with Dubois's *Pithecanthropus erectus* as host.

The aestheticisation of objects not normally regarded as beautiful – statues of ape-men and prehistoric man – was inverted in the final section of the exhibition: The Depot. This shadowy, darkened space evoked the storage area of the museum that houses thousands of artifacts not on display. The anthropomorphism of some of the primates in storage, faithfully reproducing the images of earlier centuries, complemented the animality of some of the ape-men of the Art Gallery. The presence of former taxidermists' tools, together with the natural history texts they may have consulted for their creations, gave the place the air of a workshop and not just a storage room. This aesthetic of activity was meant to mimic the way ideas are constantly being fished out of stockpiles and reworked into the debates of the moment. This constant recycling of ideas (in this case, the idea of the ape-man) enabled a connection to be made between the beginning of the exhibition (The Movies), where the problem of the interrelationship between science and popular culture was first mooted, and its end where the influence of popular (external) ideas about primates infiltrated work inside a scientific institution.

The visually impressive display of mounted prosimians, monkeys and apes developed a minor theme from the first room – a single cabinet filled with contemporary monkey toys – into a grand finale. There was some consternation among the organising committee about the effect of all these 'old monkeys': could we not achieve the same end with two or three specimens rather than two hundred? Yet the scale of the exhibition up to this point clearly required a dramatic ending of some kind. The mirroring of spectators and specimens, caught together as visitors walked the length of the gallery between the two painted *trompes-l'oeil* at each end, was in conceptual and design terms one possible response to the challenge.

PEDAGOGY

The pedagogical challenge was therefore less a matter of imparting information about human evolution, than trying to make people think about the notion of ancestry that it entails. The composition endeavoured to pose a problem about the relationship between scientific representation and popular culture (Bouquet forthcoming). This problem introduced the entire exhibition and provided a general frame within which to tell the story of Dubois: first, in the context of nineteenth- century thinking on evolution; second as a feat of sheer physical accumulation – his collection; third, as a contribution to palaeoanthropology as it has developed over the century since Dubois's discovery. The next step was to return to the problem introduced at the beginning of the exhibition by way of phylogeny. Phylogenetic diagrams and graphic depictions (such as Matternes' running men) are often used to present a simplified view of human evolution for the general public. The aim of the last three parts of the exhibition was to examine how simplifications of this sort have recourse to pre-existing genres. I only discuss the phylogeny here since it provides the clearest example of the mechanism at work, and illustrates how an anthropological perspective can inform the orchestration of a science exhibition.

I should perhaps explain that the impulse for making the phylogeny the moment of sea change in the exhibition drew upon an earlier project that also involved a kind of dislocation. That project had been concerned with the effects of teaching British kinship theory to Portuguese anthropology students in mid-1980s Lisbon, through the medium of Portuguese (Bouquet 1993a). Specialist anthropological knowledge or theorising, in the form of a number of now classic British texts from the first half of the twentieth century concerned with kinship, was produced under a set of circumstances and in contexts that have long ceased to exist. Yet the texts remain. And their precepts and concepts must be grasped by students, not only in Britain but also further afield. While they are part of anthropology's 'global' patrimony, it is none the less a patrimony to which there are differential use rights. My experience in using these texts in Portugal (and in Portuguese) taught me just how local many of the underlying assumptions were – for example, the folk idea of pedigree that underwrites the genealogical method that was so central to the development of British kinship theory.

Genealogical charts are still considered part of the ethnographer's 'minimal obligation' for making his fieldwork 'intelligible' to others (Barnes 1967). They are considered integral to an adequate description of the kinship system, which Barnard and Good could still refer to quite recently as the *sine qua non* for any British anthropologist returning home from the field (Barnard and Good 1984). Genealogical diagrams became a way of both collecting and presenting evidence of relatedness. Although genealogies are known throughout Europe and elsewhere in the world, it was Rivers who transformed the pedigree into a scientific method for ethnographic investigation around the turn of the century (Rivers 1910). Rivers' reasons for regarding the genealogy in this way reflect upon an English distinction between the animal level of biological relatedness and the social person – so much taken for granted by those writing anthropology that some have even claimed over sixty years later that the English middle class are 'kinshipless' (Fox 1970: 14). Rivers was almost certainly influenced by Darwin's ideas on descent, as well as by his frequent recourse to the idiom of genealogy and pedigree. I will return to the question this begs about the source of Darwin's inspiration below.

Interestingly enough it was Bourdieu who first called the genealogical tree into question when elaborating upon his distinction between official and practical kinship. As he put it, 'The genealogical tree compiled by the anthropologist is a spatial diagram that can be taken in at a glance, *uno intuito*, and can be scanned indifferently from any point in any direction' (Bourdieu 1977: 37–8). Bourdieu recommended a 'social history of the genealogical tool', an exploration of the relationship between the 'social' and 'scientific' use of the instrument. This, he anticipated, would require an epistemological study of the mode of investigation which is a precondition for the production of the genealogical diagram. Rivers' diagram does, of course, invert the tree: the ancestors are at the top and Ego mostly at or towards the bottom. This followed, in fact, the ordinary genealogical tree which shows ancestors in a plan of descent. There is, as Watson has pointed out, a certain conflict in so far as the metaphorical root is placed at the summit and the descendants lower down (Watson 1934: 44). The model was none the less a classic one – the pedigree as a record of descent – familiar from western Europe.

What struck and intrigued me when making the centennial exhibition and when first confronted by Dubois's 'family tree' for *Pithecanthropus erectus* and Haeckel's extraordinary trees which undoubtedly galvanised him, was a feeling of *déjà vu*. This way of rendering ancestral connections graphically concrete was familiar from elsewhere. After some reflection there seemed to be two such tree models. The first I had encountered as 'family trees' in the conventional western (European) sense of the pedigree lurking beneath the genealogical method. The second was the Tree of Jesse, popular in western Christianity since mediaeval times. The general idea of a Tree of Jesse is the 'representation of a recumbent figure from whose body rises a tree on which appear some of the ancestors of Christ, and at the summit Christ himself' (Watson 1934: 1). The earliest representations of this subject do not have an explicitly genealogical motif. This was only introduced from the twelfth century onwards when the *Arbor juris* had become thoroughly well known, and genealogies had been circulated. Before this, the *iurga Iesse* was part of a group of biblical images which prefigured the immaculate conception in mediaeval thought: the enclosed garden, the sealed fountain, the shut gate and the unspotted mirror. The Tree of Jesse was interpreted as a figurative prophecy of the Virgin: 'There shall come forth a rod [shoot] out of the stem [root] of Jesse, and a branch shall grow out of his roots' (*Et egredietur iurga de radice Iesse, et flos de radice eius ascendet*) (Isaiah x. 1–3). The root (*radix*) was David; the shoot or rod (*iurga*) was the Virgin Mary; the flower (*flos*) was Christ, in ascending order towards the spirit. It is remarkable that what was initially identified as a prophetic image of the immaculate conception, was transformed into an essentially *backward*-oriented, genealogical motif for tracing ancestry.

The time scales spanned by the various genealogical trees are extraordinarily diverse: biblical, geological, historical and ethnographic. Aesthetically, as already discussed, these differences are cancelled out by, for example, using the same species. We might, thus, range the oak trees of Haeckel, the Schaap family and the eighteenth-century Dutch Tree of Jesse alongside one another (compare Figures 2.3, 2.4 and 2.5). There is, of course, a long history of deference towards the oak tree in Europe as Frazer pointed out (Frazer 1963), but that seems a far cry from science. Watson claims that the tree is everywhere, an obvious source of symbolism: 'It embodies the idea of growth, of sequence, of decay and awakening of life' (Watson 1934: 58). This makes the discrepancy between the various projects deploying the 'same' tree as a means of representing connection through time all the more tantalising. Despite the 'revolution in ethnological time' during the nineteenth century (Trautmann 1992), and despite the redefinition of man's place in nature brought about by the spread of evolutionary ideas, the same model that had structured the biblical chronology was used to represent connections through deep time. It could be argued that aesthetic continuity served to render the revolution irrefutable, that the phylogenetic tree towered over its lesser cousins, the family tree and the tree of Jesse. But it would be equally plausible to ask whether the mere echo of those paltry time scales, however anachronistic, somehow domesticated the fantastic abysses of time that opened up in the nineteenth century.

The juxtapositioning of three trees, each referring to one of the time scales mentioned above and contrasting with a fourth non-tree, aimed at posing the problem of representational constancy across shifting temporal dimensions. This was less a matter of conveying information than placing these sharply contrastive ways of knowing in a comparative perspective. If the result was 'pure poetry', as one highly placed official in Mobil Oil remarked, that could be taken as a compliment as far as the exhibition concept was concerned.

The analogy between drawing phylogenies and drawing genealogies is in fact stunning, for all its neglected self-evidence. Still more remarkable is the fact that although evolutionary theory contested the literal interpretation of the biblical Creation story, it borrowed the very same genealogical motif to represent human kinship with the primate order through geological time that had been used to depict Christ's earthly ancestry within the biblical chronology. This replication of the genealogical motif seemed to me a very clear example of how scientific discourse is rooted in what I will call local cultural discourse. The use of this motif in the exhibition aimed to encourage visitors to think again about the story of human evolution, translating its familiarity into the unfamiliar. It facilitated the pedagogical aim of not simply instructing the public on human evolution, although that information was certainly there, but of giving pause for thought about the great steps in human evolution.

SEEING THE WOOD FOR THE TREES (DOOR DE BOMEN HET BOS NIET MEER ZIEN)

> There once was a man who said, 'God
> Must find it exceedingly odd
> If he finds that this tree
> Continues to be
> When there's no one about in the quad.'
> (Ronald Knox, Limerick)

The tree is often used emblematically today to express concern with nature; famous persons and dignitaries plant trees as a statement of engagement with environmental issues. Intrinsic to this act is the knowledge that the tree will outlive its planter. The tree regains, in this sense, some of its earlier mentioned prophetic associations although in the entirely different context of environmental concern. The trees assembled in the *Pithecanthropus* centennial Forest exhibited both kinship and confrontation between ways of knowing.

The tree thus connects two pedagogical projects: British kinship theory in Portugal, and the theory of human evolution in Holland. The kinds of claims to global understanding in each case raised (on different time scales) fundamentally local assumptions about ancestry. The controversial status of the theory of evolution in the Dutch context is worth mentioning here. The population divides between those who believe literally in the privileged creation of man by God, and those who would probably subscribe to the view that we are no more than jumped-up apes with overactive brains. The keen interest in human evolution, and more especially in the work of Richard Leakey, shown by members of the Dutch Royal Family undoubtedly imbues the scientific endeavour with an interesting measure of prestige. Religiously based resistance to the idea of apish ancestry is none the less so strong that the *Pithecanthropus* fossils had to be displayed in a bomb- and bullet-proofed vitrine. Serious concern for the safety of the fossil was expressed at various junctures during the exhibition's preparations. This situation encouraged me to try to winkle out the connections between these often emotionally polarised positions, and quite literally to put them on display.

Assumptions about ancestry nestle inside all sorts of constructs (such as genealogy), but also in the ingenuous looking diagrams used to 'simplify' and 'illustrate' arguments assumed to take place in textual form. The persuasive power of the phylogeny is well illustrated in Dubois's story. When Dubois returned from the East Indies, he presented his fossil at various scientific meetings in Europe (Leiden, Cambridge, Dublin, Berlin), drawing up a family tree for *Pithecanthropus erectus*. Dubois's biographer, Bert Theunissen, has analysed how 'Dubois followed the tradition of the German school of morphology in describing the fossils. The principal aim of the work was to describe the phylogenetic position of Pithecanthropus and to reconstruct the human family tree, as far as possible' (Theunissen 1989: 68). Theunissen contends that the 'unmistakable typological bias in Dubois's work' was 'implicit and probably even unconscious' (Theunissen 1989: 69) (see Figure 2.2).

This diagram was one of the ways in which Dubois laid claim to the intermediate position for *Pithecanthropus*, between man and a common ancestor with the apes. Dubois produced, of course, much more: dozens of articles and the life-sized reconstruction already mentioned. All this was based on what he identified as the ape-like features of the skull combined with the human-like features of the femur. It is instructive to return to what Dubois wrote in 1895:

> I am well aware of the exceptional mortality of such trees but I also know that parts of them at least often survive, from which new life emerges. One has to try to visualise the kinship relations of the forms presently known, and I know of no better means to this end than the form of a phylogenetic tree.
>
> (Dubois 1895: 737; cited in Theunissen 1989: 95)

He pursued the same metaphor in 1899 when he added,

> I cannot look upon *Pithecanthropus* but as upon a real member, the first known, in our genealogy. And even should we prefer not to regard him as a grandfather but as an uncle, still in every case he is almost venerable ape-man, representing a stage in our phylogeny.
>
> (Dubois 1899: cited in Theunissen 1989: 95)

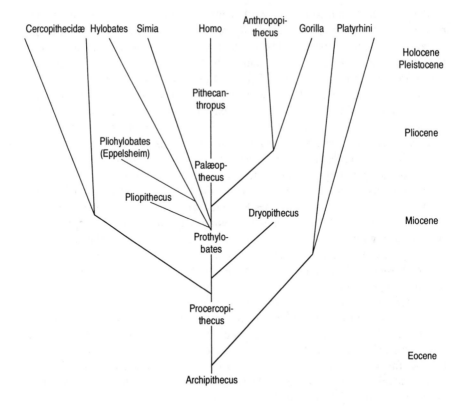

Figure 2.2 Dubois's family tree of *Pithecanthropus erectus*

Source: Theunissen 1989: 94, Figure 11 (reproduced by permission of Kluwer Academic Publishers)

Dubois was almost certainly influenced in a general way by Darwin's re-placement of formal relationships by genealogical ones (Theunissen 1989: 69). Although Darwin himself drew very few such trees, it is surely significant that the *only* illustration in *On the Origin of Species* is the famous tree diagram! Despite his own diagrammatical sparsity, his use of kinship imagery in writing about the descent of species from a common ancestor may well have inspired others in their graphic representations (see Strathern 1992: 91–2)

Dubois undoubtedly modelled *Pithecanthropus'* family tree on phylogenetic diagrams which were introduced by Haeckel in the 1860s. Haeckel viewed human descent from the apes as a proven fact that could be documented by comparative anatomy and embryology (Theunissen 1989: 74). The tree of de-scent he drew in 1874, showing *Pithecanthropus alalus* (the speechless ape-man) already in position, differs from Dubois's tree of 1895, however, in so far as Dubois referred to what he saw as his discovery of the transitional form in the fossil record.

Haeckel is widely held responsible for introducing phylogenetic trees into evolutionary discourse. Gould, for example, asserts that Haeckel made evolutionary trees into the standard iconography for phylogeny. He discusses the influence of iconography on concepts, with special reference to what he calls the 'ladder of progress' and the 'cone of increasing diversity'. 'All Haeckel's trees branch continually upward and outward forming a cone (Haeckel sometimes allowed two peripheral branches in each sub-cone to grow inward at the top, in order to provide enough room on the page for all the groups)' (Gould 1989: 263).

It is important to note that Haeckel was an accomplished artist, in addition to his scientific work (e.g. Haeckel 1899–1904; 1904–1907), and it is tempting to imagine his numerous phylogenetic trees (some with real bark and gnarled branches), as being directly inspired by nature (see Figure 2.3).

Yet it would be a mistake to regard this as unmediated inspiration drawn from nature; the route appears to have been more complicated. Haeckel saw the threefold parallel between embryological, systematic and palaeontological development of organisms as the clearest proof of evolutionary theory. He believed that the natural system of plants and animals corresponded with their 'natural, genealogical pedigree', and this he explained in the form of a widely ramifying tree, on whose branches and boughs green leaves symbolised living forms, while dead leaves signified extinct forms (Krausse 1987: 48).

Erika Krausse reports that Haeckel referred to the kinship connections between languages, already mentioned by Darwin, as evidence for human evolution. These resemblances could be demonstrated by the results of comparative linguistic studies through common descent and progressive development of languages, which could be explained and likewise depicted through genealogical trees. The influence of one of Haeckel's closest friends, the Jena philologist August Schleicher, was apparently crucial here. Schleicher read Darwin's *On the Origin of Species* at Haeckel's suggestion and immediately applied its developmental ideas to the study of language. He drafted a pedigree of the Indo-Germanic languages in an 'Open Letter' to Haeckel, entitled *Darwinian Theory and Philology* published at Weimar in 1863, and suggested designing similar ones for plant and animal families. This suggestion was consistently taken up in Haeckel's later work, where the entire realm of organisms is thus made to materialise.

If Schleicher's linguistic pedigree animated Haeckel's chosen iconography of evolution, Darwin was no less Schleicher's muse – albeit on Haeckel's own recommendation – when he sketched his linguistic *Stammbaum*. Richards has pointed to the close resemblance between Darwin's famous sketch of a descent tree, on page 36 of 'Notebook B', and Martin Barry's developmental tree of 1837 representing vertebrate and invertebrate archetypes and their developmental patterns (Richards 1992: 107–8). According to Richards, Haeckel was working within the *echt* Darwinian tradition when he used biogenetic law to reconstruct phylogenies (Richards 1992: 164). Maher, however, has observed that Schleicher's evolutionism was whole and entire long before he had ever heard of Charles Darwin (Maher 1983: xxi–xxii). He points out that the evolutionary and

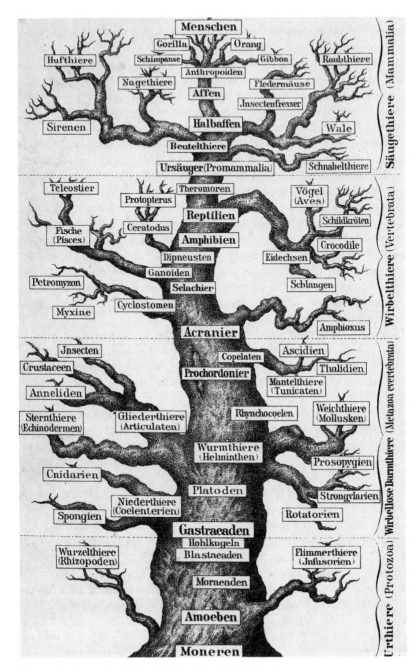

Figure 2.3 Haeckel's *Systematischer Stammbaum des Menschen*

Source: *Anthropogenie*, 1874 (reproduced with permission)

comparative method had been used by philologists in the eighteenth century. The idea of the unity of mankind and the eleventh chapter of Genesis beginning with 'the whole earth was of one language, and of one speech', followed by the confusion of Babel, prepared the ground for the explicit use of the comparative method in the linguistic field.

Wherever Haeckel's inspiration for his famous phylogenetic trees originated, it is clear that the motif had gained common currency among scientists by the time Dubois made his discovery, so that it was quite natural for him to draw up a family tree for *Pithecanthropus erectus*. But where did the genealogical motif itself originate, irrespective of the philological or palaeontological ends to which it was becoming generally harnessed? What more obvious source of inspiration could there be for the oak tree that Haeckel took as his model for the 1874 *Stammbaum des Menschen* than one of the many familiar historical genealogies (Figure 2.4)? Or again, the Tree of Jesse showing Christ's earthly ancestry – another missing link of sorts. Figure 2.5 shows this pedigree in the shape of a single oak tree, with a substantial trunk leading from Adam to Christ (Figure 2.5).

Sometimes the genealogy was subdivided as a series of individual trees, some identifiable species (for instance, bay, palm and oak) and others more stylised.

Figure 2.4 Geslacht Boom van den Heere Mr Gerard Schaap

Source: Centraal Bureau voor Genealogie, The Hague (reproduced with permission)

Figure 2.5 Geslacht Boom van Adam tot Christus

Source: Centraal Bureau voor Genealogie, The Hague (reproduced with permission)

Figure 2.6 shows the first of a series of seven by Johannes Christiaan Bendorp, dating from the late eighteenth or early nineteenth centuries.

It shows a bay tree springing from the globe, around which circles the quotation: 'De Eerste Mensche is uit der Aarde: Aardsch' ('The first man is of the earth: earthy') (I Cor. 15: 47). The inscription below reads: 'God created the whole family of man from one blood, to inhabit the entire the Earth'). Rays of sunshine illuminate Eve while Adam sleeps beneath another tree (the tree of knowledge of good and evil), to the left of the globe from which the genealogical tree of man springs. Adam and Eve figure in a landscape with an elephant, ostriches, dogs, ducks, goats, deer, rabbits and a hedgehog. A banner fluttering across the trunk proclaims: 'This is the family of Adam, the Son of God, first inhabitants of the first world.' The Flood is depicted on the right of the globe, with the Ark just going afloat while the condemned desperately struggle to climb into trees as sheets of rain gradually inundate the Earth.

Haeckel placed structureless 'moneren' at the root of his gnarled oak, mediating the transition between inorganic and organic, instead of Adam. Yet, the text used in Bendorp's first tree (from I Corinthians), that the first man is 'of the earth' could easily accommodate an evolutionary sense, as might be expected from even the sketchiest genealogy of the motif.

FINAL REMARKS

> Who assures us that your genealogical trees are anything better than the productions of your imagination?
>
> (August Schleicher, 1869: 40)

If Melanesian beliefs about animal ancestry could once be seen as 'totemic', the presence of a number of Asmat and Sepik ancestors at the exhibition turned the question back upon the identification of apish ancestors in evolutionary theory. The tree motif used to visualise evolutionary relationships between man and ape was already deeply entrenched in western European culture. Deleuze and Guattari have expressed their weariness with trees and advised us to 'stop believing in trees, roots and radicles' (Deleuze and Guattari 1988: 15). They go on to remark how odd it is that the 'tree had dominated Western reality and all of Western thought, from botany to biology and anatomy, but also gnosiology, theology, ontology, all of philosophy . . .'. They wonder whether the East, and Oceania in particular, does not offer something like a rhizomatic model, different in every respect from the western model of the tree.

Aside from whether the dichotomy can be sustained – and the prophetic sense of *iurga Iesse* as distinct from the genealogical Tree of Jesse introduces a measure of ambiguity, to say the least – what was the point of constituting a Forest in the *Pithecanthropus* centennial exhibition? The resonances between biblical, secular / historical and scientific / prehistoric accounts of ancestry, although apparently so different, looked suddenly and obviously akin under the withering gaze of

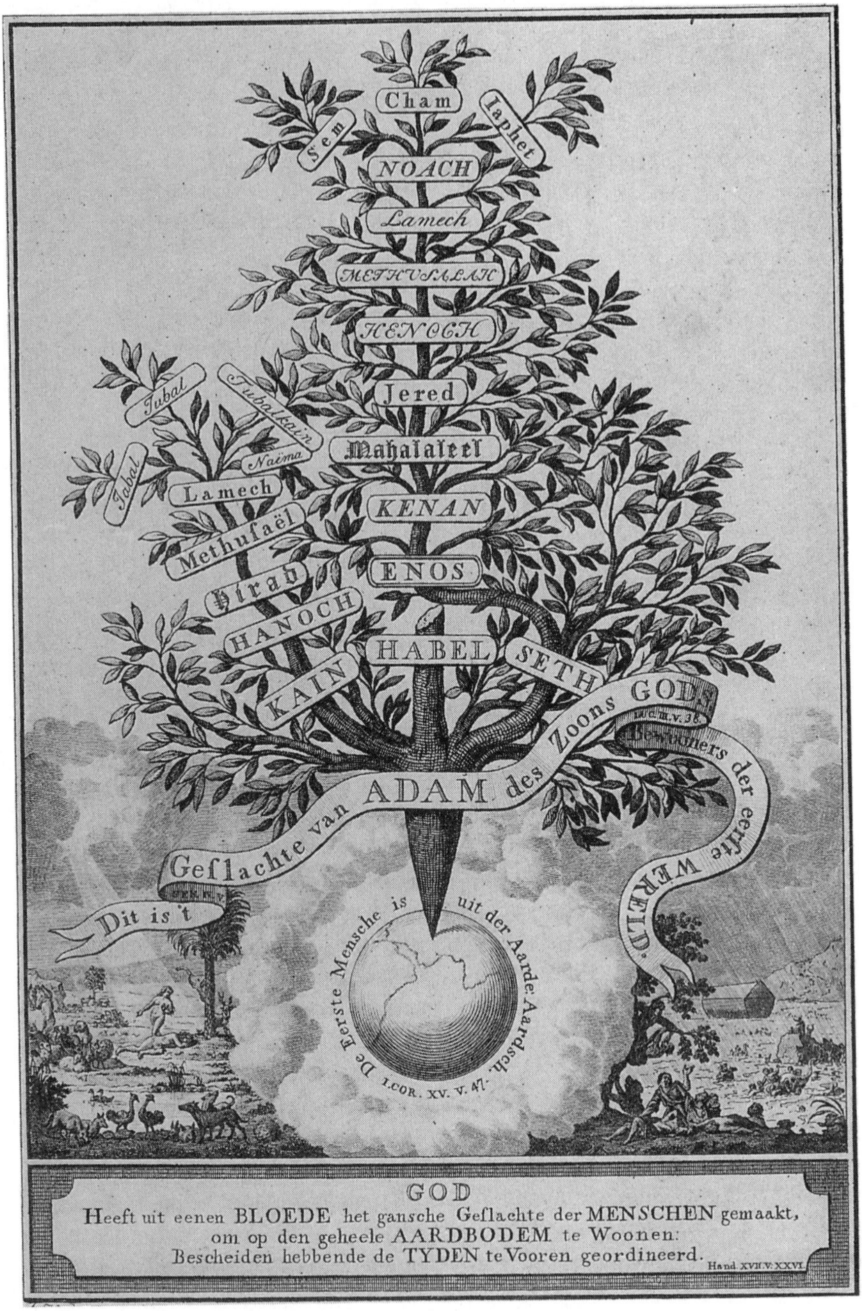

Figure 2.6 The Tree of Jesse, from Adam to Noah: first in a series of seven by J. C. Bendorp

Source: Prentenkabinet, University of Leiden (reproduced with permission)

Irian Jayan and Papua New Guinean ethnographic skulls. Contrived it most certainly was, but with the aim of promoting the kind of reflexivity that might be shared and communicated outside as well as inside the walls of conference rooms and the covers of books.

Anthropologists working outside academia may draw upon anthropological knowledge in various ways. Edmund Leach's instigation to immerse oneself, as an anthropologist, in the muddle of everyday life is inspiring, however difficult it may be to put into practice (Grimshaw 1989–90: 77). Framing an object of science, *Pithecanthropus*, with a series of different contexts or environments was an invitation to the visitor to switch perspectives. The ape-man in the exhibition was picked up in popular culture; hunted down in the history of science; concretised (and immortalised) in palaeoanthropology, and typified as an extinct human species (*Homo erectus*); positioned and connected through phylogenetic iconography to western Christian and secular conceptions of ancestry; monumentalised as art and, finally, mirrored in the anthropomorphic postures given to other members of the primate order by nineteenth-century taxidermists.

Conceiving an exhibition such as this was essentially an exercise in meddling with meanings. Meddling may, indeed, be a reasonable synonym for the kind of practical anthropology discussed in this chapter. Such interference comes about, as it does in its prototype ethnography, through arrangement and composition within given parameters, Various perspectives are afforded by juxtapositioning the normally separate, sundering the usually enwrapped, framing established sequences so as to problematise their apparent order, pursuing another tack when the story as conventionally told ought to have been concluded. There was an almost mythological intensity to the biblical, historical, evolutionary and ethnographic transpirations of the tree presented in this way. Seeing the wood for the trees of The Forest was *about* perspective, which is exactly what anthropology best affords.

ACKNOWLEDGEMENTS

I would like to thank Raymond Corbey and Bert Theunissen for being generous with their respective expertise, as well as moral support, throughout this venture. I learned much from Isabelle Galy, the designer of the exhibition and catalogue, and other colleagues at the NNM: Leslie Tjon Sie Fat, Dirk Houtgraaf, Bep van der Wilk, Wim Gertenaar, Hansjorg Ahrens, John de Vos and Chris Smeenk. I would also like to acknowledge the help of Mr N. Plomp (Centraal Bureau voor Genealogie, Den Haag), and Kees van den Meiracker (Museum voor Volkenkunde, Rotterdam). I have benefited from discussion with Sharon Macdonald, Tim Ingold, Sarah Franklin and Jeanette Edwards.

The first verse of Walter de la Mare's 'All That's Past' is reproduced with permission of the Literary Trustees of Walter de la Mare, and the Society of Authors as their representative. The limerick is reproduced with acknowledgement to Knox, R. (1972) 'Limerick', J.M. Cohen and M.J. Cohen (eds), *The*

Penguin Dictionary of Quotations, London: Penguin: 225. The publisher and author wish to state that every effort was made prior to publication to secure permission for the reproduction or the limerick. Permission has been applied for.

REFERENCES

Barnard, A. and Good, A. (1984) *Research Practices in the Study of Kinship*, London: Academic Press.

Barnes, J. (1967) 'Genealogies' in A.L. Epstein (ed.), *The Craft of Social Anthropology*, London: Social Sciences Paperbacks in association with Tavistock Publications.

Bouquet, M. (1991) 'Images of artefacts: photographic essay', *Critique of Anthropology*, 11 (4): 333–56.

—— (1992) 'Framing knowledge: the photographic "blind spot" between words and things', *Critique of Anthropology*, 12 (2): 193–207.

—— (1993a) *Reclaiming English Kinship: Portuguese Refractions of British Kinship Theory*, Manchester: Manchester University Press.

—— (1993b) *Man-ape Ape-man: Pithecanthropus in Het Pesthuis, Leiden*, Leiden: National Museum of Natural History (exhibition catalogue).

—— (1995) 'Exhibiting *Homo erectus* in 1993', in R. Corbey and B. Theunissen (eds), *Ape, Man, Apeman: Changing Views, 1600–2000*, Leiden University Department of Prehistory.

—— (forthcoming) 'Strangers in paradise; an encounter with Fossil Man at the Dutch National Museum of Natural History', in S. Macdonald (ed.), *Science as Culture* 4, Special Issue 'Science, Technology and the Politics of Display'.

Bouquet, M. and Freitas Branco, J. (1988) *Melanesian Artefacts, Postmodernist Reflections / Artifactos melanésios, Reflexões pós-modernistas*, Lisbon: IICT / Museu de Etnologia.

Bourdieu, P. (1977) *Outline of a Theory of Practice*, Cambridge: Cambridge University Press.

Deleuze, G. and Guattari, F. (1988) *A Thousand Plateaus: Capitalism and Schizophrenia*, London: Athlone Press.

Downes, N. (1993) *Big Science*, New York: AAAS Press.

Dubois, E. (1895) '*Pithecanthropus erectus*, betrachtet als eine wirkliche Uebergangsform und als Stammform des Menschen', *Zeitschrift für Ethnologie*, 27: 723–38.

—— (1899) 'Remarks upon the brain-cast of *Pithecanthropus erectus*', *Proceedings of the Fourth International Congress of Zoology*, Cambridge, 22–27 August 1898, London.

Fox, R. (1967, 1970) *Kinship and Marriage: An Anthropological Perspective*, Harmondsworth: Penguin Books.

Frazer, J.G. (1922, 1963) *The Golden Bough: A Study in Magic and Religion*, London: Macmillan & Co. Ltd (abridged edition).

Gould, S.J. (1989) *Wonderful Life: The Burgess Shale and the Nature of History*, New York: W.W. Norton & Co.

Grimshaw, A. (1989–90) 'A runaway world? Anthropology as public debate', *Cambridge Anthropology*, 13: 75–9.

Haeckel, E. (1874) *Anthropogenie oder Entwicklungsgeschichte des Menschen, Stammesgeschichte des Menschen*, Leipzig: Verlag von Wilhelm Engelman.

—— (1899–1904) *Kunstformen der Natur*, Leipzig und Wien.

—— *Wanderbilder: nach eigenen Aquarellen und Oelgemaelden*, Jena.

Haraway, D. (1989) 'Teddy bear patriarchy: taxidermy and the Garden of Eden', in *Primate Visions: Gender, Race and Nature in the World of Modern Science*, New York: Routledge.

Konrad, G., Konrad, U. and Schneebaum, T. (1981) *Asmat: Leben mit den Ahnen: Steinzeitliche Holzschnitzer unserer Zeit / Asmat: Life with the Ancestors: Stone Age Woodcarvers in Our Time*, Glashütten: F. Brückner.

Krausse, E. (1987) *Ernst Haeckel: Biographien hervorragender Naturwissenschaftler, Techniker und Mediziner*, Leipzig: BSB B.G. Teubner.

Latour, B. (1987) *Science in Action: How to Follow Scientists and Engineers through Society*, Cambridge, Mass.: Harvard University Press.

Macdonald, S. (1993) 'Reconfigurations of knowledge in science museums: ideas of the universal, the national and the individual', paper presented at the ASA Decennial conference, St Catherine's College, Oxford.

—— (1994) 'Authorizing science: public understanding of science in museums', in B. Wynne and A. Irwin (eds), *Science, Technology and Everyday Life*, Cambridge: Cambridge University Press.

Macdonald, S. and Silverstone, R. (1990) 'Taxonomies, stories and readers: rewriting the museums' fictions', *Cultural Studies*, 4 (2): 176–91.

Maher, J.P. (1983) 'Introduction', in K. Koerner (ed.), *Linguistics and Evolutionary Theory: Three Essays by August Schleicher, Ernst Haeckel and Wilhelm Bleek*, Amsterdam / Philadelphia: John Benjamin Publishing Co.

O'Hara, R.J. (1992) 'Telling the tree: narrative representation and the study of evolutionary history', *Biology and Philosophy*, 7: 135–60.

Pama, C. (1987) *Riestap's handboek der Heraldiek. Met heraldische woordenlijst in Frans, Duits, Engels en Afrikans*, Leiden: E.J. Brill.

Richards, R.J. (1992) *The Meaning of Evolution: The Morphological Construction and Ideological Reconstruction of Darwin's Theory*, Chicago and London: University of Chicago Press.

Rivers, W.H.R. (1910, 1968) 'The genealogical method of anthropological inquiry', in *Kinship and Social Organisation*, London: Athlone Press; New York: Humanities Press Inc.

Schleicher, A. (1869) *Darwinism Tested by the Science of Language*, London: John Camden Hotten.

Segalen, M. (ed.) (1991) *Jeux de Familles*, Paris: Presses du CNRS.

Strathern, M. (1992) *After Nature: English Kinship in the Late Twentieth Century*, Cambridge: Cambridge University Press.

Theunissen, B. (1989) *Eugène Dubois and the Ape-man from Java: The History of the First 'Missing Link' and its Discoverer*, Dordrecht: Kluwer Academic Publishers.

Trautmann, T. (1992) 'The revolution in ethnological time', *Man* (n.s.), 27 (2): 379–97.

Vogel, S. (1991) 'Always true to the object, in our fashion', in I. Karp and S.D. Lavine (eds), *Exhibiting Cultures: The Poetics and Politics of Museum Display*, Washington and London: Smithsonian Institution Press.

Watson, A. (1934) *The Early Iconography of the Tree of Jesse*, Oxford: Oxford University Press.

Weaver, K.F. (1985) 'The search for our ancestors', *National Geographic*, November: 560–623.

Werd, G. de (1989) 'Twee koningen uit een Boom-van-Jesse uit een Nederrijns altaar vervaardigd door Kalkarse beeldhouwer Henrik van Holt, omstreeks 1530', *Antiek*, 3, October: 156–65.

3 Building, dwelling, living

How animals and people make themselves at home in the world

Tim Ingold

This chapter is partly autobiographical, and describes my own attempts over the last few years to find a satisfactory way of understanding the relationships between people and their environments. It is incomplete, in two respects. First, it is in the nature of a preliminary sketch. Second, I cannot claim that I have yet found, or will ever find, final answers to the questions that are bothering me. Indeed, if one of the main conclusions of what I have to say is that so-called 'ends' or 'goals' are but landmarks on a journey, then this must apply as much to my own thinking and writing as to everything else that people do in the world. The most fundamental thing about life is that it does not begin here or end there, but is always *going on*. And for the same reason, environments are never complete but are continually under construction. What I shall attempt to do here is to consider the implications of this point with regard to our ideas about the similarities and contrasts between human beings and other animals in the ways in which they go about creating environments for themselves. I am concerned, in particular, with the meaning of architecture, or of that part of the environment which is conventionally described as 'built'.

In recent years, my own ideas have undergone something of a sea change, which is where the autobiographical element comes in. I began with a view that was – and indeed still is – fairly conventional in anthropology, one that sets out from the premise that human beings inhabit discursive worlds of culturally constructed significance, laid out upon the substrate of a continuous and undifferentiated physical terrain. If I differed from my colleagues, at least in social anthropology, it was in my concern to spell out the implications of this premise for the distinction between human beings and non-human animals. I felt sure that the models developed by ecologists and evolutionary biologists to account for the relations between organisms and their environments must apply as well to the human as to any other species, yet it was also clear to me that these models left no space for what seemed to be the most outstanding characteristic of human activity – that it is intentionally motivated. Human intentions, I argued, are constituted in the intersubjective domain, of relationships among *persons*, as distinct from the domain in which human beings, as biological *organisms*, relate to other components of the natural environment. Human life, I therefore proposed, is conducted simultaneously in two domains – a social domain of interpersonal relations and an ecological domain of inter-organismic relations – so that the problem is to understand the interplay between them (Ingold 1986a: 9).

Starting out from two quite reasonable propositions – that human beings are organisms, and that human action is intentionally motivated – I thus ended up with what appeared to be a thoroughly unreasonable result: that unlike all other animals, humans live a split-level existence, half in nature, half out; half organism, half person; half body, half mind. I had come out as an unreconstructed Cartesian dualist, which is perhaps not so surprising when you remember that the intellectual division of labour between the natural sciences and the humanities, and within anthropology between its biological and sociocultural divisions, rests on a Cartesian foundation. Something, I felt, must be wrong somewhere, if the only way to understand our own creative involvement in the world is by taking ourselves out of it. Eventually, it dawned on me that although the problem was an anthropological one, it would require more than an anthropological solution: what is needed is a completely new way of thinking about organisms and about their relations with their environments; in short, a new ecology. And it is towards this new ecology that I am currently groping.

In this task, I have gained inspiration from three principal sources. The first comes from biology, and consists in the work of the handful of courageous scholars, principally developmental biologists, who have been prepared to challenge the hegemony of neo-Darwinian thinking in the discipline (for example Ho and Saunders 1984; see also Oyama 1985). The second lies in what is known as 'ecological psychology', an approach to understanding perception and action that is radically opposed to the cognitivist orientation of the psychological mainstream (Gibson 1979; Michaels and Carello 1981). And the third comes from philosophical writing of a broadly phenomenological bent, above all the works of Heidegger (1971) and Merleau-Ponty (1962). Although developed independently, in the different disciplinary contexts of biology, psychology and philosophy, these three approaches have much in common. Though I cannot now explore the commonalities in detail, I want to highlight just two of them that are rather central to what I shall have to say. First, all three approaches reverse the normal order of priority – normal, that is, in the history of western thought – of form over process. Life, in this perspective, is not the revelation of pre-existent form but the very process wherein form is generated and held in place. Second, the three approaches adopt as their common point of departure the agent-in-its-environment, or what phenomenology calls 'being in the world', as opposed to the self-contained individual confronting a world 'out there'. In short, they maintain that it is through being lived in, rather than through having been constructed along the lines of some formal design, that the world becomes a meaningful environment for people.

In what follows, I refer to this position as the 'dwelling perspective', by contrast to the more conventional position from which I began, and which I shall call the 'building perspective' (Ingold 1991). Thus the movement in my own thinking has been from the building perspective to the dwelling perspective. To document this movement, I shall start by spelling out the first of these perspectives, and its implications for the way we understand the construction of the built environment, in greater depth. I shall then explain what is entailed in adopting a dwelling perspective in its place. Finally, I shall consider how this shift from a building perspective to a dwelling perspective bears upon the concept and meaning of architecture.

CONSTRUCTING ENVIRONMENTS AND MAKING WORLDS

Our initial problem may be framed by juxtaposing two statements, the first of which will be familiar to anthropological readers, the second much less so. 'Man', Clifford Geertz has declared, 'is an animal suspended in webs of significance he himself has spun' (1973: 5). One is led to suppose that non-human animals are not so suspended. Spiders spin webs, and do indeed suspend themselves in them, but their webs are tangible objects – they catch flies, not thoughts. But now consider this passage from the delightful but little known text of Jakob von Uexküll, 'A stroll through the worlds of animals and men': 'As the spider spins its threads, every subject spins his relations to certain characters of the things around him, and weaves them into a firm web which carries his existence' (1957: 14). Now the subjects of which von Uexküll speaks are not merely human, nor even close to human. Indeed he begins his stroll with a particular species of parasitic tick! If, as it would seem, what Geertz says of humankind applies equally to ticks, then what – if anything – *does* distinguish human from non-human environments?

Though it might be said, with Nelson Goodman (1978), that human beings are makers of worlds, this only begs the question of how human acts of world-making differ from the processes whereby non-human animals fashion their environments. It was this question that initially led me to focus on the meaning of the built environment: not, that is, on what a built environment means, but on what it means to say that an environment is built. How can we distinguish an environment that is built from one that is not? It is all very well to define the built environment, as do Lawrence and Low in a recent review, to include 'any physical alteration of the natural environment, from hearths to cities, through construction by humans' (1990: 454). But why should the products of human building activity be any different, in principle, from the constructions of other animals? Or to phrase the same question in another way, by what right do we conventionally identify the artificial with the 'man-made'? And where, in an environment that bears the imprint of human activity, can we draw the line between what is, and is not, a house, or a building, or an instance of architecture?

My first efforts to deal with these questions all hinged on a crucial distinction, which I thought quite unproblematic at the time, between design and execution. The argument ran roughly as follows: imagine a mollusc shell, a beaver's lodge and a human house. All have been regarded, at one time or another, as instances of architecture. Some authors would restrict architecture to the house, others would include the lodge – as an example of 'animal architecture' (von Frisch 1975) – but exclude the shell, others would include all three forms. The usual argument for excluding the shell is that it is attached to the body of the mollusc, whereas for something to count as an artifact it must be detached from the body. The shell, it is said, 'just grows' – there is nothing the mollusc can or need do about it. The beaver, by contrast, works hard to put its lodge together: the lodge is a product of the beaver's 'beavering', of its activity. Likewise the house is a product of the activities of its human builders. In their respective forms, and levels of complexity, they need not be that different (Figure 3.1). Should we, then, conclude that the lodge is beaver-made just as much as the house is man-made?

To this question I answered in the negative (Ingold 1986b: 345–6; 1988: 90). Wherever they are, beavers construct the same kinds of lodges and, so far as we know, have always done so. Human beings, by contrast, build houses of very diverse kinds, and although certain house forms have persisted for long periods, there is unequivocal evidence that these forms have also undergone significant historical change. The difference between the lodge and the house lies, I argued, not in the construction of the thing itself, but in the origination of the *design* that governs the construction process. The design of the lodge is incorporated into the same programme that underwrites the development of the beaver's own body: thus the beaver is no more the designer of the lodge than is the mollusc the designer of its shell. It is merely the *executor* of a design that has evolved, along with the morphology and behaviour of the beaver, through a process of variation under natural selection. In other words, both the beaver – in its outward, pheno-typic form – and the lodge are 'expressions' of the same underlying genotype. Dawkins (1982) has coined the term 'extended phenotype' to refer to genetic effects that are situated beyond the body of the organism, and in this sense, the lodge is part of the extended phenotype for the beaver.

Human beings, on the other hand, are the authors of their own designs, constructed through a self-conscious decision process – an intentional selection of ideas. As Joseph Rykwert has recently put it: 'unlike even the most elaborate animal construction, human building involves decision and choice, always and inevitably; it therefore involves a project' (1991: 56). It is to this project, I maintained, that we refer when we say that the house is *made*, rather than merely constructed. I even went so far as to extend the argument to the domain of toolmaking, criticising students of animal behaviour for their assumption that wherever objects are manifestly being modified or constructed for future use, tools are being made. They are only being made, I claimed, when they are constructed in the imagination prior to their realisation in the material (Ingold 1986a: 40–78). But if the essence of making lies in the self-conscious authorship of design, that is in the construction of a project, it follows that things can be made without undergoing any actual physical alteration at all. Suppose that you need to knock in a nail but lack a hammer. Looking around the objects in your environment, you deliberately select something best suited to your purpose: it

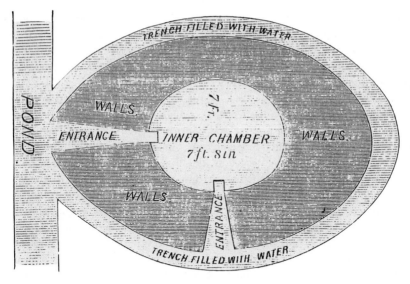

Figure 3.1a Ground plan of beaver lodge
Source: Morgan 1868: 142

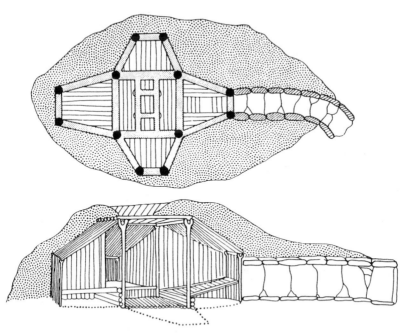

Figure 3.1b Floor plan and cross-section of Eskimo house, Mackenzie region
Source: Mauss and Beuchat 1979: 41

must be hard, have a flat striking surface, fit in the hand, and so on. So you pick up an appropriate stone. In this very selection, the stone has 'become' a hammer in that, in your mind's eye, a 'hammer-quality' has been attached to it. Without altering the stone in any way, you have made a hammer out of it. In just the same manner, a cave may come to serve as a dwelling, a stretch of bare flat land as an airstrip, or a sheltered bay as a harbour.

To deal with situations of this kind, I chose the term *co-option*. Thus the stone was co-opted, rather than constructed, to become a hammer. It follows that there are two kinds of making: co-optive and constructive. In co-optive making an already existing object is fitted to a conceptual image of an intended future use, in the mind of a user. In constructive making this procedure is reversed, in that the object is physically remodelled to conform more closely to the pre-existing image. Indeed it seemed that the history of things – of artifacts, architecture and landscapes – could be understood in terms of successive, alternating steps of co-option and construction. We press into service what we find around us to suit our current purposes, we proceed to modify those things to our own design so that they better serve these purposes, but at the same time our objectives, or adaptive requirements, also change so that the modified objects are subsequently co-opted to quite other projects for which they are perceived to come in handy, and so on and on. Exactly the same model has been applied to account for the evolution of organisms; Darwin himself used it in his book on orchids (1862: 348). To adopt terms suggested by Gould and Vrba (1982), structures *ad*apted for one purpose may be *ex*apted for another, subsequently undergoing further adaptation, etc. The difference is just that in the case of organic evolution, the selection involved is natural rather than intentional (Ingold 1986b: 200–2).

It was in searching around for ways to express these ideas that I came across the writings of Jakob von Uexküll, Estonian-born aristocrat and a founding figure in the fields of both ethology and semiotics, to whose 'A stroll through the worlds of animals and men', first published in 1934, I have already referred. Reacting against the mechanistic biology of the day, von Uexküll argued that to treat the animal as a mere assemblage of sensory and motor organs is to leave out the subject who uses these organs as tools, respectively, of perception and action:

> We who still hold that our sense organs serve our perceptions, and our motor organs our actions, see in animals . . . not only the mechanical structure, but also the operator, who is built into their organs, as we are into our bodies. We can no longer regard animals as mere machines, but as subjects whose essential activity consists in perceiving and acting. . . . All that a subject perceives becomes his perceptual world and all that he does, his effector world. Perceptual and effector worlds together form a closed unit, the *Umwelt*.
> (1957: 6)

For von Uexküll, the *Umwelt* – that is, the world as constituted within the specific life activity of an animal – was to be clearly distinguished from the environment, by which he meant the surroundings of the animal as these appear to the indifferent human observer. We human beings cannot enter directly into the *Umwelten* of other creatures, but through close study we may be able to imagine what they are like. But the reverse does not hold: the non-human animal, because it cannot detach its consciousness from its own life-activity, because it is always submerged within its own *Umwelt*, cannot see objects as such, for what they are in themselves. Thus for the animal, the environment – conceived as a domain of 'neutral objects' – cannot exist (Ingold 1992a: 43).

Towards the end of his stroll, von Uexküll invites his readers to imagine the manifold inhabitants of an oak tree. There is the fox, who has built its lair between the roots; the owl, who perches in the crotch of its mighty limbs; the squirrel, for whom it provides a veritable maze of ladders and springboards; the ant, who forages in the furrows and crags of its bark; the wood-boring beetle who feeds and lays its eggs in passages beneath the bark, and hundreds of others (Figures 3.2 and 3.3). Each creature, through the sheer fact of its presence, confers on the tree, or on some portion of it, a particular quality or 'functional tone': shelter and protection for the fox, support for the owl, a thoroughfare for the squirrel, hunting grounds for the ant, egg-laying facilities for the beetle. The same tree thus figures quite differently within the respective *Umwelten* of its diverse inhabitants. But for none of them does it exist *as a tree* (von Uexküll 1957: 76–9). Now consider the forester, who is measuring up the tree to estimate the volume of timber it will yield. For him, the tree figures as a potential source of valuable raw material, whereas for the little child – again to follow von Uexküll's example (ibid.: 73–5) – it seems to be alive and to reveal a frightening aspect. But these different perceptions are not tied, as they are for non-human animals, to the *modus operandi* of the organism. Human beings do not construct the world in a certain way by virtue of what they are, but by virtue of their own conceptions of the possibilities of being. And these possibilities are limited only by the power of the imagination.

Herein, it seemed to me, lay the essential distinction I was seeking between the respective ways in which the subjective existence of human and non-human animals is suspended in 'webs of significance'. For the non-human, every thread in the web is a relation between it and some object or feature of the environment, a relation that is set up through its own practical immersion in the world and the bodily orientations that this entails. For the human, by contrast, the web – and the relations of which it consists – is inscribed in a separate plane of mental representations, forming a tapestry of meaning that *covers over* the world of environmental objects. Whereas the non-human animal perceives these objects as immediately available for use, to human beings they appear initially as occurrent phenomena to which potential uses must be affixed, prior to any attempt at engagement. The fox discovers shelter in the roots of a tree, but the forester sees timber only in his mind's eye, and has first to fit that image in thought to his perception of the occurrent object – the tree – before taking action. Or to take another example, suggested recently by Maurice Bloch, the 'swidden plot' exists as an image in the mind of the horticulturist, who has to match that image to an

Figure 3.2 Fox, owl and oak tree

Source: von Uexküll 1957: 76–7, illustrations by G. Kriszat (reproduced by permission of International Universities Press)

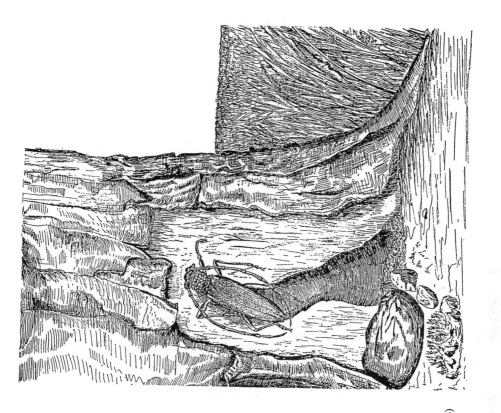

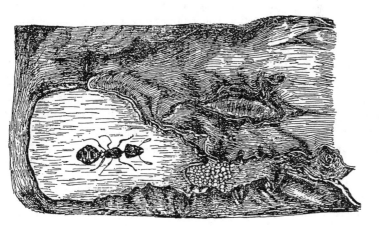

Figure 3.3 Ant, bark-boring beetle and oak tree

Source: von Uexküll 1957: 78–9, illustrations by G. Kriszat (reproduced by permission of International Universities Press)

observed stand of uncut forest prior to transforming it into a field (Bloch 1991: 187). As mental representations, the timber and the swidden plot belong to the 'intentional worlds' (cf. Shweder 1990: 2) of the forester and the farmer; as occurrent phenomena, the oak tree and the stand of forest belong to the physical environment of 'neutral objects'. It has been conventional, in anthropological and other writings of western academic provenance, to refer to these worlds, of human values and purposes on the one hand, and of physical objects on the other, by means of the shorthand terms, culture and nature, respectively. And in a paper written in 1987, I concluded that 'making is equivalent to the cultural ordering of nature – the inscription of ideal design upon the material world of things' (Ingold 1989: 506). This statement, I confess, is now a source of considerable embarrassment.

THE BUILDING PERSPECTIVE

In my defence, I can only say that I was singing a tune that has been sung by most anthropologists in one form or another, for decades, in the context of an encounter with students of animal behaviour whose theories had no place for agency or intentionality at all, except as an epiphenomenal effect of innate predisposition. This tune is what I earlier called the 'building perspective', and I should now like to elaborate on this perspective with reference to anthropological work other than my own. For a founding statement, we could turn once again to Geertz, and to his assertion that culture – or at least that kind of culture taken to be the hallmark of humanity – consists in 'the imposition of an arbitrary framework of symbolic meaning upon reality' (1964: 39). Reality, that which is imposed upon, is en-visioned here as an external world of nature, a source of raw materials and sensations for diverse projects of cultural construction. Following from this, a distinction is commonly made between the 'real' environment that is given independently of the senses, and the 'perceived' environment as it is recon-structed in the mind through the ordering of sense data in terms of acquired, cognitive schemata. Other conventional oppositions that encode the same distinc-tion are between 'etic' and 'emic', and between 'operational' and 'cognised'. The starting point in all such accounts is an imagined *separation* between the perceiver and the world, such that the perceiver has to reconstruct the world, in the mind, prior to any meaningful engagement with it.

Here, then, is the essence of the building perspective: that worlds are made before they are lived in; or in other words, that acts of dwelling are preceded by acts of world-making. A good example of this approach comes from the intro-duction to Maurice Godelier's book, *The Mental and the Material* (1986). Here, Godelier is concerned with the proper translation of the Marxian concepts *Grundlage* and *Überbau*, usually rendered in English as 'infrastructure' and 'superstructure'. He likens the *Überbau* to a building: 'The *Überbau* is a construction, an edifice which rises on foundations, *Grundlage*; and it [the *Überbau*] is the house we live in, not the foundations' (pp. 6–7). Human beings, then, inhabit the various houses of culture, pre-erected upon the universal ground of nature, including the universals of *human* nature. For another example, I would like to turn to Peter Wilson's *The Domestication of the Human Species* (1988). In this book, Wilson argues that the most significant turning point in human social evolution came at the moment when people began to live in houses. Roughly speaking, this marks a division between hunters and gatherers, on the one hand, and agriculturalists and urban dwellers, on the other. 'Hunter-gatherers', Wilson writes, 'create for themselves only the flimsiest architectural context, and only the faintest line divides their living space from nature'. All other societies, by contrast, 'live in an architecturally modified environment', inhabiting houses and villages of a relatively enduring kind, structures that – even when abandoned – leave an almost indelible impression on the landscape. In essence, Wilson is distinguishing between societies with architecture and societies without it.

This is a bold generalisation, and like all such, it is an easy target for empirical refutation. That is not my concern, however. I am, rather, concerned to expose the assumptions entailed in making the distinction between an 'architecturally modified environment' and what is simply called 'nature'. For it is on this distinction that Wilson's entire argument rests. One objection to it immediately comes to mind. To be sure, the physical arrangement and formal properties of a hunter-gatherer encampment may be very different from those of a permanent village settlement. By way of example, compare the plan, shown in Figure 3.4, of the Mbuti Pygmy camp of Apa Lelo, in the Ituri forest of Zaire, with the plans shown in Figure 3.5 of the ancient Mesopotamian village site of Tell es-Sawwan. In the first case the spatial structure of settlement is loose, informal, and sensitive to the changing state of interpersonal relations between cliques, hosts and visitors. In the second it is tightly packed, geometrically regular, and appears to impose fairly tight constraints on the disposition of people and activities. Moreover, compared with the substantial buildings of the village settlement, the constructions of the hunter-gatherers are scarcely more than shades and windbreaks. Most of life, for hunter-gatherers, goes on around dwellings rather than in them. Nevertheless, the fact remains that hunter-gatherers do build shelters of various kinds. So who are we to say that they have no architecture? And if they do not, how are we to comprehend their building activity?

The answer that emerges from Wilson's account is that among hunter-gatherers, erecting shelters is one of a suite of activities, along with food-collecting, cooking, toolmaking and repair, childminding, and so on, that constitute the daily round for these people. Thus building activity is part and parcel of life in an environment that is already *given* in nature, and that has not itself been artificially engineered. With village architecture, by contrast, nature has to a degree been covered over or transformed, so that what immediately confronts people is not a natural environment but – in Wilson's words – 'an environment of their own making, the cultural' (1988: 8). If hunter-gatherers build as part of their adaptation to the given conditions of the natural environment, villagers adapt to the conditions of an environment that is already built.

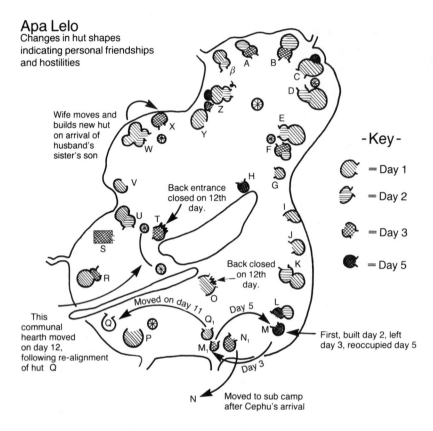

Apa Lelo
Changes in hut shapes
indicating personal friendships
and hostilities

Wife moves and
builds new hut
on arrival of
husband's
sister's son

Back entrance
closed on 12th
day.

Back closed
on 12th
day.

This
communal
hearth moved
on day 12,
following re-alignment
of hut Q

Moved on day 11

Day 5

Day 3

First, built day 2, left
day 3, reoccupied day 5

Moved to sub camp
after Cephu's arrival

- Key -

= Day 1

= Day 2

= Day 3

= Day 5

Figure 3.4 The Mbuti Pygmy camp of Apa Lelo

Source: Turnbull 1965: 357

Either way, the environment is given in advance, as a kind of container for life to occupy. Where, as among hunter-gatherers, building is a part of everyday life, it is not supposed to have any lasting impact on the environment; where, as among villagers, the environment has been manifestly built, the buildings are apparently made before life begins in them. This, of course, is the architect's perspective: plan and build the houses, then import the people to occupy them.

What, then, of the dwellings of nomadic pastoralists? A recent study comparing pastoral tent dwellings and village houses in Turkey and Iran by the archaeologist, Roger Cribb (1991), found that despite differences in the building materials used and the flexibility they afford, the tent and the house were virtually identical in their underlying organisational templates. What really distinguished the house from the tent was the degree to which the imposed cultural design – shared by villagers and nomads alike – is actually translated into enduring, material structures. For such structures do not get built overnight; they grow

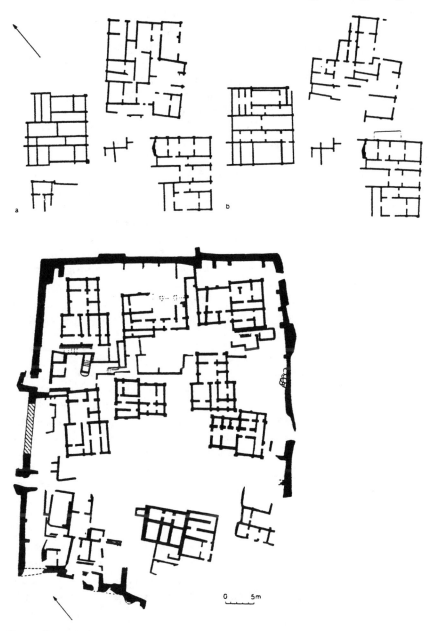

Figure 3.5 Building plans of three periods from the ancient Mesopotamian site of Tell es-Sawwan

Source: Maisels 1990: 162

cumulatively in the course of a settlement's continuous occupation, such that 'each new alteration or addition builds on a series of existing structures'. But in the case of a pastoral nomadic camp, 'each occupation is a fresh event', so that the camp 'has no such history but remains permanently retarded in the initial stages of the normal developmental cycle [of the settlement]' (1991: 156). Thus, although pastoralists carry a basic organisational template with them, there is little opportunity for its enduring physical realisation before the camp picks up and moves off somewhere else, where the occupation process starts all over again. In such cases, building never proceeds beyond the first phase of temporary habitation (Ingold 1992b: 795–6).

In a statement that epitomises the building perspective, Amos Rapoport writes that 'the organisation of space cognitively precedes its material expression; settings and built environments are thought before they are built' (1994: 488). In the case of villagers, the environment is ready-built. In the case of nomadic pastoralists, it would seem, the environment, though thought, is never more than partially built. And as for the hunter-gatherers, it appears that the building hardly gets started at all: indeed Rapoport refers to the camp sites of Aboriginal people of the Australian Central Desert as exemplars of the situation where the environment is thought but *never* built. On these grounds they are supposed to inhabit a 'natural' rather than an 'artificial' environment. Wilson spells out the contrast in the following passage:

> The hunter/gatherer pins ideas and emotions on to the world as it exists: the landscape is turned into a mythical topographic map, a grid of ancestor tracks and sacred sites, as is typical among Australian Aborigines. . . . A construction is put upon the landscape rather than the landscape undergoing reconstruction, as is the case among sedentary peoples, who impose houses, villages, and gardens on the landscape, often in place of natural landmarks. Where nomads read or even find cosmological features in an already existing landscape, villagers tend to represent and model cosmic ideas in the structures they build.
>
> (1988: 50)

THE SEARCH FOR ORIGINS

Having spelled out the essence of the building perspective, let me now return to my earlier observation, comparing the forms of the beaver's lodge and the human house, that the first is tied, as it were, to the nature of the beaver itself, whereas the second is both historically and regionally variable. Among non-human animals, it is widely supposed, there can be no significant change in built form that is not bound to evolutionary changes in the essential form of the species. With human beings, by contrast, built form is free to vary independently of biological constraint, and to follow developmental pathways of its own, effectively decoupled from the process of evolution. In his famous paper of 1917, on 'The super-organic', Alfred Kroeber declared: 'Who would be so rash as to affirm that ten thousand generations of example would convert the beaver from what he is into a carpenter or a bricklayer – or, allowing for his physical deficiency in the lack of hands, into a planning engineer!' (1952: 31). Yet human beings, through practice, example and a good measure of ingenuity, coupled with their ability to transmit their acquired know-how across the generations and to preserve it in long-term memory, have learned all these trades, and many more besides.

However, this argument implies some kind of threshold in the evolution of our own kind, at which point our ancestors were sufficiently endowed with the qualities of intelligence and manual dexterity to become the authors of their own projects of building. From this point the history of architecture must have 'taken off', leading from the earliest dwellings to the modern construction industry, without entailing any further change in the species-specific form of the human organism. But what *was* the earliest dwelling? According to Kenneth Bock, an event in the history of architecture – such as the construction of a Gothic vault – differs from an event in the evolution of species 'in that the former involves formation of intent or purpose on the part of an actor while the latter does not' (1980: 182). The same idea is implied by Joseph Rykwert when he suggests that the essence of architecture lies in 'taking thought about building' (1991: 54). But how did it come about that, at some decisive moment, our ancestors began to think about what they built?

As Rykwert shows, in his study of the notion of the 'primitive hut' in the history of architecture, this is a question that has long exercised the minds of western thinkers. And the title of his book, *On Adam's House in Paradise* (1972), nicely conveys the mythic quality of the many speculative answers that have been proposed. Reproduced in Figure 3.6 is one of the more delightful images of 'the first hut', taken from the work of the great French architectural theorist, Eugène Viollet-le-Duc, *Histoire de l'habitation humaine*, published in 1875 (Viollet-le-Duc 1990: 26). Architecture began, for Viollet-le-Duc, when the problem of the need for shelter was met through the procedures of rational planning. In his tale of the building of the first hut, the secret is revealed to a hapless primitive tribe, the Nairitti, by a progressive time-traveller by the name of Epergos, an earlier incarnation of our own Dr Who, as a gift of his superior intelligence. For Viollet-le-Duc, as for many others, Rykwert notes, it was 'the difference of conception, the attachment of meaning to his task, that distinguishes man's first attempts [at building] from those of the instinctually driven beasts' (1972: 22). These attempts may have been decidedly inferior to the constructions of animals, but nevertheless they marked the turning point at which humanity was set upon the road to culture and civilisation.

The search for the first building continues to this day, though it is informed by a much better knowledge both of the archaeological traces left by early human or hominid populations, and of the behaviour of those species of animals – namely the great apes – most closely related to humankind. One of the most peculiar and distinctive aspects of the behaviour of chimpanzees, gorillas and orang-utans is their habit of building so-called 'nests'. In functional terms, they are not really

Figure 3.6 The first hut

Source: Viollet-le-Duc 1990: 26

nests at all: every individual animal builds its own nest afresh, each evening, and uses it for the sole purpose of sleeping. Nor does the nest site mark any kind of fixed point in the animal's movements; it may be built anywhere, and is abandoned the next morning (Groves and Sabater Pi 1985: 23). Nevertheless, assuming that the common ancestor of apes and humans would have had a similar habit, attempts have been made to trace an evolutionary continuum from this nesting behaviour to the residential arrangements of prototypical human groups (of which the camps of contemporary hunter-gatherers have frequently been taken as the closest exemplars, on the grounds of the presumed similarity of ecological context).

Comparing the nesting patterns of apes with the camping patterns of human hunter-gatherers, Colin Groves and J. Sabater Pi note some striking differences. The human 'nest', if we may call it that, is a fixed point for the movements of its several occupants, and a place to which they regularly return. In other words, it has the attributes of what the ethologist, Heini Hediger (1977: 181), would call 'home': it is a 'goal of flight' and a 'place of maximal security'. There is a difference, too, in the respective ways in which apes and humans go about building their accommodation. For one thing, apes use material that comes immediately to hand, normally by a skilful interweaving of growing vegetation to form an oval-shaped, concave bed; whereas humans collect suitable materials from a distance, prior to their assembly into a convex, self-supporting structure. For another thing, the ape makes its nest by bending the vegetation around its own body; whereas the human builds a hut, and then enters it (Groves and Sabater Pi 1985: 45). There is a sense, as Hediger remarks, in which apes build from the 'bottom up', seeking support for rest and sleeping, whereas humans build from the 'top down', seeking shelter from sun, rain or wind (1977: 184). Yet there are also remarkable similarities between ape and human living arrangements, in the overall number and layout of nests or huts and in the underlying social organisation, and on the grounds of these similarities, Groves and Sabater Pi feel justified in arguing that human campsites are but elaborations of a generalised ape pattern. All the critical differences – the functioning of the site as a home-base, the collection of material prior to construction, the technique of building from the outside – can be put down, they think, to one factor, namely the human ability 'to visualise objects in new configurations, and to bring these configurations into being on the basis of that mental picture' (1985: 45).

Though in substance based on fact rather than fantasy, the form in which this argument is cast is virtually identical to that of Viollet-le-Duc's tale of the building of the first hut. Equipped, albeit by natural selection rather than providential intervention, with foresight and intelligence, the first builders set to work to execute a plan that was already formed as a picture in their imagination. They had solved the problem of shelter in their minds, prior to putting the solution into practical effect. It is in this light that we can understand the extraordinary significance that has been attached to the so-called 'stone circle' discovered at the famous site of Olduvai Gorge in Tanzania, and dated to some 1.75 million years ago (Figure 3.7). In her interpretation of the circle, Mary Leakey writes that in its general appearance, it 'resembles temporary structures often made by present-day nomadic peoples who build a low stone wall round their dwellings to serve either as a windbreak or as a base to support upright branches which are bent over and covered with either skins or grass' (1971: 24). A photograph of such a dwelling, from the Okombambi people of Southwest Africa, is provided to substantiate the comparison. As always in these matters, the specific interpretation has been challenged. What has not been challenged, however, is the frame of mind that leads us to suppose that if the interpretation were correct, we would have at last discovered the *real* 'first hut', and with it not just the origins of architecture, but the point of transition to true humanity.

For it is the structure of our thought, not the patterning of the archaeological record, that sets up a point of origin at the intersection of two axes, one of evolutionary change – leading from ancestral pongid and hominid forms to what are known in the trade as 'anatomically modern humans', the other of historical change – leading from Palaeolithic hunter-gatherers to modern industrial science and civilisation (Ingold 1992b: 791). To explode the myth of the first hut thus requires nothing less than the dissolution of the dichotomy, which in modern scholarship separates the biological sciences from the humanities, between

Figure 3.7 The 'stone circle' from Bed I of Olduvai Gorge

Source: Leakey 1971, Figure 7 (reproduced by permission of Cambridge University Press)

evolution and history, or between the temporal processes of nature and culture. Before indicating how this might be done, I need to introduce what I have called the 'dwelling perspective'.

THE DWELLING PERSPECTIVE

For this purpose I turn to Martin Heidegger's evocative essay, 'Building dwelling thinking', on which I have drawn for my title (1971: 145–61). In this essay, Heidegger asks what it means to build and to dwell, and what the relation is between these two – between building and dwelling. He begins with what might be taken as the orthodox view, as enshrined in the discourse of western modernity. This is that building and dwelling are separable but complementary activities, related as means to ends. We build houses so that we may dwell in them (or, as is usual in industrial society, some people build houses for other people to live in). To dwell, in this sense, means merely 'to occupy a house, a dwelling place'. The building is a *container* for life activities, or more strictly for certain life activities, since there are other kinds of activity that go on outside houses, or even in the open air. Yet, Heidegger asks, 'do the houses in themselves hold any guarantee that *dwelling* occurs in them?' (1971: 146). To clarify matters, let us call the physical structure, the building in itself, the *house*; and the setting within which people dwell the *home* (cf. Lawrence 1987). Heidegger's question can then be rephrased as follows: what does it take for a house to be a home? Merely to pose the question in this form suggests that there must be more to dwelling than the mere fact of occupation. What, then, does it mean, 'to dwell'?

Heidegger tackles the issue through an exercise in etymology. The current German word for the verb 'to build', *bauen*, comes from the Old English and High German *buan*, meaning 'to dwell'. Though this original meaning has been lost, it is preserved in such compounds as the English 'neighbour', meaning one who dwells nearby. Moreover, this sense of dwelling was not limited to one sphere of activity among many – to domestic life, say, as opposed to work or travel. Rather it encompassed the whole manner in which one lived one's life on the earth; thus 'I dwell, you dwell' is identical to 'I am, you are'. Yet *bauen* has another sense: to preserve, to care for, or more specifically to cultivate or to till the soil. And then there is the third sense: to construct, to make something, to raise up an edifice. Both these modern senses of building – as cultivation and as construction – are thus shown to be encompassed within the more fundamental sense of dwelling. In the course of time, however, this underlying sense has fallen into disuse, such that *bauen* has come to be reserved exclusively for cultivation and construction. Having forgotten how the latter activities are grounded in dwelling, modern thought then *rediscovers* dwelling as the occupation of a world already built.

In short, where before, building was circumscribed within dwelling, the position now appears reversed, with dwelling circumscribed within building. Heidegger's concern is to regain that original perspective, so that we can once again understand how the activities of building – of cultivation and construction – belong to our dwelling in the world, to the way we are. 'We do not dwell because we have built, but we build and have built because we dwell, that is because we are dwellers. . . . To build is in itself already to dwell. . . . *Only if we are capable of dwelling, only then can we build*' (Heidegger 1971: 148, 146, 160, original emphases). I take this to be the founding statement of the dwelling perspective. What it means is that the forms people build, whether in the imagination or on the ground, arise within the current of their involved activity, in the specific relational contexts of their practical engagement with their surroundings. Building, then, cannot be understood as a simple process of transcription, of a pre-existing design of the final product on to a raw material substrate. It is true that human beings – perhaps uniquely among animals – have the capacity to envision forms in advance of their implementation, but this envisioning is itself an activity carried on by real people in a real-world environment, rather than by a disembodied intellect moving in the subjective space delimited by the puzzles it sets out to solve (Ingold 1993a: 466). In short, people do not import their ideas, plans or mental representations into the world, since that very world, to borrow a phrase from Merleau-Ponty (1962: 24), is the homeland of their thoughts. Only because they already dwell therein can they think the thoughts they do.

To argue that the forms of buildings arise as a kind of crystallisation of human activity within an environment clearly puts paid to my initial dichotomy between design and execution. No longer can we assume, with Christopher Alexander, that form is 'the ultimate object of design' (1964: 15), as though the one issued quite automatically and unproblematically from the other. To the contrary, a dwelling perspective ascribes the generation of form to those very processes whose creativity is denied by that perspective which sees in every form the concrete realisation of an intellectual solution to a design problem. Where, then, does this leave the constructions of non-human animals? The argument is equally damaging to the conventional biological account, which holds that the outward, phenotypic form – not just of the animal itself, but of the constructions making up its 'extended phenotype' – is the realisation or expression of an inner design specification, the genotype, that the animal is supposed to receive as a 'biological endowment' at the point of conception, coded in the materials of heredity – the genes. That design is thus imported into the organism, as a kind of 'evolved architecture' (Tooby and Cosmides 1992), prior to the organism's development within an environmental context, is one of the great delusions of modern biology.[1] To be sure, every organism begins life with its complement of DNA in the genome, but on its own, DNA 'specifies' nothing. There is no 'reading' of the genetic code that is not itself part of the organism's development in its environment. And of course, the organism does not begin life only with DNA. What is literally passed on from one generation to the next, as Susan Oyama has pointed out, 'is a genome and a segment of the world' (1985: 43). Together these constitute a developmental system, and it is in the unfolding of this system, in the course of the life-cycle of the organism, that form emerges and is sustained.

The implications of this argument for evolutionary theory are profound. It means that animals, through their own activities, can participate actively in the evolutionary process by establishing the environmental contexts of development for their successors. For example the beaver incorporates in its own bodily orientations and patterns of activity a set of relations with an environment that has been cumulatively shaped by the activities of its predecessors, and that it will shape in turn. And indeed the same goes for human beings. Human children, like the young of many other species, grow up in environments furnished by the work of previous generations, and as they do so they come literally to carry the forms of their dwelling in their bodies – in specific skills, sensibilities and dispositions. But they do not carry them in their genes, nor is it necessary to invoke some other kind of vehicle for the inter-generational transmission of information – cultural rather than genetic – to account for the diversity of human living arrangements. It is the very notion of information, that form is *brought in* to environmental contexts of development, that is at fault here. For as we have seen, it is within such contexts, in the movement of human beings' (or non-human animals') practical engagement with the components of their surroundings, that form is generated.

We can now see how, by adopting a dwelling perspective – that is, by taking the animal-in-its-environment rather than the self-contained individual as our point of departure – it is possible to dissolve the orthodox dichotomies between evolution and history, and between biology and culture. For if history be understood as the process wherein people, through their own intentional and creative activities, shape the conditions of development for their successors, then it is but a specific instance of a process that is going on throughout the organic world. And if by cultural variation we mean those differences of embodied knowledge that stem from the diversity of local developmental contexts, then far from being superimposed upon a substrate of evolved human universals, such variation is part and parcel of the variation of all living things, which has its source in their involvement within a continuous field of relations. We do not, then, need to invoke one theory, of biological evolution, to account for the transition from nest to hut, and another, of cultural history, to account for the transition from hut to skyscraper. Once we come to recognise that history is but the continuation of an evolutionary process by another name, the point of origin constituted by the intersection of evolutionary and historical continua disappears, and the search for the first hut – for the beginnings of architecture, history and true humanity – becomes a quest after an illusion.

THE HOUSE AS ORGANISM

Let me conclude by returning to von Uexküll's oak tree. Suppose that it stands, not in the forest, but in the precincts of a house. Now at first glance we might have no hesitation in regarding the house, but not the tree, as a building, or an instance of architecture. For surely the house, as Godelier puts it, belongs to 'that part of nature which is transformed by human action and thought [and] owes its existence to conscious human action on nature' (1986: 5). The tree, on the other hand, has no such debt to humanity, for it has grown there, rooted to the spot, entirely of its own accord. On closer inspection, however, this distinction between those parts of the environment that are, respectively, built and unbuilt seems far less clear (Ingold 1993b). For the form of the tree is no more given, as an immutable fact of nature, than is the form of the house an imposition of the human mind. Recall the many inhabitants of the tree: the fox, the owl, the squirrel, the ant, the beetle, among countless others. All, through their various activities of dwelling, have played their part in creating the conditions under which the tree, over the centuries, has grown to assume its particular form and proportions. And so, too, have human beings, in tending the tree's surroundings, or even more directly, in pruning its branches.

But the house also has many and diverse animal inhabitants – more, perhaps, than we are inclined to recognise. Sometimes special provision is made for them, such as the kennel, stable or dovecote. Others find shelter and sustenance in its nooks and crannies, or even build there. And all, in their various ways, contribute to its evolving form, as do the house's human inhabitants in keeping it under repair, decorating it, or making structural alterations in response to their changing domestic circumstances. Thus the distinction between the house and the tree is not an absolute but a relative one, relative, that is, to the scope of human involvement in the form-generating process. Houses, as Suzanne Blier notes (1987: 2), are living organisms. Like trees, they have life histories, which consist in the unfolding of their relations with both human and non-human components of their environments. To the extent that the influence of the human component prevails, any feature of the environment will seem more like a building; to the extent that the non-human component prevails, it will seem less so. Thus does the house, following its abandonment by its human occupants, become a ruin.

Building, then, is a process that is continually going on, for as long as people dwell in an environment. It does not begin here, with a pre-formed plan, and end there, with a finished artifact. The 'final form' is but a fleeting moment in the life of any feature, when it is matched to a human purpose, likewise cut out from the flow of intentional activity. As the philosopher Alfred North Whitehead once remarked, 'from the moment of birth we are immersed in action, and can only fitfully guide it by taking thought' (1938: 217). And this applies, with equal force, to 'taking thought about building', the definitive characteristic of the architectural attitude. We may indeed describe the forms in our environment as instances of architecture, but for the most part we are not architects. For it is in the very process of dwelling that we build.

ACKNOWLEDGEMENTS

This is the latest in a long series of attempts to write this paper. Earlier versions were presented to the workshop on 'Constructing Environments', organised by the RAI Biological and Social Anthropology Committee in January 1991, to the graduate seminar of the Department of Social Anthropology at the University of Bergen, and to the seminars of the International Centre for Contemporary Cultural Research and the Department of Architecture at the University of Manchester. I am grateful for the many helpful comments received from participants on all these occasions. Needless to say, and despite the efforts of all these people, I still haven't got it right.

NOTE

1 I have shown elsewhere, and cannot go into the reasons here (cf. Ingold 1995), that the genotype exists nowhere except in the imagination of biologists, as a context-independent specification of organic form derived by abstraction from the observed characteristics of organisms as they actually appear.

REFERENCES

Alexander, C. (1964) *Notes on the Synthesis of Form*, Cambridge, Mass.: Harvard University Press.
Blier, S.P. (1987) *The Anatomy of Architecture*, Cambridge: Cambridge University Press.
Bloch, M. (1991) 'Language, anthropology and cognitive science', *Man* (n.s.), 26: 183–98.
Bock, K. (1980) *Human Nature and History*, New York: Columbia University Press.
Cribb, R. (1991) *Nomads in Archaeology*, Cambridge: Cambridge University Press.
Darwin, C. (1862) *On the Various Contrivances by which British and Foreign Orchids are Fertilised by Insects*, London: John Murray.
Dawkins, R. (1982) *The Extended Phenotype*, San Francisco: Freeman.
Frisch, K. von (1975) *Animal Architecture*, London: Hutchinson.
Geertz, C. (1964) 'The transition to humanity', in S. Tax (ed.), *Horizons of Anthropology*, Chicago: Aldine.
—— (1973) *The Interpretation of Cultures*, New York: Basic Books.
Gibson, J.J. (1979) *The Ecological Approach to Visual Perception*, Boston: Houghton Mifflin.
Godelier, M. (1986) (1st edn 1978) *The Mental and the Material: Thought, Economy and Society*, trans. M. Thorn, London: Verso.
Goodman, N. (1978) *Ways of Worldmaking*, Brighton: Harvester Press.
Gould, S.J. and Vrba, E.S. (1982) 'Exaptation – a missing term in the science of form', *Palaeobiology*, 8: 4–15.
Groves, C.P. and Pi, J.S. (1985) 'From ape's nest to human fix point', *Man* (n.s.), 20: 22–47.
Hediger, H. (1977) 'Nest and home', *Folia Primatologica*, 28: 170–87.
Heidegger, M. (1971) *Poetry, Language, Thought*, trans. A. Hofstadter, New York: Harper & Row.
Ho, M.-W. and Saunders, P.T. (eds) (1984) *Beyond Neo-Darwinism: Introduction to the New Evolutionary Paradigm*, London: Academic Press.
Ingold, T. (1986a) *The Appropriation of Nature: Essays on Human Ecology and Social Relations*, Manchester: Manchester University Press.
—— (1986b) *Evolution and Social Life*, Cambridge: Cambridge University Press.
—— (1988) 'The animal in the study of humanity', in T. Ingold (ed.), *What is an Animal?* London: Unwin Hyman.
—— (1989) 'The social and environmental relations of human beings and other animals',

in V. Standen and R.A. Foley (eds), *Comparative Socioecology*, Oxford: Blackwell Scientific.

—— (1991) 'Against the motion (1)', in T. Ingold (ed.), *Human Worlds are Culturally Constructed*, Manchester: Group for Debates in Anthropological Theory.

—— (1992a) 'Culture and the perception of the environment', in E. Croll and D. Parkin (eds), *Bush Base: Forest Farm*, London: Routledge.

—— (1992b) 'Foraging for data, camping with theories: hunter-gatherers and nomadic pastoralists in archaeology and anthropology', *Antiquity*, 66: 790–803.

—— (1993a) 'Technology, language, intelligence: a reconsideration of basic concepts', in K.R. Gibson and T. Ingold (eds), *Tools, Language and Cognition in Human Evolution*, Cambridge: Cambridge University Press.

—— (1993b) 'The temporality of the landscape', *World Archaeology*, 25: 152–74.

—— (1995) '"People like us": the concept of the anatomically modern human', *Cultural Dynamics* 7 (2): 187–214.

Kroeber, A.L. (1952) *The Nature of Culture*, Chicago: University of Chicago Press.

Lawrence, D.L. and Low, S.M. (1990) 'The built environment and spatial form', *Annual Review of Anthropology*, 19: 453–505.

Lawrence, R.J. (1987) 'What makes a house a home?' *Environment and Behavior*, 19: 154–68.

Leakey, M.D. (1971) *Olduvai Gorge*, vol. 3, Cambridge: Cambridge University Press.

Maisels, C.K. (1990) *The Emergence of Civilization*, London: Routledge.

Mauss, M. and Beuchat, H. (1979) *Seasonal Variations of the Eskimo*, trans. J.J. Fox, London: Routledge & Kegan Paul (first published 1904–5).

Merleau-Ponty, M. (1962) *Phenomenology of Perception*, trans. C. Smith, London: Routledge & Kegan Paul.

Michaels, C.F. and Carello, C. (1981) *Direct Perception*, Englewood Cliffs, N.J.: Prentice-Hall.

Morgan, L.H. (1868) *The American Beaver and his Works*, New York: Burt Franklin.

Oyama, S. (1985) *The Ontogeny of Information*, Cambridge: Cambridge University Press.

Rapoport, A. (1994) 'Spatial organisation and the built environment', in T. Ingold (ed.), *Companion Encyclopedia of Anthropology: Humanity, Culture and Social Life*, London: Routledge.

Rykwert, J. (1972) *On Adam's House in Paradise: The Idea of the Primitive Hut in Architectural History*, New York: Museum of Modern Art.

—— (1991) 'House and home', *Social Research*, 58: 51–62.

Shweder, R. (1990) 'Cultural psychology – what is it?', in J.W. Stigler, R.A. Shweder and G. Herdt (eds), *Cultural Psychology: Essays on Comparative Human Development*, Cambridge: Cambridge University Press.

Tooby, J. and Cosmides, L. (1992) 'The psychological foundations of culture', in J.H. Barkow, L. Cosmides and J. Tooby (eds), *The Adapted Mind: Evolutionary Psychology and the Generation of Culture*, New York: Oxford University Press.

Turnbull, C.M. (1965) *Wayward Servants: The Two Worlds of the African Pygmies*, London: Eyre & Spottiswoode.

Uexküll, J. von (1957) 'A stroll through the worlds of animals and men: a picture book of invisible worlds', in C.H. Schiller (ed.), *Instinctive Behavior: The Development of a Modern Concept*, New York: International Universities Press.

Viollet-le-Duc, E. (1990) *The Architectural Theory of Viollet-le-Duc: Readings and Commentary*, ed. M.F. Hearn, Cambridge, Mass.: MIT Press.

Whitehead, A.N. (1938) *Science and the Modern World*, Harmondsworth: Penguin.

Wilson, P.J. (1988) *The Domestication of the Human Species*, New Haven: Yale University Press.

4   Transformations of identity in Sepik warfare

Simon Harrison

A sequence of violent incidents precipitated, and accompanied, the establishment of Australian colonial rule over the Manambu people of the middle Sepik in Papua New Guinea. I argue that the two parties in this encounter operated with different conceptions of sociality and, in particular, with contrasting theories of violence. To the Australian authorities, the events I shall describe indicated a Hobbesian state of nature in which social ties between the protagonists were non-existent or tenuous. The Manambu, on the other hand, conceived of violence as necessarily predicated on the prior existence of social ties between the opponents, and as remaining always embedded and encompassed within these ties. Their warfare, for instance, required enemies temporarily to abrogate their human form, and transform themselves by means of special ritual and body-decoration into approximations of dangerous spirit-beings; the end of hostilities required a reverse transformation of the fighters back into ordinary men. Hence, the Manambu found the hostile actions of the first Europeans unintelligible as autonomous actions of the Europeans themselves. Rather, Manambu accredited the strangers' aggression to their traditional enemies, the Western Iatmul, of whom they assumed these newcomers to be the instruments and, indeed, the transfigured forms.

SOCIALITY AND ENMITY IN MELANESIA

Tribal society is often described as structured in such a way that 'sociability' decreases with social distance. The strongest moral conventions, the most powerful normative constraints, apply to close kin and neighbours. Weaker constraints apply to more distant kin, and the weakest of all apply to strangers (Evans-Pritchard 1940: 155–62; Gluckman 1956; Sahlins 1972; Wedgwood 1930). Beyond a certain, limited range of social relationships, the fundamental condition of tribal society is thus one of Hobbesian 'Warre' (Sahlins 1968).

Yet this stereotype does not seem to apply well to many societies in Melanesia. It is true that some Melanesian peoples made war over long distances, against communities socially remote from them. The Marind-Anim, for instance, raided distant strangers for heads and regarded their victims as subhuman, existing only as a source of trophy-skulls (van Baal 1966: 695–6). But there seems to be no necessary association between violence and social distance in Melanesia. Rather, violence in these societies is much more often associated with close social proximity.

Among the Mae Enga, for instance, the fiercest military conflicts take place between neighbouring groups related by descent (Meggitt 1977). Violence among the Tauade is more frequent within a tribe than between tribes (Hallpike 1977: 119–21, 202). In the eastern Highlands, wars are most common between closely related groups (Berndt 1962: 203; Read 1952). Characteristically in Melanesia, as Barth (1975: 145) observes of Baktaman warfare, attacker and victim are 'known to each other as social persons. . . . [E]very victim is seen as a social alter' (see also Brown 1979; Schieffelin 1977). A striking example of this association between violence and sociality is provided by the Gebusi (Knauft 1985, 1987), among whom a strong ethic of good fellowship, affection and social effervescence alternates with episodes of uncontrolled killing of suspected sorcerers. The Gebusi have an exceptionally high homicide rate by any standards whatsoever, yet these chronic outbreaks of killing occur almost wholly among close kin and neighbours, whose relations are governed by very strong norms of amity and non-violence.

Violence is very much a concomitant of sociality among the Manambu, a people of the middle Sepik River. Before pacification, they fought constantly with neighbouring peoples and at the same time had strong ties of trade and totemic clanship with all of them. Their main traditional enemies are their downriver neighbours, the Western Iatmul or Nyaule. A river-people like the Manambu themselves, the Nyaule have a very similar mode of adaptation and are, as it were, adapted to the same ecological niche. Most Manambu men can speak their language, which is closely related to their own. The Nyaule outnumber the Manambu and for many generations have been trying to expand into Manambu territory because of population pressure on their own resources. Attempts by the Nyaule to expand into Manambu territory have not only been military. They have also taken the form of peaceful attempts to exploit their ties of clanship with the Manambu: to immigrate into the Manambu villages, intermarry with them, and gain rights to their lagoons and other resources on the grounds of kinship and co-residence. At times, some of the Manambu villages have welcomed these overtures and have had close ties with the Nyaule. At other times, they have sought to assert their separate identity, rejecting the Nyaule with fierce hostility.

To the Manambu, the most significant of the Nyaule villages has always been Japandai, their immediate downriver neighbour. At times, Japandai has been their closest Nyaule ally, and at other times their deadliest enemy. At some stage before European contact, a faction from Japandai migrated upriver and settled among the Manambu (see Bragge 1990; Staalsen 1965; Townsend 1968: 93–108). The migrants purchased land from the two Manambu villages of Malu and Yuanamb with women and wealth. But they quarrelled with Yuanamb over women, and over gardening and fishing rights, and after about a generation the

Yuanamb people attacked their settlement and drove them back to Japandai with the help of Malu and some Kwoma allies (Bragge 1990: 41; Staalsen 1965: 186). After some retaliatory raids against Malu and Yuanamb, Japandai made peace with them, and were eventually invited by Yuanamb to return on condition that they caused no further trouble and assimilated into the Yuanamb community instead of having their own separate settlement (Bragge 1990: 42). The motive of Yuanamb in allowing their return is unclear, though according to one of Bragge's informants (ibid.: 40) the motive for allowing the first migration had been to improve the terms of trade with the people of Japandai itself, who were important trading partners.

At any rate, Japandai agreed to the conditions and paid Yuanamb pigs and other wealth, as well as giving their hosts women in marriage (Staalsen 1965: 187). But once resettled, the immigrants attracted increasing numbers of their fellow Nyaule, to the growing alarm of the Yuanamb villagers. The immigrants and their hosts began quarrelling openly. The Nyaule settlers, Yuanamb people say, were having affairs with their women, stealing fish from their fish-traps and yams from their gardens, and disputing their ownership of fishing lagoons. These grievances came to a head in 1923, when the Yuanamb men massacred their guests with the help of allies from the Manambu villages of Malu and Avatip, and from the Kwoma and the Nyaule villages of Nyaurenggai and Japanaut. Sixty-eight of the immigrants were killed. It is clear that some of the Manambu made attempts to protect and hide some of the Nyaule, but others discovered and killed them. No women or children were spared because it was feared that they would always remain more loyal to their own people than to the Manambu (Bragge 1990: 42). Casualty figures reflect the indiscriminateness of the killing, being more or less evenly distributed between men and women, adults and children (ibid.: 46).

The news of this massacre reached Australia, and was reported there in the press. It was raised in Parliament, and the Australian Government established Ambunti Patrol Post near Malu village in 1924 in order to pacify the area and bring it under Government control. In 1926 or 1927, the survivors once again sought to migrate upriver. This time, with the help of the newly established Patrol Officer, they bought land from the Yessan-Mayo people, just upstream of the Manambu, and established the village of Brugnowi (Bragge 1990: 46; Staalsen 1965). This is now the most westerly of all the Nyaule settlements, separated from the others by the whole of Manambu territory.

Let me make some points about the massacre. The problem for the Manambu was that the Nyaule immigrants had become too numerous, and too assertive, for them to assimilate, and indeed perhaps threatened to assimilate *them*. They therefore sought to *separate* the two groups and re-establish the social boundaries between them by violence. To Europeans at the time, the massacre was indicative of savagery, of an urgent need to impose order and control (see Bragge 1990: 44–5). But in actuality, the violence occurred between two groups long and very closely associated; it was an act of aggression meant precisely to split them apart, to *create* social distance between them. The scale and ferocity of the massacre, far from being the result of an absence of social ties, were a reaction to an excessive closeness and intimacy, a too intense sociability, that the killers perceived as having developed between the two sides.

The relations of the Manambu villages with their Nyaule neighbours continue even nowadays to be characterised by violent and abrupt swings between sociability and aggression. Let me contrast this with their relations with people on the remotest fringes of their social universe.

The longest headhunting expedition made by Manambu men along the Sepik was against the Eastern Iatmul village of Timbunke and took place around the turn of the century. This village is some two days downriver from Manambu territory by canoe, or three days if returning upstream against the current. Except for this one encounter, the Manambu had no direct contact with Timbunke in pre-contact times, and possibly had no knowledge of its existence up until this raid. In other words, it was not so much regarded as either friendly, hostile, or even neutral, as outside of the categories of friend or enemy altogether.

An alliance of Nyaule villages had combined to attack Timbunke and managed to recruit one war canoe from the Manambu village of Avatip into their fleet. Avatip men say that when the fleet arrived at Timbunke, one of the war-leaders of that village came out on to the river in a canoe and asked his enemies who the Avatip men were. My informants say that, on being told, he addressed a speech to them, the gist of which was as follows:

> You are my pig Yambunmawndu ['Upriver-source-man': the name of a mythological pig, a totemic ancestor of his clan] and I cannot fight you because I drink your urine and faeces in my river-water. I have never killed you before, nor have you ever killed us. Go home. I do not know your names or your faces. If these Nyaule had come alone I would fight them and kill them all today. But they have brought you strange men from far upriver, whom I cannot fight.

And with that, he turned his back dismissively on the attackers and paddled back to his village, and the Nyaule and their Avatip allies went home, highly dismayed that no battle had taken place. The point I want to make is that what the Timbunke leader did, in effect, was to accuse the attackers of a kind of solecism or impropriety. From his point of view, men of a remote, unknown tribe, spirit-beings of his own clan come out of the world of myth, had presumed to enter into a feuding relationship with his own village, and it was that violent *social relationship* being proffered to him that he was rejecting. There was nothing between his people and those of Avatip except their common membership of the pan-human totemic clan system. In his view, these distant foreigners had overreached themselves. Ever since this battle *manqué*, Avatip have regarded the Eastern Iatmul as their friends, on the grounds that they are both enemies of the Nyaule.

The attempt by Avatip to engage the Eastern Iatmul village of Timbunke in a feuding relationship failed because, as far as Timbunke was concerned, the two groups were too distant, their sociality too tenuous, for an antagonism to be formed between them. To put it differently, they were not close enough to need to create a social division between them by acts of violence. It is only close neighbours who *have* to be preoccupied with the maintenance of their shared boundaries. For these peoples, social distance may indeed imply an absence of peaceful interactions; but it also implies an absence of hostile interactions as well.

MASKING AND BODY-DECORATION IN MELANESIAN WARFARE

What seems common to these Melanesian societies is that violence is not a concomitant of social distance but of close and intense sociality. In other words, in these societies violence and peaceful sociability are often aspects of the *same* social relationships, and it is the *same* actors who are violent and sociable toward one another in different contexts. Their basic assumption is not that there are radically distinct categories of people (friends and enemies, kin and strangers, in-group and out-group) but that there are radically distinct modalities of action. These – amity and enmity, peace and war, help and harm – are contrasting aspects under which the same persons present themselves to one another. They do not belong to different domains of social relations, but are antithetical ways of envisioning, and acting within, the 'whole' of social relations. To shift from one modality of action into the other is therefore also to redefine one's identity contextually, to undergo a temporary transformation of the self.

Let me try to elucidate the nature of this transformation. Although Manambu men value and admire aggression, they do not conceive of human nature as inherently violent, nor assume that homicidal aggression is in some sense natural or innate. Rather, headhunting raids required special magic, which placed the fighters in a trance-like state of dissociation and relieved them of accountability for their actions. It was supposed to make them capable of killing even their own wives and children. The magic is said to have been so dangerous that it could not be administered until after the raiders had set out from their home village, and it had specifically to be removed before the raiders could return. The ability to kill had to be imparted by magic and ritual, and deliberately withdrawn at the end of raids. But for so long as the magic was in effect, the capacity to kill was quite indiscriminate and turned the fighters into a dangerous menace to all other people, including their own families. These representations of aggression are not of a natural drive held in check by internalised norms, but of a temporary ritual transformation of the self.

The outward, visible sign of this transformation was self-decoration. For war, Manambu men wore special fighting regalia, and the same attire is still worn nowadays for rituals: black face-paint (*nggəl*), a head-dress of cassowary plumes (*səpamənd*); a woven forehead band decorated with nassa and cowrie shells (*kasəsəra angk*); armbands decorated with conus shell disks (*sa'an*); and a bailer shell (*kapi*) hung around the neck. Daggers (*aka'aw*) of cassowary thigh-bone used to be worn in the arm-bands point-downwards on friendly visits to other villages, to indicate peaceful intentions. In war they were worn point-upwards to indicate hostility. The symbolic focus of the attire is a chest-ornament in the shape of a face, called a *kwa'aləsapi*. When a man went into combat, he held this ornament in his teeth by a tag at the back, so that it masked his face. The whole decoration-set is meant quite explicitly to make the wearer unrecognisable and is spoken of as pervaded by, or containing, his life-force (see Harrison 1985a, 1985b, 1993). In war, the magical power of the attire is supposed to have struck fear into the enemy and to have protected the wearer from spears and arrows.

The association of aggression with special modes of body-decoration is widespread in Melanesia. Among the Kwoma, neighbours of the Manambu, the captured souls of homicide victims were said to live specifically in the adornments worn by their killers (Bowden 1983: 105). The Ilahita Arapesh, another nearby Sepik society, had ambivalent attitudes toward war. They regarded it as useful or unavoidable at times, but did not glorify war nor was homicide a major means to prestige for men (Tuzin 1976: 50–3). Homicides accordingly were credited to the village as a whole and to its cult-spirits rather than to individual men. As is true for the Manambu, what is perhaps implied here is that warlike aggression is a relation between cults, rather than between individual men (see below). Significantly, warfare required special costumes creating a bizarre and frightening transformation of the fighters' appearance (Tuzin 1976: 47–8).

Mount Hagen men, in the Papua New Guinea Highlands, decorated themselves for war with black body-paint and dark head-dresses, intended to make themselves look large, frightening, and anonymous. The decorations were also said to indicate the presence of ancestral ghosts on the men's faces, implying that the men's individual identities were submerged in the corporate identity of the clan (Strathern and Strathern 1971: 101–6, 137–8, 154): 'when enemies fight, they no longer "see one another's faces", but blacken their faces with charcoal to make themselves anonymous. When they wish to "see the faces" again, they make peace' (A. J. Strathern 1984: 31). Again, what seems to be implied here is that it is specifically groups that are hostile, while people themselves are sociable. To fight, men must mask themselves behind a collective identity and transmute themselves, by means of self-decoration, from distinct persons into depersonalised refractions of a group.

The men of another Highland people, the Wahgi, wore costumes in war similar to those of the Hageners, of black cassowary plumes and specially bespelled charcoal body-paint. The charcoal in particular was said to indicate the presence and support of the fighters' ancestral ghosts, and to make the men look unbearably frightening. At the same time 'Wahgi stress the extent to which charcoal conceals the individual identities of those who wear it. . . . The wearers appear as *dulom ding* (a single group [whose members cannot be told apart])' (O'Hanlon 1989: 89). This is a society, like many in the Highlands, in which men of the same clan are divided among themselves by strong loyalties to affines and uterine kin in other clans (ibid.: 12). Clansmen have a keen sense that their group is a fragile entity, constantly threatened by betrayals from within, always in danger of fragmenting because of its individual members' internal rivalries and their personal relationships with outsiders and enemies (ibid.: 56–70). The success of all clan enterprises, such as warfare and the staging of festivals, depends on making a spectacular outward demonstration of solidarity and unity of will. The clansmen's war-costumes are meant quite explicitly to assert that they identify wholly with their clan (ibid.: 31–2); that it is, in a sense, their clan itself that is acting. When the fighters displayed before a battle, spectators would advise them not to fight if their appearance was judged ineffective by the canons of indigenous aesthetics, as a poor appearance was an omen of disunity and defeat (ibid.: 109).

In the southern New Guinea Lowlands, Asmat men wore special ornaments in war which, as at Avatip, were regarded as magical weapons, making the wearer intimidating and fierce. On a visit to another village, men were not supposed to wear them if their intentions were friendly; to do so was a deliberate provocation and an invitation to attack (Zegwaard 1968: 439). Again, aggression is, as it were, something on the outer surface of the self that can be worn or shed.

A particularly striking example of the association of aggression with costumery and self-disguise comes from the Ilahita Arapesh. The male initiation ceremonies of these people required a special act of ritual homicide. The man appointed to carry this out had to don a particular body-mask, and he temporarily 'became' the spirit which the mask represented and housed. In this state, he was indiscriminately homicidal, even towards his own kin (Tuzin 1980: 50–4). His victim was preferably an enemy, but often it was someone of his own village: for instance, a woman or non-initiate who had in some way offended against the men's cult. The assassination was carried out secretly, and was attributed publicly to the spirits of the cult (ibid.: 229–30).

Indeed, homicide formed part of the performance of men's rituals in many Melanesian societies, particularly those of the Lowlands, and was often an integral episode of male initiation (Bowden 1983: 16, 105; Herdt 1981: 53; Tuzin 1980: 50–4, 229–30; van Baal 1966; Whiting and Reed 1938/9: 195, 208). Among the Manambu, for instance, when a new ceremonial house was built, an enemy head had to be taken and put in the main central post-hole as an offering to the cult-spirits, and the post dropped in on top of it. Nowadays, the blood of a fowl or pig is sprinkled on the post after it has been set in place.

At the end of every initiation, the ritual enclosure (a screen erected around the cult-house to hide the ritual from women and non-initiates) could not be removed until one or more victims had been killed and eaten as sacrifices to the cult-spirits. Nowadays, a pig hunt is held instead, and wild pigs are substituted for human victims. The only exception to this is one of the third-stage initiation rites, Maiyir, which has had to be abandoned because it absolutely required a human victim. The last time an enemy was killed and eaten at Avatip was at the end of the last full-scale performance of the scarification ritual there in 1936. This was early in the Australian Administration, and the homicide was carried out secretly to avoid punishment by the authorities. The victims did not need to be enemies as such, but simply people from outside Avatip. The last victim was a man from a friendly bush village on the Amoku River. He was enticed into a canoe by some Avatip trade friends among the crew, and taken off to be killed. In other words, the ritual did not require an actual raid or combat. What was important was simply to obtain the sacrificial victim, and any means were permissible, including guile.

When plans were being laid during the 1970s to resurrect the Maiyir ritual, it seems that a secret murder of this sort was seriously being contemplated. Men explained to me privately that it would be an easy matter nowadays, when people go about in the forest unarmed, to ambush and secretly kill someone there. What men stressed was the randomness of their choice of victim: any outsider would do. Certainly, Avatip in the past saw it as justified to repay one death with another, and in that sense engaged in feud with their enemies. But in these symbolically most important acts of homicide, what seems to have been significant as a demonstration of power in those 'arbitrary' ritual killings of outsiders, was precisely the intentionally provocative arbitrariness and the irrelevance of 'rightful' motives of vengeance. These killings were meant to violate even the conventions of feud. They were acts of war against the world at large.

After the victim was killed, the body would be taken to a yam garden, where a war magician and his wife would butcher it. The remains were then taken to the village where the tongue, penis, and the muscles of the arms, legs and back were cooked and eaten in the enclosure by the novices and their initiators. This cannibal meal, in which the participants were meant to absorb the victim's strength, was called *kəndjəm*. The rest of the body was burnt along with the initiatory enclosure, except for the head which was treated in the normal way as a trophy. This was the only circumstance in which the Manambu practised cannibalism. Unlike some other Melanesian peoples they were not gastronomic cannibals. For some men, especially the younger ones and the novices taking part for the first time, the practice was too repellent, and they could not keep themselves from vomiting. Clearly, this meal violated a deeply felt taboo. But it was a source of 'power' precisely because it deliberately and radically transgressed the villagers' conceptions of normal human behaviour.

An intriguing survey of the literature on cannibalism (Arens 1979) has argued that most, if not all, accounts of cannibalism are fictions. Many peoples define other cultures or communities as man-eating simply so as to denigrate them. Cannibalism is thus a myth that anthropologists themselves have helped to perpetuate. Arens' thesis that cannibalism is wholly a cultural fantasy projection is indefensible, but it nevertheless makes an important point, and one central to the interpretation of the *kəndjəm* meal: namely, that the idea of cannibalism is an almost universal symbol of 'otherness'. But one needs to remember that ritual often involves inversions of everyday behaviour, and that people may seek to live out their images of otherness in ritual. By eating human flesh, Manambu men demonstrated that in ritual they were not bound by normal human conventions. Shared violations can be powerful means of creating group identity (see Bock

1980: 114, 200; Erikson 1963: 337; Freud 1950) and this, I think, was the effect of ritual cannibalism. It *implicated* the younger men in these violations and established between them and their initiators a bond of complicity. What it created was not a sense of Durkheimian moral solidarity, but a shared experience of transgressing norms, and a kind of exciting and, for some men, frightening, collective culpability.

Through this act of cannibalism men identified with their cult spirits. For in Manambu myth, the totemic ancestors not only created the natural environment and instituted the rituals of the men's cult, but also fought and killed each other, murdered and ate their own uterine kin, and committed many other outrages. They are spoken of as fierce, wild and powerful, but also as dangerous and only partially social. The spirits most closely associated with the men's cult, such as the flute-spirits, are as hostile and lethal to women, children and the uninitiated, as they are to enemies. They do not embody the common interests and collective identity of the community, nor function in some sense as a symbolic representation of 'society'. They are an idealised image, projected by the adult male community, of one particular conception of their own selves. It is this specific conception men sought in the old days to realise in the *kəndjəm* meal, when they temporarily became cannibal beings like their totemic ancestors.

My approach to the ritual practices associated with Manambu warfare begins from the observation that all their warfare was carried out against outsiders with whom the community had many social ties, and that the warfare inevitably violated these ties. To make acts of homicide an organisational requirement of the community's ritual system relieved men of accountability for their own violence. That is to say, these ritual homicides were a model for *all* acts of killing; and the implication of this model was that, when men kill, it is not ultimately they who kill but their cults that kill through them.

In this respect, one might describe Manambu conceptions of war as fundamentally realist rather than nominalist. For them, war does not have its origins in the inner aggressive urges of the individual, but in the mutually hostile collectivities to which individuals belong. These collectivities are the men's cults. In the old days, all the spirit-beings associated with the cult were believed to go into battle with the men and fight invisibly alongside them. They protected the men by deflecting spears and arrows, and struck fear and confusion into their enemies. They would seize any victims who tried to escape and drag them back to the raiders. They would make the fighters' sight especially keen so that they could detect any victims who tried to hide themselves.

I suggested earlier that men conceptually assimilate their own identities to these spirit beings. This identification is in fact a quite literal one. For the names of all of a subclan's forest-spirits, secret flutes, slit-drums and so forth are its hereditary property, and are the personal names borne by its human members (see Harrison 1990). All people are named after their ancestral spirits and, in the past, men *fought under these beings' names*. The powers that made war alongside them as their invisible alter egos were the raiders' own namesakes. From the villagers' perspective, different wars may be fought as one generation succeeds another, but men wage them always under the same immutable aliases. The fighters themselves change as they grow old and die and younger ones replace them. But the identities under which they fight are always the same identities and transcend the individual men who bear them. Men can therefore imply that it is not entirely they themselves who killed in war but those beings who killed through them. Individual men were the human forms through which the powers of their cult acted.

These attitudes towards war are still evident nowadays in the football matches and other sports contests which villages arrange with each other, and which have become something of a modern substitute for headhunting raids. Many of the ritual preparations for raids are nowadays carried out before these games. When a team sets off from Avatip in their canoes, Təpəyimbərman (the tutelary spirit of the village) is said to go at the head of all the legions of supernatural beings that accompany the team, sometimes taking the form of a crocodile playing in the water, and leads the whole expedition as it travels to the games. In 1977 a team from the nearby village of Chambri came to Avatip for a football match, which resulted in a goalless draw. Afterwards, as the visitors were setting off for home, two birds were seen setting off in the direction of Chambri as well. These, it was decided, were the spirits of Mount Aibom and Mount Chambri (two hills in the Chambri area) which the visitors had invoked to assist them. These two beings had fought a prolonged and violent battle with Təpəyimbərman while the game was taking place, but had been unable to overcome him, and therefore the two teams had drawn. To the men, the 'real' contest – the one that really determined the outcome – was between the spirit-beings of the two sides. The match itself, as an event, was only the outward, phenomenal reflection of a contest taking place between the power of the two sides' ritual systems.

Many of the practices in Melanesian ritual seem intended not only to prepare men for war but also, effecting a reverse transformation at the end of raids, to protect men from the dangerous supernatural consequences of having fought and killed. Godelier, for instance, speaks of initiation rituals among the Baruya 'intended to prepare youths for war, to prepare them to kill and to handle the blood of enemies, to protect themselves from the pollution of the blood and the vengeance of the victims' spirits' (1986: 196). When a Manambu man killed an enemy, he entered a particularly perilous state of pollution, in which he was not only in danger himself from the victim's ghost but also posed a danger to the whole community. The village shamans had to perform a special ritual to cleanse the killer of his victim's 'blood' and reintegrate him into human social life.

Mead (1935) describes the Mountain Arapesh as a non-violent culture in which warfare is very rare. But if a fight between communities does break out, and if

> as sometimes happens, someone is killed in one of these clashes, every attempt is made to disavow any intention to kill: the killer's hand slipped; it was because of . . . sorcery. . . . Almost always those on the other side are called by

kinship terms, and surely no man would willingly have killed a relative. If the relative killed is a near one, an uncle or a first cousin, the assumption that it was unintentional and due to sorcery is regarded as established, and the killer is commiserated with and permitted to mourn wholeheartedly with the rest.

(1935: 24–5)

Accordingly, Arapesh attitudes to murder and to killing in war are essentially the same, and both require special rituals to purify the killer (Mead 1935: 23). Rituals of purification for men who have killed in war were formerly very common in Melanesia (see for instance Barth 1975: 151; Hogbin 1970: 95; Landtman 1927: 160–1; Tuzin 1976: 50), and seem extremely widespread in tribal societies in general (see Ferguson 1988: vi). Freud observed this long ago, and attributed the rituals to emotional ambivalence, to what he saw as the complex mixture of friendship and hostility that enemies feel towards each other (Freud 1950: 41; see also Bock 1980: 30–1).

Kennedy (1971) has made a similar argument, interpreting the elaborate rituals often associated with war in tribal societies as cultural defence mechanisms against guilt. Perhaps these practices may have served such functions for some individuals, but I do not consider this to be an adequate explanation for their existence. It is rather that Melanesians do not represent violence as belonging to some 'natural' substratum on which peaceful sociality is built, as a background against which sociality exists as an artifact having always to be safeguarded from reverting to disorder. Rather, they take sociality for granted (M. Strathern 1980; 1988). For them, aggression is an undertaking that requires a ritually transformed self; and violent acts appear as artifices upon a taken-for-granted background of sociality.

AVATIP AND THE COLONIAL ENCOUNTER

My reason for having discussed these indigenous conceptions of war is that I wish now to describe how they affected the first encounters the Manambu had with Europeans, whose conceptions were of course very different from their own. One of the first contacts with the colonial order, probably in the early 1920s, was with a labour recruiter who was signing up men from villages along the Sepik in a ship with native police. The ship called at Malu, where his Nyaule interpreter ordered the villagers to bring them pigs and other food, betel-nut, and women, and threatened to have the village shelled and burned if they failed to do so. A man from Avatip happened to be visiting Malu at the time, and he returned to Avatip bringing word of this event. When the ship reached Avatip, all the women and children had been sent into hiding in the bush. Their menfolk were lying concealed in the long grass along the foreshore, decorated and armed, except for one man standing alone in the open next to one of the ceremonial houses.

The Nyaule interpreter called out to him demanding two girls. The man asked them which specific girls they wanted, and the interpreter gave their names. The man replied that they could not have those two, and sardonically offered his own daughter whom he described as disfigured by ringworm, and a long banter ensued. One of the ship's crew climbed up one of the canoe mooring-poles to see if he could spot any men in hiding, and was hit by a spear. The Avatip men then waded out, some with firebrands to try to set fire to the ship, others with poles to try to push it off downstream. Three of these were shot and killed by police firing through the portholes.

In reprisal, the Australian Naval and Military Expeditionary Force, at the time administering New Guinea, made a punitive expedition against Avatip (Rowley 1958: 202–3; Townsend 1968: 100), although the villagers themselves claim that two such raids in fact took place. A gunboat arrived and stood off from the village shelling it. Most of the shells seem in fact to have been aimed at coconut palms, but one hit a house and killed two women. One group of villagers, mainly the women and children, fled west along the riverbank. Most of the men escaped inland with the police in pursuit, but the men split up and vanished into the swamps. The police then retraced their steps and began to follow the women and children, but one of the police was speared as he climbed over a fallen tree and the others retreated carrying him. In the course of this pursuit two, or possibly three, of the villagers were shot and killed. The police then burned the village house by house and left.

According to the villagers, a second punitive raid took place about a year later. There was a particularly severe flood season at the time, and the villagers were able to escape by canoe into the flooded swamps. The police did not try to follow them but just burned the village once again. When it was dark, the men returned and stood at the back of the village watching the houses smoulder, while the ship stood off with all the crew and police aboard and eventually left. In fear of further attack, everyone now abandoned the village, and the community split into small groups living in temporary camps and shelters on the Amoku River and inland on the lagoon just south of Avatip. Eventually they returned and rebuilt the village, and some time after this the first Avatip men were taken by ship to the coastal town of Madang to work as indentured labourers.

The point to make is that Avatip people see these attacks as wholly the work of the Nyaule. In fact, the native police who took part are often described nowadays as Nyaule men, though this seems unlikely to have been the case. But in relating these events, men represent Europeans as simply new, powerful allies the Nyaule had recruited in their attempts to destroy Avatip. In traditional warfare, allies were assembled through the totemic clan system, often from villages quite distant from those of both the attackers and the victims (see Harrison 1993). The experience of having one's enemies bring along remote strangers to attack one's village was not new. Though Europeans were and are strangers even more distant than the Nyaule, there seems to be no notion that these newcomers were at the time necessarily hostile simply by virtue of being strangers. They only acted toward Avatip with hostility because they had been prevailed upon by the Nyaule to do so. In other words, the village's utterly traumatic first encounter with colonialism is seen as simply one episode in a longstanding private feud between Avatip and its Nyaule neighbours. Europeans appear in this feud as just the passive instruments of the traditional enemies of Avatip, as though these white newcomers were simply a neutral force of nature that the Nyaule had somehow managed to harness for their own insidious ends.

The same conceptions reveal themselves in the villagers' attitudes toward the Japanese, with whom Avatip had a short-lived but violent encounter during the Second World War. Toward the end of the war, a group of Japanese soldiers based themselves at Avatip. A number of the river villages hosted Japanese units: apparently, the soldiers used to promise the villagers, in return for their help, that once the war was won Japan would give them aircraft and factories, and inter-marry with them. The only criticism Avatip villagers nowadays make of their Japanese guests concerns the rapacious appetites and disgusting eating habits they are supposed to have had, evidenced by their boiling unripe pawpaw, but there is no doubt that the community must at the time have found the soldiers a burden on its food supply. On the other hand, older men recall the Japanese with admiration for their discipline, which they consider both far stricter and more even-handed than that of the Australians; Japanese officers, they say, were just as ready to have their own men flogged as Avatip men. But the soldiers were soon on first-name terms with many Avatip men, who had obviously gained their trust, with fatal consequences for the Japanese themselves.

At the time, which was probably mid-1945, some Avatip men were in secret contact with an Australian unit operating on the Amoku River, who informed them that unless the villagers killed the Japanese soldiers, they themselves would mount an attack, which would inevitably involve casualties among the villagers. The Japanese were having the villagers build a fenced enclosure at Avatip for some purpose, and the Avatip men made an arrangement among themselves to stage a surprise attack on the Japanese while this work was being done. The agreed signal for the attack was that one of the Avatip men would ask the officer for his sword on the pretext of needing to split a piece of bamboo. The men carried out all the magical and ritual preparations which traditionally preceded a headhunting raid. On the appointed day they killed the soldiers with their axes and machetes, taking their heads as trophies, apart from the officer whom they took up the Amoku River and handed over to the Australians.

The fact that the village was more or less coerced by the ultimatum of Australian guerrillas into making this attack does not figure in most versions of the story as these are told nowadays. It does not seem to be known to many of the villagers, apart from the men who were directly involved in the negotiations with these Australians. Nowadays, when the story is related, the attack is described as having been motivated by concern over the making of the fenced enclosure. The villagers are said to have suspected that the Japanese were planning to imprison them in this and kill them all, and that the Japanese had been induced by the Nyaule to do so. These apprehensions may indeed have been a genuine factor at the time: earlier in the war, Japanese soldiers had executed the male population of Timbunke, incited, Avatip people say, by the traditional enemies of Timbunke who wanted its womenfolk. Perhaps the Avatip villagers genuinely feared that a similar fate was in store for them. But in any case, the killing of the Japanese is nowadays certainly portrayed as the village's spontaneous reaction to a violent Nyaule plot. It was Japanese men that they actually killed. But whenever the story is told it is Nyaule, in the outward guise of Japanese, that the teller and his audience kill in their imaginations.

CONCLUSION

The contrast between Manambu attitudes to their Nyaule neighbours, and to distant strangers such as Eastern Iatmul, Europeans or Japanese, could not be more striking. These latter peoples are certainly more remote socially than the Nyaule. But they are resources of power that any group can establish relations with, and use as weapons in its conflicts with its neighbours. Like the dangerous wild boars and crocodiles that are outward forms in which enemy sorcerers conceal themselves, these distant outsiders may act in inimical ways but it is always old, familiar enemies that lie behind and direct their hostility. Europeans, Japanese, wild animals, and indeed the powers of sorcery itself, are powerful but morally neutral forces that enemies compete to recruit or harness to use against each other. The acts of these beings are interpreted as not ultimately their own acts but those of enemies close to home. They are just signs behind which enemies may discern each other's malign intentions.

In other words, Manambu do not expect hostility (at the level either of social attitudes or of actual behaviour) necessarily to increase with social distance. On the contrary, it is neighbours that fight and expect to fight. Those beings on the remote fringes of their shared social world, if drawn into these conflicts at all, participate not as enemies but as the weapons with which enemies fight.

In Manambu oral history, the first Europeans have over time become partially assimilated in this way to the Nyaule, and the imposition of the colonial order has been assimilated to the old enmity between the Manambu and Nyaule. It is as though, for these people, there was no 'first contact' (cf. Connolly and Anderson 1987), in the sense of a wholly unprecedented encounter, a confrontation of peoples having no prior relationship. There was just the continuation of an old feuding relationship between the Manambu and Nyaule in a new form, and Europeans were simply novel manifestations of old, familiar enemies.

Europeans, of course, brought very different expectations to this encounter. For they assumed the initial situation they confronted to be a 'state of nature'. For them, all that existed in the Sepik was anarchy, both between the various Sepik tribes and between them and the whites. They represented themselves as having come to Papua New Guinea precisely to bring this state of nature to an end, to impose the authority and sovereignty of a state where there had previously been none (cf. M. Strathern 1985). For Europeans, the massacre of Nyaule settlers by their Manambu hosts, or the fight between Avatip and the labour recruiter, exemplify such a state of nature. These were exactly the sorts of events to be expected in what were officially called uncontrolled or semi-controlled areas, in the absence of a framework of law. Hence the European justification for their own presence in Papua New Guinea: it was precisely such a framework of law that the Australian administration had the duty to impose.

Manambu too are familiar with the idea that men can act toward each other in ways ungoverned by norms, and recognise no accountability to one another. But theirs is very far from the European conception of a 'state of nature'. It is the form men assume who have disguised and bespelled themselves for war, and transfigured themselves ritually into spirits, or into something very like spirits. To put it differently, I do not think Manambu people can easily conceive the possibility of a people with whom they have no social relationships. Hobbesian 'Warre', or the nearest equivalent of it in their conceptions, can arise only between persons *already in social relationships*. For it is defined by the deliberate transgression of taken-for-granted norms; it is made by persons already bound by common moral conventions contextually placing themselves outside the ambit of these conventions by means of a ritual self-transformation, and presenting themselves to each other as alien and estranged. Social distance is, for them, something that can only be brought into being from *within* a pre-existing relationship. 'Enemies' are simply consociates disguised and transformed; 'strangers' are just deceptive appearances assumed by figures close to home.

Marilyn Strathern (1990; 1992) has suggested that many Melanesian peoples did not react to the advent of the first Europeans as a unique and unprecedented event, but as a kind of performance or display enacted by familiar beings in disguise. I think that the reactions of the Manambu were very much of this sort. For however brutally the first European newcomers on the Sepik may appear to have acted, the Manambu could not interpret the violence, as the newcomers themselves might have done, as arising from a quite literal absence of any previous ties of sociality. The Manambu could only imagine the violence as *intended to conceal or deny a pre-existing sociality*. For them, the problem the visitors posed was never how the two sides might in some sense 'establish' social relationships with one another, since these relationships were assumed. All that was problematic was *who* precisely it was that these interactions were taking place with: to identify the true authors of the powerful and violent newcomers' actions, and unmask familiar faces behind the alien forms.

REFERENCES

Arens, W. (1979) *The Man-Eating Myth*, Oxford: Oxford University Press.
Barth, F. (1975) *Ritual and Knowledge among the Baktaman of New Guinea*, New Haven: Yale University Press.
Berndt, R. (1962) *Excess and Restraint*, Chicago: Chicago University Press.
Bock, P.K. (1980) *Continuities in Psychological Anthropology: a Historical Introduction*, San Fransisco: W. H. Freeman.
Bowden, R. (1983) *Yena: Art and Ceremony in a Sepik Society*, Oxford: Pitt Rivers Museum.

Bragge, L. (1990) 'The Japandai migrations', in N. Lutkehaus *et al.* (eds), *Sepik Heritage: Tradition and Change in Papua New Guinea*, Durham, NC.: Carolina Academic Press.

Brown, D.J.J. (1979) 'The structuring of Polopa feasting and warfare', *Man* (n.s.), 14: 712–33.

Connolly, B. and Anderson, R. (1987) *First Contact: New Guinea Highlanders Encounter the Outside World*, Harmondsworth: Penguin.

Erikson, E.H. (1963) *Childhood and Society*, New York: Norton.

Evans-Pritchard, E.E. (1940) *The Nuer*, Oxford: Clarendon Press.

Ferguson, R.B. (1988) *The Anthropology of War: a Bibliography*, New York: Harry Frank Guggenheim Foundation.

Freud, S. (1950) [1913], *Totem and Taboo*, New York: Norton.

Gluckman, M. (1956) *Custom and Conflict in Africa*, Oxford: Blackwell.

Godelier, M. (1986) *The Making of Great Men*, Cambridge: Cambridge University Press.

Hallpike, C.R. (1977) *Bloodshed and Vengeance in the Papuan Mountains*, Oxford: Clarendon Press.

Harrison, S.J. (1985a) 'Concepts of the person in Avatip religious thought', *Man* (n.s.), 20: 115–30.

—— (1985b) 'Ritual hierarchy and secular equality in a Sepik river village', *American Ethnologist*, 12: 413–26.

—— (1990) *Stealing People's Names: History and Politics in a Sepik River Cosmology*, Cambridge: Cambridge University Press.

—— (1993) *The Mask of War: Violence, Ritual and the Self in Melanesia*, Manchester: Manchester University Press.

Herdt, G.H. (1981) *Guardians of the Flutes: Idioms of Masculinity*, New York: McGraw-Hill.

Hogbin, I. (1970) *The Island of Menstruating Men: Religion in Wogeo, New Guinea*, Scranton: Chandler.

Kennedy, J.G. (1971) 'Ritual and intergroup murder: comments on war, primitive and modern', in M.N. Walsh (ed.), *War and the Human Race*, New York: Elsevier.

Knauft, B.M. (1985) *Good Company and Violence: Sorcery and Social Action in a Lowland New Guinea Society*, Berkeley: University of California Press.

—— (1987) 'Reconsidering violence in simple human societies: homicide among the Gebusi of New Guinea', *Current Anthropology*, 28: 457–82.

Landtman, G. (1927) *The Kiwai Papuans of British New Guinea*, London: Macmillan.

Mead, M. (1935) *Sex and Temperament in Three Primitive Societies*, New York: William Morrow.

Meggitt, M.J. (1977) *Blood is their Argument*, Palo Alto: Mayfield.

O'Hanlon, M. (1989) *Reading the Skin: Adornment, Display and Society among the Wahgi*, London: British Museum Publications.

Read, K.E. (1952) 'Nama Cult of the Central Highlands, New Guinea', *Oceania*, 23: 1–25.

Rowley, C.D. (1958) *The Australians in German New Guinea, 1914–1921*, Melbourne: Melbourne University Press.

Sahlins, M. (1968) *Tribesmen*, Englewood Cliffs: Prentice-Hall.

—— (1972) *Stone Age Economics*, London: Tavistock.

Schieffelin, E.L. (1977) *The Sorrow of the Lonely and the Burning of the Dancers*, St Lucia: University of Queensland Press.

Staalsen, P. (1965) 'Brugnowi: the founding of a village', *Man*, 65: 184–8.

Strathern, A.J. (1984) *A Line of Power*, London: Tavistock.

—— and Strathern, M. (1971) *Self-decoration in Mount Hagen*, London: Duckworth.

Strathern, M. (1980) 'No nature, no culture: the Hagen case', in C. MacCormack and M. Strathern (eds), *Nature, Culture and Gender*, Cambridge: Cambridge University Press.

—— (1985) 'Discovering "social control"', *Journal of Law and Society*, 12: 111–34.

—— (1988) *The Gender of the Gift*, Berkeley and Los Angeles: University of California Press.

—— (1990) 'Artefacts of history: events and the interpretation of images', in J. Siikala (ed.), *Culture and History in the Pacific*, Helsinki: Transactions of the Finnish Anthropological Society.

—— (1992) 'The decomposition of an event', *Cultural Anthropology*, 7: 245–54.

Townsend, G.W.L. (1968) *District Officer: From Untamed New Guinea to Lake Success, 1921–46*, Sydney: Pacific Publications.

Tuzin, D.F. (1976) *The Ilahita Arapesh*, Berkeley: University of California Press.

—— (1980) *The Voice of the Tambaran: Truth and Illusion in Ilahita Arapesh Religion*, Berkeley: University of California Press.

van Baal, J. (1966) *Dema: Description and Analysis of Marind-Anim Culture (South New Guinea)*, The Hague: Martinus Nijhoff.

Wedgwood, C. (1930) 'Some aspects of warfare in Melanesia', *Oceania*, 1: 5–33.

Whiting, J.W.M. and Reed, S. (1938/9) 'Kwoma culture: a report on fieldwork in the Mandated Territory of New Guinea', *Oceania*, 9: 170–216.

Zegwaard, G.A. (1968) 'Headhunting practices of the Asmat of Netherlands New Guinea', in A.P. Vayda (ed.), *Peoples and Cultures of the Pacific*, New York: Natural History Press.

5   Human rights and moral knowledge

Arguments of accountability in Zimbabwe

Richard Werbner

The central issue of this chapter is the extent to which social knowledge of the past is moral knowledge.[1] Much has been written about the orientation to the past which glorifies it (as in nationalist myths), laments a loss (as in nostalgia), legitimises (as in social charters), recovers a silenced history (as in the ethnic 'search for roots') (Hall 1991; Kapferer 1988; Robertson 1990; Strathern 1995; Thompson 1985). This chapter foregrounds knowledge of the past as violation; my emphasis is on the legacy of debt that is kept alive in the present through an ongoing argument which is moral, ritual and political. Whether to bury the past or to expose it is openly debated, as is the choice between reconciliation and confrontation. At one scale, this is an argument about personal responsibility within a Kalanga family in western Zimbabwe. At another scale, it reaches to the most inclusive public sphere and the accountability for state terror and ethnic violence.[2] Over time, the arguments of accountability both separate the local and the global and also fuse them in historical narrative.

In its most recent moment, the argument of accountability gains force, in the public sphere, from what are perceived to be even broader, international pressures towards democratisation in Africa. International aid is now routinely linked, at least officially, to good governance, political conditionality, and to the safeguarding of basic human rights (Stirrat 1993). It is not merely that western scholars represent the argument in terms of a problematic nexus between state and civil society (Lemarchand 1992). It is that protagonists themselves assert that they are consciously acting to realise a civic culture, to compel the state to guarantee the rights of individuals *qua* citizens (Moyo 1992; *The Insider*, February 1994).[3]

Underlying the argument about the past and accountability are quite disparate assumptions, distinguishable for purposes of analysis but which may be brought to bear by the same people at different times in different situations. Lemarchand suggests a useful distinction framed, first, in terms of Lockean ideas, a version of social contract theory, reflected in the rhetoric of civic culture and citizens' rights, and, second, in terms of Edmund Burke's notion of moral partnership, regarded as enduring and not perishable, 'between those who are living, those who are dead and those who are yet to be born' (Lemarchand 1992: 178, citing Burke). The Burkean and Lockean notions need not be seen, at least in

Zimbabwe, as exclusive alternatives displacing each other. Social contract theory is increasingly salient in debates within the public sphere (in newspapers, in parliament, in litigation) about the state and its agents. The premise of moral partnership is equally stressed, and in the past decade increasingly so, where political accountability is extended to comprehend what is perceived to be a disturbance in the cosmos. Here people convert their awareness of the past, as violation of the person or even the earth, into ritual debt, redeemable only through the performance of rites of personal healing and of cleansing the earth from bloodshed. An intensification of arguments of accountability has meant the increasing salience of debates about the social contract in the public sphere (Moyo 1992) and an efflorescence of ritual practice recognising and attempting to assuage ritual debt (Ranger 1992).

THE POLITICS OF MORAL ACCOUNTABILITY

At the height of the recent crisis over Zimbabwe's worst drought in living memory, the search for fresh water sources in abandoned mines unearthed mass graves. Bulldozers bringing up water also dredged up human bones. The bones had been dumped in the mines located in the southwestern part of the country, following massacres committed by the elite Fifth Brigade of Zimbabwe's national army in the mid-1980s. While the discoveries were being made, a former commander of the Fifth Brigade, Air Marshall Perence Shiri, was appointed Commander of Zimbabwe's Air Force. In the outcry that followed, the Minister of Defence appealed to the nation not to open up 'old wounds' by invoking the history of post-independence violence.

One immediate response, not only to the discovery of the bones but to the Zanu–PF regime's attempt to bury the history, was unambiguous. It was a groundswell of protest, both local and national. It heightened civic debate about the government, criticism of which had become widespread and increasingly more vocal in the late 1980s. The popular demands were carried forward in a stream of newspaper letters and columns. Many urged that the regime must accept moral and legal responsibility for the atrocities carried out in Matabeleland by the Fifth Brigade and the Zimbabwean Central Intelligence Organisation.[4]

At the national level, *The Financial Gazette*, an independent newspaper, published a debate about the significance of the atrocities. 'Horrors of the Fifth Brigade can not be forgiven nor forgotten' is the title of an article by Welshman Ncube, a professor of law at the University of Zimbabwe and himself from the western region where the atrocities had been committed. Ncube rejects the calls for reconciliation; he opposes the appeal for healing of the social wounds of war; he argues that the priority has to be the public acknowledgement of guilt by the government and compensation for the families of victims:

> I believe that we should neither forgive or [*sic*] forget for there is no reason to forgive. Those who lost their loved parents, spouses, brother and sisters,

children, relatives and friends, at the hands of soldiers constituted to protect them have absolutely no reason to forgive. Why should there be forgiveness of a Government which refuses to accept responsibility for its atrocities?

(*The Financial Gazette*, 15 October 1992: 4)

Ncube's article is an outspoken challenge, coming from within a nascent social movement. This movement, intended to create public opinion demanding that the government be made accountable to the people, has become increasingly more salient since the mid-1980s. At present somewhat marginal to this movement, although initially at its forefront, are a number of leading politicians from Matabeleland, including the recently appointed Minister of Home Affairs, Dumiso Dabengwa.[5] These politicians, formerly of the disbanded opposition party ZAPU, have joined the government, under the unity agreement with the ruling party. They 'prefer to deal with the past in such a way that it consolidates the present alliance between the two parties' (Ranger 1993: 4, citing *Southscan*). By contrast, 'Human rights activists' is the label currently used in Zimbabwe for some prominent campaigners within the nascent movement who continue to opt 'for a public, confrontational approach' (ibid.).

This is a confrontation between the rule of law and the role of the Central Intelligence Organisation as a political apparatus of the ruling party and its regime. The argument is as much about the present and the future as it is about the past. The terms used, including 'human rights', and that master term 'democracy', come from a global discourse of human rights which the movement has localised, giving it new and specific meanings (Appadurai 1990: 300–1).

Such localisation of a global discourse of human rights is reflected in the recent report of the *Sunday Times* (of Zimbabwe) on the decision of the Attorney General not to prosecute the deputy director and other officials of the CIO on charges of abduction and murder. The unfinished case follows the disappearance of Rashiwe Guzha in Harare on 30 May 1990. The *Sunday Times* on 19 July 1992 reports the protest of, among others, the Dean of Law at the University of Zimbabwe, Kempton Makamure:

> In a democratic society the government should resign where it fails to protect the lives of its citizens. The Guzha case is a sad episode in the legal history of Zimbabwe and it clearly means that no one's life can be safe or guaranteed any more. Why should blacks in this country have a government? They were murdered by Smith and they are being murdered by this government – the so-called government of freedom fighters – what freedom do we have?

To prove the answer, others have contested the silence about earlier 'disappearances'. Even before the discovery of the bones, a group of women from Silobela in Midlands Province had been pursuing a case to get a High Court ruling on the deaths of their husbands who 'disappeared' after being abducted at night by security forces in early 1985 (*Censureship News* 17: 3). They are only one group among the many families of the bereaved seeking death certificates officially acknowledging murder by the security forces. Most recently, according to the *Sunday Mail* (of Zimbabwe) of 6 December 1992, Dumiso Dabengwa as Minister of Home Affairs,

> reviewed the registration system to enable the children of people who disappeared during the post-independence political disturbances in Matabeleland to get birth certificates. . . . Children of missing persons could now be issued with birth certificates as long as there was someone to testify before the registrar that their parents disappeared.
>
> (cited in Ranger 1993: 5)

But the nascent social movement is not merely a campaign to make the government accountable to individuals *qua* citizens. Nor does it merely reflect a wider discontent with economic mismanagement and corruption. It is most critically a struggle against what is seen to be an attempt to evade public responsibility, both moral and legal, for making the security forces the means of state-sponsored ethnic violence. Ncube argues,

> Mr. Mahachi [the Minister of Defence] and his government will not own up to these atrocities. They would rather we all shut up and pretend that the Fifth Brigade did not engage in what can only be described as ethnic genocide.
>
> (*The Financial Gazette*, 15 October 1992)

The demand is that ethnic violence be recognised and acknowledged as the criminality of the regime whose forces perpetrated it. If there is to be healing, there must be reconciliation with the state, and not only between Zimbabweans asserting opposed super-tribal identities as 'Shona' and 'Ndebele'.

A moral debt is seen to be at issue, one that many Zimbabweans are unwilling to renounce without reparation. Such a moral debt is, I shall argue here, like an unfinished narrative, which motivates people to call again and again for a resolution.

The stress on the making of historical narrative has been salient in recent discussions of the politics of identity (Friedman 1992; Hall 1991; Tonkin, McDonald and Chapman 1989). The re-invention of the past or the recovery of lost histories – 'the search for roots' (Hall 1991: 52) – is seen to be a condition for empowering current identities and group causes, such as mobilisation in particular struggles. In line with this, Friedman, for example, argues that 'the people without history are, in this view, the people who have been prevented from identifying themselves for others' (1992: 837). What many of these discussions miss, however, is the point that the politics of representation is a politics of moral accountability in which the past is unfinished, festering in the present. It is not a 'search for roots' which is at stake but a demand for *rights* as a basis for a healing of open wounds. As Ncube contends:

> Unconditional and unqualified acceptance of responsibility by the government

would be an important step towards healing the wounds, that so many in government want not to be re-opened as if they were ever closed.

(*Financial Gazette*, 15 October 1992: 4)

THE POLLUTION OF THE LAND

The moral debt is widely perceived as more than a debt to the people themselves. It is perceived to be a ritual debt offending the dead and God. The disappearance of victims of the Fifth Brigade left their surviving kin in an ambiguous predicament. Not only were they unable to get the needed death certificates, and birth certifi- cates for children of the dead, but they were unable to work out their bereavement through burials and funerals. Many felt they were suffering from the restless dead, aggrieved, violated and unburied. As individuals, the sufferers turned, in an efflorescence of healing ritual, to Christian churches, diviners, and cult healers offering personal relief and personal cleansing (Reynolds 1990; Werbner 1991; Ranger 1992).[6] For whole communities there was an awareness of a disturbance in the cosmic order. The earth had been polluted by the massacres.

Even beyond that, there was a recognition that the spilling of blood in the war of liberation itself had left the land and the people as a whole in need of cleansing. From the perspectives of priests and followers of the Mwali Cult of God Above, Southern Africa's largest indigenous regional cult centred in Matabeleland (Ranger 1967, 1991, 1992; Werbner 1977, 1989), Joshua Nkomo and Robert Mugabe as the leaders of the victorious guerrilla armies were at fault; they had not authorised messengers to come together on their behalf at a central shrine and make sacrifice to God Above for restoring the peace of the land.

In 1989, early in the drought and before the worst of it, Mandikangangwa, a very senior and elderly *wosana* (an initiated adept possessed in the Mwali cult) reflected on the liberation war and 'the war of Mugabe', which was the civil war fought against 'dissidents' by the Fifth Brigade as an army of occupation. The *wosana* told me:

Nkomo himself in that war with Europeans was not saying that he would kill the Europeans off. He was saying, 'They are giving us a public order [*mthetho*] which is oppressing us, but let us all live together.' But that one [Mugabe] said, 'I am going to kill until I finish and remain alone.' He wants everyone, whether Europeans or Matabele, to be killed off, so that only he and the people of his home remain.[7]

(Mandikangangwa, 24 July 1989)

If limited war might be right, the unlimited war, and what Ncube calls genocide, must be wrong because it denies that the world was created for many different peoples, rather than for one only.

The *wosana* continued,

Recently, it has been a little better because Joshua pleaded with Mugabe that they should all be together and rest from all those things, Mugabe had been opening his war to kill us. The soldiers came saying these are the footsteps of dissidents. But the dissidents were really his, Mugabe's [invention]. He said, 'I am not letting the day pass until you kill 3,000 people in Matabeleland. Stop at 3,000.' Now that is what has been done and it is finished.[8]

As himself a Kalanga from Bango Chiefdom in the southwest, the *wosana* expressed an opinion widespread in Matabeleland. First, he conveyed that the regime in power, like the armies, is personified by the leader, who is held ultimately responsible for the abuse of power.[9] Second, he insisted that the violence was a deliberate, unprovoked campaign launched by the head of state. But the wosana went further to disclose the religious significance in God's coming judgement of collective responsibility.

If I understand the *wosana's* transcendental and universalistic perspective rightly, it assumes two critical conjunctions defining the moral universe in the regional cult's cosmology. One is between the cosmos, as an ordered universe, and sociality, which is at once human and beyond humanity. Sociality lies both between different peoples, and between these peoples and each of the various species of all living creatures. The other aspect of this moral universe is the relation between human hubris and God's retribution. As put by my interlocutor, sociality is universal in that the universe is composed of many peoples, *all* of whom are empowered by God and *none of whom can presume to be alone.* Such a presumption denies that there is a God above them. To act against universal sociality is to act against the cosmos, the very order wherein all upon which life ultimately depends comes from God Above. Human hubris, epitomised by the overreaching arrogance of great and powerful temporal leaders, brings its nemesis in God's collective retribution. The *wosana* said:

Mugabe does not know that Mwali (God Above), who created below, created for them, too, and for each and every people to live well. God hears what this man says. The way it is we thank God for the power that he gave this man [we do not complain against God for empowering Mugabe], but it [his having power] is not good. And whether you will make it right, God, we do not know. But it will come after this [he gave an ironic, bitter laugh] that the Master of the Sun (God, the Master of the Day) will 'despise and reject' (*sodza*), having looked closely and kept silent. He won't say, 'You, what have you done? You are spoiling.' He will go, 'Whh, whh (blow the wind, keeping silent).' [This wind sweeps away pollution, despised by God, and it also drives away rain, desired by people.] If you say you are going to do something, he allows it, 'All right (let it be your responsibility).' But one day, ahh! It will reach a measure that is enough for the day of 'I [Mwali] will come here.' Just as he has said, 'I will bring the clouds [of rain]', so too he stops them saying, 'You go ahead and pour out, get rain for yourselves; and if you can't, it is your own affair. I am the one who put you in your place. If you do not respect me, and seize each and everything for yourself, then you can make your own, by yourself [if you arrogate all power to yourself, do not expect help from God].'

The *wosana's* fearful anticipation of God's judgement hinted further at an apocalyptic image of impending drought so terrible that it would be decimating in loss of cattle, goats, even chickens and so much loss of human life that there would be no one to bury anyone else. His remarks assume a meta-history; it is that underlying philosophy of the succession of regimes and God's will which Terence Ranger's work illuminates (1989). God's punishment, 'the stick that beat your fathers', as *wosana* speak of it, was widely perceived in the length and extreme severity of the subsequent drought.[10]

The public demands for acknowledgement of wider political and moral responsibility intensified during the drought. It is an important message of the cult, Ranger argues, that 'individual cleansing must be accompanied by rituals in which the whole society comes to terms with the violence of its past' (1992: 706), including all people within the wider society, whites as well as blacks. The assertion is that public accountability and the admission of responsibility for violence must be inclusive; it must extend beyond the liberation war to the colonial conquest.

In his autobiography, Nkomo reflected upon this inclusive representation and advanced it in his disclosure of a prophecy made to him at a central shrine (Dula) in 1953 (Nkomo 1984). On that occasion, a witness told me in 1989, he had accompanied Joshua Nkomo to the shrine and had heard the oracular Voice weeping about blood spilt in the first war against the whites (at the end of the nineteenth century). 'I am made to withdraw by that blood', the Voice said and then explained why the people would have to wait thirty years for their own country (see also Ranger 1989; Nkomo 1984). In the cult's continuing and unfinished narratives, the violence of the past has been represented as leaving a trace which still affects the well-being and welfare of people in the present. Responsibility cannot be narrowed down. It must make demands beyond the temporal interest of the immediate moment.

This inclusive representation itself has a very wide resonance. It is echoed in a recent column by the Catholic priest Father Oskar Wermter entitled 'Time to choose':

> The dead will not go away. They claim their right. Now Matabeleland is yielding up its dead, shattering the official silence. The Minister of Defence, Moven Mahachi, appeals to the spirit of reconciliation so that he can quickly throw his blanket of silence once more, and this time for good, over those bones. . . . But even the dead of the first Chimurenga [the Shona name for the nineteenth-century war against the whites] are not at peace. Zimbabwe must be cleansed of a century of violence, say the ancestors.
>
> (cited in Ranger 1993: 3)

What I propose here is that the people's creation of historical narratives, especially about the violence of a collective past, is more than mere legitimation, more than the construction of a past charter in present struggles. Historical narratives of responsibility are unfinished moral narratives, in which traces of past faults impinge on the present and compel people to act. The dead claim *their* right. Such historical narratives gain even greater moral force amidst complaints in the public sphere, amounting to very widespread and far-reaching political criticism, about the regime's broken promises, mismanagement, corruption and self-enrichment. This is the conjuncture in the finding of historical fault and current failure which characterises the present crisis of legitimacy of the Zanu–PF regime under Mugabe. The arguments of accountability are activating an emerging civic culture and from it, in turn, gain further momentum.

GUERRILLA WAR – THE HERITAGE OF AMBIVALENCE

With this crisis of legitimacy and the nascent movement for accountability has come a growing public reaction against the purely heroic representation of the liberation war. It is a reaction which increasingly brings into public discourse much of the personal, familial and private discourse among civilians in the countryside. In some ways the atrocities endured during the post-independence period were, for members of the family I know best, Lupondo's family, a continuation of the suffering experienced during the liberation war (Werbner 1991). The home of Lupondo's family is in Bango Chiefdom, southwestern Matabeleland. In both periods, family members and other local people continued to be caught between two forces, subjected to arbitrary torture and humiliation and, in extreme cases, brutally murdered without provocation. In both, the people had been compelled to become informers and betray members of their community: during the war of liberation, accused them under threat or out of alleged self-interest of being 'sell-outs', and in the post-independence period of having helped the 'dissidents' or knowing their whereabouts.

By the time I returned to the family in 1989, after almost a thirty-year absence, family members were engaged in questioning themselves about how they had survived. They had a year of relative peace following the Amnesty of 1988, but many were still uncertain whether the violence of the early 1980s would return. They were all too aware, often enough, that in order to save themselves they had to betray someone in their community, and they were trying to come to terms with this. At the same time, the women in the family also told stories about their own heroism, about how they stood up to soldiers or rescued children; about how they were the ones who had managed to feed and clothe the guerrillas.

Both periods had left family members with unsettled debts to the dead, debts which expressed themselves in afflictions by abused ghosts or grieving spirits. To ease, if not fully settle the debt, rituals had to be performed. It was not a matter simply of cleansing individuals. There was a concern with putting to rest the restless presence of past moral violation, of which the wandering ghost is the forceful embodiment. Relatives and neighbours had to be brought together in shared sacrifices of cattle or goats. These sacrifices, felt to be demanded by the dead, re-created moral communities, communities much wider than the family itself. They did not merely alter the personal condition of the afflicted as individuals. Their practice reflects their concern with the moral responsibility of healing. Healing is here an essentially social process.

But besides the carrying forward of moral and spiritual debt for collective as well as individual purposes, there were also very real differences in the narratives about the two periods. Family members conveyed that the horror of the post-independence period had been beyond anything they had thought possible, or could have imagined before. They told about the massacres of nearby people who had been stuffed into the mines, the rapes and starvation which this time left no one untouched. As I have argued in my account of the family, some of the nightmarish quality of their experience came from a virtually surrealist re-enactment during the later period of terror of certain parts created in the liberation war. The Fifth Brigade soldiers were the merciless enforcers of collective punishment by the state, re-enacting the part of the Rhodesian forces, yet they represented themselves also as having the moral authority of the people who had liberated Zimbabwe and made it free, and they demanded displays of support of the kind they had known as freedom fighters (see Werbner 1991: 169).

Looking back upon the senselessness and futility of the post-independence terror, family members conveyed that they had been able to make more sense of their suffering during the war of liberation. They saw themselves as parents protecting guerrillas just as they expected other parents elsewhere to protect their children, and they accepted that their own children had gone to fight a war to win the country from the whites. At the same time, the very recognition of a moral relationship between civilians and guerrillas – and both sides expressed expectations of actual performance as parent and child (clothes, food, shelter) – made the ambivalence of the actual relationship between them all the more problematic.

It is important that this ambivalent relationship must not be reduced to a matter of mere coercion as Norma Kriger (1992: 109–15) would have it. Kriger's approach dissipates our understanding of the moral contradictions with which people have to wrestle in guerrilla war. Instead, the analysis must get right the very pervasiveness of the appeal to 'kinship', and the forceful ambivalence it entailed, when the appeal came along with the ill-controlled threat and, all too often, the actuality of physical coercion. Such an appeal to a parent–child relationship runs not only through the narratives I recorded, but also through the life histories of many of the Zimbabwean women in *Mothers of the Revolution* (Staunton 1990).[11] In no way does this deny the arbitrariness in the victimisation of civilians in guerrilla violence. It is a reality in moral contradiction to which my interlocutors in Lupondo's family insisted I bear witness on their behalf.

Having survived the suffering and brutalisation of both wars, family members and their neighbours remembered the liberation war not as in any way a heroic period for the combatants. Nor did they create a narrative of unified struggle against an external enemy. Theirs was not the triumphalist history of the kind produced for schools as an official, government-endorsed version of the war, extolling the heroism of (especially ZANLA) freedom fighters, (Seidman, Martin and Johnson 1982). Instead, family members and their neighbours gave diverse accounts, and from different perspectives, which reflected the suspicions, divisions, mistrust, as well as the loyalty, support and courage among themselves. They stressed in their stories how they had come through ordeals and confronted them. Survival was itself heroic.

The recent ordeals, which were still fresh in their minds, overshadowed earlier ones. They talked about the wars as distinct periods of suffering and drew comparisons between them. Their overriding emphasis for the second period was on evil; on the threat to annihilate all the people; on the sense parents had of an absurd twist in which their children came back to them, having survived the war, only to be once again in danger of their lives, under suspicion of being 'dissidents' and thus enemies of the very Zimbabwe they had fought to liberate. The war of liberation was remembered in moral terms as a far more ambivalent experience. And, in the light of the later ordeals, many family members had to ask themselves: was their suffering in vain?

THE CHANGING FOCUS OF MORAL NARRATIVE

To create a world of moral understandings among themselves, members of a family such as Lupondo's have to manage a tension between the global and the local. How far the global is to interpenetrate with the local is a matter that has to be managed actively. It is not a given of geography, a matter of physical or ethnic isolation, or even of a necessary articulation in a world capitalist system. It is a dynamic condition which can be negotiated and renegotiated.

In the early accounts of their lives which members of Lupondo's family gave me in 1960–61, the local dominated over the global. This was so despite the fact that the family had to re-create home and all that it meant to them in the face of colonial encroachment. Dislocation was imposed upon them from without, and repeatedly. They had to move from place to place, dispossessed of their land by white settlers, until their Chiefdom of Bango was re-established to the remote south in a 'Special Native Area', at the beginning of the 1940s. Their local relations of production and consumption were embedded in the wider capitalist economy. They took part in the increasing circulation of labour migrants between countryside and town, at times reaching very high rates of migration. From generation to generation, and even within generations, they moved through very different work careers, distinctive both in the short and long term. They became involved in the defence of their settlement against the modernising and enframing thrust of the late colonial state. Of all that wider movement, however, relatively little emerged from the background in their early personal narratives.

It might be suggested that there is a simple explanation for their inward focus in this pre-war period: withdrawal in defence of autonomy. Having gone through successive dislocations from the early colonial period till the 1940s, a whole generation enjoyed a period of reconstruction, from the 1940s to the late 1950s.

Benign or not-so-benign neglect, in effect *laissez-faire*, was the colonial policy in their part of the district. This practical limit on official intervention freed them to follow their own social strategies for settlement. They recovered vital connections with neighbours; they reconstituted neighbourhoods of their own choosing. In other words, their localism as an inward focus on kin and neighbours would simply appear to be an expression of relief from the press of the outside world, and most importantly the press of white settlers and colonial officials.

But why did members of other families nearby not share this inward focus? After all, others at that time did give me accounts full of reflection on and consciousness about colonial rule (see Werbner 1991: 47–64). And why was this inward focus that of a prominent family sustaining themselves together in the largest concentration of family homesteads? The point is that Lupondo's family cannot be taken as 'typical' or even representative of others in their chiefdom. Nor can they be regarded as reflecting some dominant mode of consciousness. Here we can see why the suggestion about reconstruction takes us only part of the way. That is because it neglects the crucial specificity of family narratives. It is a matter of this family, not another, and not the whole chiefdom. This is pertinent to my own argument.

Lupondo's family did not start off from a shared reality. Instead, they had a discourse within which they negotiated their understandings and argued with and against each other. What they shared was the argument, not the representations of themselves and others in some consensual interpretation of events in everyday life. They were engaged with, and committed to, each other, even despite themselves. The self-absorption, the disattention to the colonisation and the dislocation on the land were constitutive of the defence of autonomy *at a specific phase* of the development of the family. It was the phase in which what was at issue was not only the transfer of leadership from the founder's generation to his sons' but also the very existence of the family as a residentially nucleated group. The family was about to split. It was a cause of much anguish and uncertainty. No one in Lupondo's family took the emerging split as a matter of course, as if it were natural and unavoidable.

Motivated by concerns about their future commitments to each other, members of the family were drawn to engage in an intense moral argument about character and the blame for misfortune. This was the argument about recourse to sorcery within the family. I found that the names given to children were a register around which versions of family history were read. Once given in full, and not as abbreviated nicknames, 'the names speak', as one family member told me when she gave the following nicknames: 'Mind your manners'; 'The village is mine'; 'You make us vomit', and so forth. The names express recriminations and counter-recriminations among and between the various wives. For me this register was one key to family genres of personal narrative. What characterises different genres are the ways family members position themselves morally within or outside quarrel stories.

In relation to the ongoing moral argument, the personal narratives that were told to me fall into four genres. At one extreme is the genre of romance in which the narrator completely distances herself from quarrel stories. She makes her life out to be a glorious romance, without conflict or hostilities – a quest for the right man, the finding of a husband, and now the idyllic marriage. It is especially artful as a representation understood against the background of the voices of other family members speaking of her blame in family quarrels. Partial disengagement from quarrel stories characterises the second genre, that of nostalgia. In old age the moralising narrator looks back upon a radical break from good to bad times. The quarrel stories come from after the break, and the narrator longs for the good times when he was himself central in the life around him, and not yet peripheralised in elderhood on the verge of ancestorhood.

At a further extreme from romance is the genre of cautionary realism in which the quarrels are cautionary moments. These are told as it were objectively; the warnings about people and their dispositions are less openly stated than implied in the elaboration of circumstantial detail. The narrator fully engages with telling quarrel stories but places herself as a witness, somewhat at the periphery, virtually never as a heroine or at the centre. Finally, in this spectrum, comes the genre of heroic adventure. It is apt for leading sons who give the self-accounts of purposeful and resolute heroes. The narrator represents himself as justified, as deserving of his rightful place, as standing up to the tests of his rivals and enemies within the family. In the quarrel stories, his virtues emerge more or less explicitly by contrast to their wrongs and shortcomings.

In their personal narratives as in the rest of their ongoing moral argument, family members had strong views about malice and the destructive capacities of human beings. They took it as an unquestionable truth that human character is profoundly inscrutable and liable to reveal unsuspected evil. They spent a great deal of time backbiting, gossiping, making moral judgements, defending and assassinating each other's characters. Direct violence was rare. Admittedly, the campaigns of sorcery accusations, while controlled from exploding into violence against the accused, did arouse hostilities. Such campaigns evoked the passion for vengeance and further embittered rivalries. But restraint was called for in response to attacks of sorcery. Moreover, much was said and done with the explicit intent of containing the destructive capacity of human beings.

If the local can be said to have dominated the global in the pre-war personal accounts and moral argument of Lupondo's family, the reverse is more true immediately after the liberation and civil wars. Family members continued to focus on the moral concerns of family members, of course, but these, like the imposed terror and violence, could not be imagined as limited to local events. Their narratives, commenting upon Mugabe, inflation, trends and changes in the wider sense, foreground their ordeals with outsiders primarily, rather than their internal quarrel stories. Family members felt compelled to bring the wider scene into perspective.

To pursue the significance of this displacement in global–local relations these family narratives have to be positioned in a wider context that includes a changing public discourse about violence.

FAMILY NARRATIVES AND PUBLIC DISCOURSE

During the liberation war the white Rhodesian press had carried endless reports of atrocities allegedly committed by the 'ters' (terrorists) against the civilian population in rural areas (see Frederikse 1982). Afterwards, there was a run of post-war reminiscences by Rhodesians. Remarkably matter-of-fact about their part in massacres and in the campaign of terror, even their use of poisoned clothing, many of the Rhodesians displaced moral blame (see Ranger 1992, citing Flower 1987). Within post-independence Zimbabwe there was, moreover, a muting in the public discourse, the media and press, of civilian suffering as a moral outrage. This was so, I would suggest, because the ambivalence around the suffering could be negotiated in moral terms (the war was held to be a just war and it could be argued that civilians often do suffer in wars), and because blame could not be allocated singly to any one group or leader. The grounds were found for a public agreement to bury enough of the past to allow a *modus vivendi* under the country's negotiated settlement. Much concern was expressed about the safety of the business community, the avoidance of a flight of foreign capital, and the need for reconciliation with whites in order not to disrupt the economy. For the liberation war, unlike the post-independence civil war, there was no single social agency, ethnic group or political movement perceived to be overwhelmingly responsible for the atrocities. No political interest group dared make moral capital out of the atrocities by politicising them; that was true even when the mass graves left by the Rhodesian regime were discovered.

It was thus possible to reconstruct and re-imagine the war as one of heroic struggle and suffering of the nationalist kind memorialised at Heroes' Acres, the national cemetery at Harare. At first there was little or no attempt to create a monument to civilian sacrifice, or to seek a way to honour and appease the civilian dead in national ceremonial at the capital or in the countryside. Debate in the press raised the question of the absence at the memorial site of any heroines, women combatants. Even beyond that, *heroism* was politicised. Heroism was appropriated by the ZANU–PF regime for its guerrilla army, ZANLA. As Kriger has argued, the exclusion of ZAPU's claimed heroes of their army, the Zimbabwe People's Revolutionary Army (ZIPRA), was part of a wider appropriation of the symbol of The National Hero by the new ruling elite (Kriger 1990, cited in Brickhill 1992). The regime created a hierarchy of heroes, Kriger suggests: at the top, the national heroes buried at the capital in costly and glorious funerals paid for by the state; at the bottom, the local heroes from among the rank and file whose own communities pay for their burial.

This appropriation, and the symbolic hierarchy along with it, was contested by ZAPU and its leaders. It is a contestation that was at first suppressed, along with ZAPU, during the post-independence struggle of the early 1980s. The unity agreement between the parties allowed former ZAPU leaders to found the Mafela Trust (Mafela, the Fallen One, after the *nomme de guerre* of ZIPRA's last wartime commander). At first the intent was to commemorate ZIPRA's war dead in their own home areas. Eventually, the Trust began to extend its concern to other 'forgotten heroes', the civilians themselves. Brickhill contends, as a founder of the Mafela Trust, 'The contribution of the Mafela Trust to this contestation is to argue for a return of the historical legacy of the war to the rural people who fought and sacrificed most for the liberation war of Zimbabwe' (1992: 11).

Initially, straight after the war, there was entrenched resistance to any public criticism minimising the glory of the guerrilla war. More recently, however, there has been a countersurge of literary, academic and other publications in the public sphere. The literature confronts the sufferings of civilians in the war and the atrocities they had to bear. Thus Ranger comments on the concern with violence and terror emerging from the material on the war now being published in Zimbabwe:

> At first, after the 1980 victory, the war was portrayed in terms of the triumph of heroic virtues and bravery both in narrative accounts and in novels. Today both compel the reader to confront and think through terror.
>
> (Ranger 1991: 11)

He reports that at a conference of writers he attended in Zimbabwe in 1990, many writers said that 'they felt it to be *their duty* to record the brutality and insanity of the war and the nitty-gritty of guerrilla life' (1991: 12, emphasis added); they felt 'a compulsion to confront and understand' the horror they felt about it (1991: 13). The writers as intellectuals are moved to create the art of an embracing civic and popular culture. It is one that brings into the widest public sphere the painful moral contradictions with which so many individuals and communities have long been wrestling. This is more than a demystification of the past. The thrust is towards a radical disenchantment which rejects the politics of secrecy and authoritarianism.[12]

Clearly the past refuses to be buried. This, despite the fact that there is no *ethnic* political interest in sustaining popular memories of the liberation war's atrocities – they do not provide a legitimating charter for any present political struggles between ethnic groups. Indeed, these popular memories cannot be appropriated, and thus reduced to the 'truth' of a single group. They are intractable memories for any regime that claims political legitimacy by disguising the terror of the past. The burial of terror is the birth of disenchantment.

MORAL KNOWLEDGE AND GLOBAL–LOCAL DISPLACEMENTS

My discussion raises the problem of the dialogic nature of social life. Even at the most minute scale, social life is dialogic – argument, disagreement, contradiction, divergence of perspectives, competing interpretations and representations of reality flourish. The question is the extent to which there is interpretation from one scale to another, so that the *same* concerns may come to dominate *throughout* the different scales. This question of scale leads on to others about crisis, narrative, and social memory. How and why are shifts in scale produced by or in crisis? What force can moral narrative have, when a crisis increases towards flashpoint? How is the now global discourse of human rights localised by the social memory of knowing the past as violation, as an unforgettable moral debt?

It follows from the raising of these questions, no less than from my main discussion earlier, that social knowledge of the past cannot be made at will, forgotten or retained simply in terms of current interests. The late colonial and early post-colonial experiences of too many people obviate that. Knowledge of the past in narratives of moral debt feeds the passion for commitment in present crises; and, in turn, being crisis-driven, it recovers its grip on popular imagination. The relation is dialectical. The terror and atrocities of the past move unavoidably into the foreground of social memory when a crisis escalates to include moral judgements publicising a whole series of disparate failures by the wielders of public authority and power – in Zimbabwe, failures such as economic corruption, the breach of promise to return the land to the people and to secure justice and human rights under a rule of law. In turn, such foregrounding further escalates the crisis.

In no way does that imply holding or being held hostage to the past. The conjuncture in moral knowledge of the past and the present during a crisis of legitimacy remakes the past. It gains the prescriptive force of a moral imperative. The past as moral narrative has to be theorised in relative terms. My discussion pursues the question of how the making of moral narratives effects and is effected by the displacement of global–local relations from one period or context to another.

Despite the now well-established recognition in anthropology and sociology that moral knowledge is a distinct form of knowledge, too little attention has been paid to the social pragmatics of this knowledge, to the distinctive types of argument that constitute it, both locally and globally. The local only makes sense in relation to the global, of course. But what is the local conceived of in terms of moral knowledge? At one period, what defines the local is put in moral argument which is relatively closed, impermeable, and self-referential. Such argument backgrounds, even obscures, events and actions which an outside observer might recognise to be critically determinative. At another period, the once-backgrounded is so pervasive and interventionist that the former closure, the old rules of moral relevance, can no longer be sustained. Nevertheless, the local does not disappear. Protagonists do not cease to focus upon their personal relationships, such as within a family or regional cult. In evaluating these relationships, however, they find that they have to pass judgement also on 'the global', on actions and events of which they have a fragmentary, sometimes indirect knowledge but which remain well beyond their control. At the same time, what had been 'the local' comes to be globalised: it is cited in the press, re-imagined in novels, re-presented in ethnography, and made the subject of national and international commissions of inquiry. The globalisation of the local is a critical process in the making of citizenship and in the creation of a civic culture.

NOTES

1 Earlier versions of this chapter were presented to seminars of the Institute of Commonwealth Studies in the University of London, the Satterthwaite Colloquium on African Religion and Ritual, the Centre for Southern African Studies at York University, and the African Studies Centre, University of Oxford. I am grateful to seminar participants for their helpful comments. Above all, I wish to thank Pnina Werbner and Jocelyn Alexander for their constructive criticism.

2 In highlighting new directions for the analysis of 'Political accountability in African history', Lonsdale anticipates the present growth of interest in the subject, by comparison to past neglect. 'The idea of accountability seems noticeable for its comparative absence from the field of African studies' (1985: 127).

3 Comaroff (in press) highlights a continuity from the colonial discourse of rights in South Africa to the present, as the new South African post-colony emerges. On the force of new religions in the recognition of human rights in Africa, see Jules-Rosette (forthcoming).

4 The argument was not all on one side, of course. Also popular, and expressed in an opposed stream of public opinion were ethnic counter-appeals, calling upon an earlier past for justification. The nineteenth-century raids by 'Ndebele' against 'Shona' were often mentioned. If the government was to redress the wrongs against Ndebele, so a popular counter-argument ran, it would also have to put right the earlier wrongs about 'Shona'. The recent wrongs (by 'Shona' against 'Ndebele') were represented as just retribution for the earlier ones (by 'Ndebele' against 'Shona').

5 On some of the public opinion about Dabengwa, and his importance for the debates about human rights issues, I quote from *The Insider*, a muckraking and populist monthly. I give the quotation at some length because it documents, forcefully, the moral tenor and the political substance of current public debate in Zimbabwe about human rights and state power.

> The Law and Order (Maintenance) Act which was introduced by the Ian Smith regime in the early 1960s to control public gatherings of black nationalist leaders has been in force for more than three decades. It is now being used by the government to curb the activities of opposition parties or organisations that are considered unfriendly to the government. Dabengwa was himself a victim of the Act. He was detained for four years under the Act after being acquitted by the Supreme Court in 1983 of treason charges following the discovery of arms caches at properties owned by the then ZAPU. The scrapping of the Law and Order (Maintenance) Act could spell the end of an era of oppression. Already the government has lifted the State of Emergency and the Emergency Powers Regulations. For Dabengwa it would be a personal triumph over a decadent law that denied him and several other Zapu supporters freedom. Last year, he hinted that the Act might be scrapped but nothing has been done since. People will also be closely watching the case as Dabengwa's stance will clearly show whether he has softened up and joined the government bureaucracy or not. As a victim, he has no reason to defend the Act, but as a Minister he has a duty to do so. The question will be can he afford to ignore the four bitter years he suffered in detention to retain a law he does not seem to agree with. If he does, this could also spell the political doom for him. Most people now believe that Dabengwa has abandoned the hard-line stance he took after his release and when he was still deputy Minister of Home Affairs, to join the bandwagon of 'yes-men' in the cabinet.
>
> (*The Insider*, February 1994: 3, 12)

6 How far, and in which respects, such healing was itself politicised is a moot point. Jocelyn Alexander argues that the view I have been putting forward is too generalised:

it needs to be qualified in the light of a post-war restoration of power relations undermined during the war. Alexander's hypothesis is that 'some healing was about reasserting control over women and young people who had gained power during the war, about stigmatising them as mad or possessed or, with regard to women, as prostitutes' (personal communication).

7 On Nkomo's contested efforts to identify with, capture and even re-invent the cult as a focus of national pilgrimage, see Ranger 1989; Nkomo 1984.

8 This perception of dissidents as Mugabe's invention is a moral judgement; and I do not report it as a statement of plain fact. Against that is the available evidence on banditry, insurgency, and the escalation of violence, involving ex-guerrillas apparently from ZIPRA (see Alexander 1991: 584–8).

9 Ultimate responsibility does not mean exclusive responsibility, of course. Popular opinion in the provinces of Matabeleland also blamed the Minister of Defence Enos Nkala and other Matabeleland ZANU–PF politicians. Some of the most important among these, including Defence Minister Nkala, were eventually driven from office following what came to be known as the 'Willowvale scandal' (Alexander 1991: 603, and personal communication).

10 I have benefited from discussions with Mr Nthoi about his recent fieldwork on the cult of Mwali during the drought.

11 Among the numerous references are the following: pages 5, 83, 100, 109, 116, 162, 170, 209.

12 This literature of disenchantment gains some of its impetus from the conjuncture of historical fault and current failure in the present crisis of legitimacy. See above also on the cumulative increase in criticism raised against the government.

REFERENCES

Alexander, J. (1991) 'The unsettled land: the politics of land distribution in Matabeleland, 1980–1990', *Journal of Southern African Studies*, 17: 581–610.

Anon (1992) 'Zimbabwe: attacks on freedom of expression', *Censureship News*, 17: 1–14.

Appadurai, A. (1990) 'Disjuncture and difference in the global cultural economy', *Theory, Culture and Society*, 7: 295–310.

Brickhill, J. (1992) 'Making peace with the past', paper presented to the conference on 'Religion and war in Zimbabwe and Swedish relationships', Uppsala: University of Uppsala.

Comaroff, J.L. (in press) 'The discourse of rights in Colonial South Africa: subjectivity, sovereignty, modernity', in A. Serat (ed.), *The Paradox of Rights*.

Diamond, L. (1993) 'The pro-democracy movement in Africa', *Times Literary Supplement*, 2 July.

Flower, K. (1987) *Serving Secretly: An Intelligence Chief on Record; Rhodesia into Zimbabwe, 1964–1981*, London: John Murray.

Frederickse, J. (1982) *None but Ourselves: Masses vs Media in the Making of Zimbabwe*, Harare: Ravan Press and Zimbabwe Publishing House.

Friedman, J. (1992) 'The past in the future: history and the politics of identity', *American Anthropologist*, 94: 837–59.

Hall, S. (1991) 'Old and new identities, old and new ethnicities', in A.D. King (ed.), *Culture, Globalisation and the World-System*, London: Macmillan Education Ltd.

Jules-Rosette, B. (forthcoming) *Human Rights and Religion in Africa*.

Kaarsholm, P. (1991) 'From decadence to authenticity and beyond: fantasies and mythologies of war in Rhodesia and Zimbabwe, 1965–1985', in P. Kaarsholm (ed.), *Cultural Struggle and Development in Southern Africa*, London: James Currey.

Kapferer, B. (1988) *Legends of People, Myths of State*, Washington: Smithsonian Institution Press.

Kriger, N. (1990) *In Search of a National Identity: The Politics of War Heroes*, unpublished manuscript, cited in Brickhill 1992.

—— (1992) *Zimbabwe's Guerrilla War*, Cambridge: Cambridge University Press.

Lemarchand, R. (1992) 'Uncivil states and civil societies: how illusion became reality', *Journal of Modern African Studies*, 30: 177–91.

Lonsdale, J. (1985) 'Political accountability in African history', in P. Chabal (ed.), *Political Domination in Africa*, Cambridge: Cambridge University Press.

Moyo, J. (1992) 'State politics and social domination', in *Journal of Modern African Studies*, 30: 305–30.

Ncube, W. (1992) 'Horrors of the Fifth Brigade can not be forgiven nor forgotten', *The Financial Gazette*, 15 October: 4.

Nkomo, J. (1984) *Nkomo, The Story of My Life*, London: Methuen.

Ranger, T. (1967) (2nd edn 1979) *Revolt in Southern Rhodesia 1896–7*, London: Heinemann.

—— (1989) 'The politics of prophecy in Matabeleland', paper presented to the Colloquium on African Religion and Ritual, Satterthwaite.

—— (1991) 'The meaning of violence in Zimbabwe', paper presented to the Conference on Terror and Counter-Terror, Trinity College, University of Cambridge.

—— (1992) 'War, violence and healing in Zimbabwe', *Journal of Southern African Studies*, 18: 698–707.

—— (1993) *Britain Zimbabwe Society Review of the Press*, 67.

Reynolds, P. (1990) 'After war: healers and children's trauma in Zimbabwe', *Africa*, 60: 1–38.

Robertson, R. (1990) 'After nostalgia? Wilful nostalgia and the phases of globalization', in B.S. Turner (ed.), *Theories of Modernity and Post-Modernity*, London: Sage Publications.

Rukuni, C. (1994) 'Dabengwa's day of reckoning', *The Insider*, 26 February: 3, 12.

Seidman, G., Martin, D. and Johnson, P. (1982) *Zimbabwe: A New History*, Harare: Zimbabwe Publishing House.

Staunton, I. (1990) *Mothers of the Revolution*, Harare: Baobab Books.

Stirrat, R.L. (1993) 'Developing Africa?', *African Affairs*, 92: 294–300.

Strathern, M. (1995) 'Nostalgia and the new genetics', in D. Battaglia (ed.), *The Rhetoric of Self-Making*, Berkeley and Los Angeles: University of California Press.

Sunday Times (Zimbabwe) (1992) 'Rashiwe: shock, anger and fear', 19 July.

Thompson, L. (1984) *The Political Mythology of Apartheid*, New Haven and London: Yale University Press.

Tonkin, E., McDonald, M. and Chapman, M. (1989) *History and Ethnicity*, ASA Monographs 27, London: Routledge.

Werbner, R. (1977) *Regional Cults*, London: Academic Press.

—— (1989) *Ritual Passage, Sacred Journey*, Washington: Smithsonian Institution Press.

—— (1991) *Tears of the Dead*, Edinburgh: Edinburgh University Press.

6 Globalisation and the new technologies of knowing

Anthropological calculus or chaos?

Angela P. Cheater

Anthropologists are, perhaps, the prototype for Ulf Hannerz's (1990) 'cosmopolitans'. Recently, without really intending to, I have become part of this category, shuttling wearily between two peripheral homes as well as into northern centres, after a brief contract elsewhere in the periphery. Yet I have come very late and somewhat unwillingly to the divided cultural worlds of long-distance migrants, already examined in detail (especially in Southern Africa) for 'others' by so many anthropologists, even if their explorations, unlike those of Rushdie, Said and Naipaul (Paine 1992: 193–4, 200, 205), were not set in global or regional contexts.

Mine is now the as-yet-imperfectly globalised world of itinerant cosmopolitans, so far little examined from within by anthropologists. This is Appadurai's (1990: 301ff.) world of deterritorialising, denationalising global interdependence, expressed in regular inter-continental travel, often inconvenienced by airline workers' strikes; of 'frequent flyer' relationships with specific airlines, in which their computers give preferential treatment against the better judgement of their human staff; of plastic cards negating notional currency boundaries; of fax, disk, electronic mail as normal modes of uncensored communication; of standard English in many distinct idioms, as well as communication in other languages. It is also Toffler's (1990) individualising world of 'demassification' and 'customisation', of increasing heterogeneity driven by personal choice, which is encouraged as well as enabled by the new communications technology.

It is a world also of different professional emphases, even different types of anthropology in different nation-states; of a repeating divergence, though differently detailed in each case, between local and central colleagues about what is thought anthropologically significant within peripheral states themselves. This aspect makes me acutely aware of the ever-increasing technological and knowledge divide which separates peripheral cosmopolitans like myself from peripheral locals (cf. Tong 1989). In my information-technologised world, unlike theirs, both time and space stressfully compact upon each other to de-articulate my multiple identities[1] and responsibilities. Perhaps I manage my identities badly; but Barth (1978: 180, original emphasis) indicates that this stress arises from structural rather than personal reasons. 'Diversity between the repertoires of different persons increases the complexity of networks . . . the more diversity between repertoires, the more persons will *not* be possible alters for certain kinds of interaction.'

Is there anything new in my situation? Probably not. But 'having been there' allows me one last opportunity to examine globalising processes in the late twentieth century as one of Paine's (1992: 202) bystanders, a status which is, appropriately in the light of my later argument, accidental, stochastic and sufficiently expensive to lie beyond normal research funding. It is a useful vantage point from which to address problems specific to anthropological knowledge in Toffler's (1990) powershifting interface between the global and the local, and to examine the impact of globalising processes on anthropologists as well as on the subject-matter of anthropology.

The profession was born in the world's greatest era of homogenising competitive imperialism. Yet it could be argued that early analyses deliberately ignored, or even mystified this globalising reality, as 'other cultures' were problematised first within the framework of evolutionary and diffusionist theories, and then within 'the island model' of clearly bounded, isolated, functionally integrated societies. Radcliffe-Brown (1952) noted the limitations of such models in 1940; but even after this explicit recognition, the multiple links of arbitrarily bounded units of study to encompassing structures were rarely investigated by anthropologists. Norman Long (1992: 28–9) has recently deemed it necessary to reiterate this point:

> My background as a social anthropologist gave me the wherewithal to describe and analyse micro-processes but did not provide much of a theoretical framework for dealing with the ways in which these processes were locked into larger-scale economic and political systems.

Attempting to plug this hole in professional knowledge and to explain such linkages is both essential and very difficult, for today's heterogeneous 'global village' is *not* just a scaled up version of a local village writ large. Its many diversities (linguistic, cultural, social) introduce to the same urban street, farming settlement, refugee camp, previously unknown complexities and uncertainties in interaction among neighbours. Paine (1992: 201–3) has recently doubted whether our traditional research techniques lend themselves to investigating such polyethnic situations. Moreover, mobile people with their fleeting interactions are difficult to find in one place long enough to study using normal anthropological techniques. Global processes thus present us as anthropologists with *two* discipline-threatening crises: one conceptual and theoretical, the other methodological. Such crises are familiar, so let us not panic; but how do we investigate the global and its relations with local realities? In the context of the new information technologies, I think that we should identify two inseparable parts to answering this question. On the one hand, what is the relationship of 'global' to 'local' anthropologists and anthropologies? On the other, how do our local subjects relate to cosmopolitans, and our cosmopolitan subjects to locals; and how do both categories relate to globalising processes?

The new, intelligence-augmenting information technologies include: satellite-linked telecommunications; internationally mobile personalised telephones, usable even in aircraft; computers; digital information storage on optical discs;[2] digital networks for electronic mail,[3] publication,[4] and information retrieval;[5] computer-aided design (CAD) and manufacturing (CAM); computer-intelligent photography and creative photo-restoration using fuzzy-logical pixel shifts; inter-active video; 'virtual reality' as 'a structure of seeming' in the 'consensual hallucination' of 'cyberspace' (Rheingold 1991: 177, 16), including 'virtual billboards' and mobile holograms; and, finally, what Tong (1989; 68) has called 'intelligence technology' (computerised artificial intelligence and knowledge engineering). Almost all of these technologies are visualised and, as Bridgeman (1993: 316–17) notes, 'evidence from several sources indicates that two distinct representations of visual space mediate perception and visually guided behav-iour, respectively. . . . In designing spatial displays, the results mean that "what you see isn't necessarily what you get".' Human scepticism of *what* is 'seen' has already been reflected in American jurors' distancing of video evidence of behaviour from the motivation, or intent, behind that behaviour.[6]

In the near future, apparently, all forms of satellite telecommunications (television, phone, fax, e-mail) will be combined with personal computers into 'single-box' interactive systems based on fibre-optic cabling, which will permit – among many other things – interactive computerised shopping and TV chat-shows as well as individually chosen, menu-driven news construction from a continually updated central database.[7] In this future, we as customers will be able to select and screen our own information of choice on television, in effect to compile our own programmes. Will we then choose to witness disturbing scenes (for example of poverty and violence) from other parts of the globe? More generally, will this technology be used to reinforce existing dominant percep-tions, representations and systems of distribution, within academic professions such as anthropology as well as in society more generally? Or will there emerge a new democratisation of information, based on individualised self-selection rather than on past patterns of social choice exercised by constituted broadcasting and censoring authorities?

It is clear that the new communications technologies, in their currently separ-ated forms, already structure human perception, compress the time-frame of decision-making, and have the capacity to distance human responsibility for their results from decisions themselves. They can be used merely to amplify and perhaps extend existing relationships. Pornography is now available on CD–ROM and accessible on computer by a phone–modem link.[8] Defamation and sexual harassment by e-mail, though not quite the same as harassment in person, are already problems in Australian (and probably other) universities.[9] Likewise, new faculties or schools of information science research are unlikely to alter existing models of university organisation.

But the new communications technologies may also 'change the way people live, perceive, believe' and 'bring new political regimes, new social institutions, new economic opportunities, new mental diseases' (Rheingold 1991: 247, 219). In the cabled future, for example, university campuses may well be replaced by 'interactive multi-media communication'. Virtual Campus already exists.[10] However, changing the form of capital investment in social and educational organisation is likely to be available mainly if not exclusively to cosmopolitans. Our local colleagues, especially those on the global periphery, are and will remain largely excluded from the new perception-structuring technologies.

So among cosmopolitan but not local anthropologists, these new ways of knowing are likely to call into question past analytical, theoretical, epistemological, even ontological certitudes. They will return the already well-endowed section of the profession to questions of the structure of perception and the creation of 'knowledge'; to issues of the definition of meaning in new technological contexts and matters of representation (Strathern 1994; in press); to what Bateson (1979) called matters of 'mind' – based on an ancient, unresolved, but now newly significant definitional problem: what are the differences among knowledge, information and intelligence? Why might such hair-fine distinctions be important to anthropology in a globalised world?

If it ever was, 'knowledge' may no longer be synonymous with 'information'. 'To know' requires no object: etymologically knowledge is essentially personalised, as sensory or mental constructs. In contrast, 'to inform' must take an object to make sense. Logically, then, though this is rarely made explicit, 'knowledge' can only be individualised and by English definition is impossible to transmit, as many teachers attest! 'Information', on the other hand, requires sharing. But since 1937, in the context of 'information science', 'information' has become dehumanised, being that which is

> separated from or without the implication of reference to, a *person* informed: that which inheres in one of two or more sequences, arrangements, etc., that produce different responses in something, and which is capable of being stored in, transferred by, and communicated to *inanimate* things.
>
> (*OED* 1989, vol. 7, my emphases)

This dehumanised information is increasingly being used to create an artificial sensory reality experienced by humans. Architectural and personalised anatomical simulations are already beyond the experimental stage. We can 'walk' through virtual buildings that exist only as computerised projections; and 'travel' through our own body tissue. Three-dimensional maps of tissue and its pathology allow surgeons to practise removal techniques on screen rather than on patients. When projected on to the site of operation, such information permits 'virtual surgery' and computer-controlled 'surgery-at-a-distance' is currently under test.

Moreover, information,

> as a mathematically-defined quantity, now especially one which represents the

degree of choice exercised in the selection or formation of one particular symbol, sequence, message, etc., out of a number of possible ones . . . is defined logarithmically in terms of the statistical probabilities of occurrence of the symbol or the elements of the message.

(OED 1989, vol. 7)

This meaning, from 1948, has been regarded in information theory as synonymous with entropy *(OED,* 2nd edn, 1989, 7: 1069), but is today probably better regarded as chaotic in the mathematical sense (see later), not least in the context of gatekeeping filters and screening-out devices in electronic communications networks; information pollution and computer viruses; and the development of intelligent, self-adaptive and thinking computers.

So what we mean, in the future, by 'knowledge' may be closer to the older, now rare referent of 'intelligence' ('the action or fact of mentally apprehending something; understanding, knowledge, cognisance, comprehension'; *OED* 1989, 7: 1069) than to 'information' as 'the act of informing' a person about something specific. What might the uses of such personalised, customised intelligence be, to whom, with what effects? And what will the future be for 'collective' knowledge, a categorical form developed under conditions of modernity and the basis of existing disciplines? Will collective anthropological 'knowledge' – as tacitly understood in the past – be possible under the domination of information technology, or did the discourse of post-modernist authorial fracture really represent the shape of things to come?

One vexed question concerns what, exactly, we may be studying when attempting to investigate the relations between what, in the past, have been conceptualised in good binary fashion as dichotomised 'knowledges', often implying a global versus local split. Friedson (1986: 3), as one example, distinguishes sacred from profane, theoretical from practical, elite from popular or mass, higher from lower 'knowledges', describing the 'formal' knowledge of modern, western societies as theoretical, abstract, rationalised, institutionalised and professionalised, despite 'originally [being] rooted in arcane lore and texts in ancient languages'. But such knowledge still practises 'techniques of discourse opaque to outsiders' (ibid.). Similarly, van der Ploeg (1989) contrasts 'scientific' knowledge with local 'art de la localité'. I suspect that such classifications tell us less about the 'knowledges' in question than about the epistemological assumptions of the authors concerned. The problem, as I see it, is who gets to define 'knowledge'. And that, in turn, is partly an issue of power. We are all familiar with the aphorism attributed to Francis Bacon (1597, *De Haeresibus*), in the pre-modern era when both were personalised: 'knowledge itself is power'. But today there is an epistemologically more accurate counter-claim, according to English definitions, from the contemporary third world. 'Knowledge itself is not power; its power lies in use and innovation' (Tong 1989: 76), specifically in its use in the new information technologies, which are little used by locals.

Both quotations suggest that to those who can make definitions stick comes power of some sort. Passive reception of cosmopolitan 'knowledge' entails local subordination. But even the intellectual authority of the global centre that defines 'knowledge' may eventually be shaken from within by new interpretations of existing data (Kuhn 1970; Stewart 1989). Indeed, as natural scientists have recognised the limitations of their understanding of complex natural systems, they at least have renounced rationalist hegemony.

There is no absolute knowledge. All information is imperfect.

(Bronowski 1973: 353)

[S]ystems obeying immutable and precise laws do not always act in predictable and regular ways. Simple laws may not produce simple behaviour. Deterministic laws can produce behaviour that appears random. Order can breed its own kind of chaos.

(Stewart 1989: 2)

So we should logically ask: in a globalised world, can there possibly be *one* anthropology, defined by some putative centre; or will there be many anthropologies, responding to the exigencies of local history and politics in relation to globalised ideas? In the context of the transmission of 'knowledge' via the new technologies, what is 'global' and what is 'local' anthropology? These questions are not new: Gudeman and others (1982, 1989) first raised them over a decade ago. But they are becoming more urgent, in our rapidly globalising world, because they reflect the problem of identity, as well as the (ab)uses, of knowledge.

As Gellner (1987: 162), among others, has observed: 'knowledge is not a simple echoing of facts, of confrontation with reality'. At all levels, and especially in global interface contexts, knowledge is constructed against opposition from different systems of knowledge and from those who 'know' differently (Long and Long 1992). Hence the dichotomies. Nor are the new technologies of information transmission, with their specific angles, emphases and omissions, simply devices to relay, more quickly than in the past, pictures or echoes of 'reality'. That transmission itself has its own facticity (as well as the potential for iterative distortion, reification and virtuality), grounded in the potentially chaotic impact on the human memory of visually imaged action-gestalt, so much more mobile, complex, difficult to comprehend and yet easier to remember than neatly ordered letters or characters on a page. But what will that facticity 'mean', if 'what you see isn't necessarily what you get' (Bridgeman 1993: 316–17)?

If anthropology is to make theoretical sense of what Appadurai (1990) calls these 'imagined worlds' and their ongoing information processes, we should heed his observation that understanding globalisation and relations between the global and the local (however these categories may ultimately be defined) will require recourse to similar principles to those of chaos theory in mathematics (1990: 20).

Chaos theory has already excited Abrahams (1990) in a form of *déjà vu*, but (as Brown (1992) has also pointed out) it ranges well beyond oscillating equilibria, being concerned with the real world's dynamic structure of patterned irregularity, its interplay between regularity and randomness, its 'stochastic behaviour occurring in a deterministic system' (Stewart 1989: 17). Emphatically, chaos is unitary, as is the physical world which it attempts to model.

> [M]athematicians are beginning to view order and chaos as two distinct manifestations of an underlying determinism. And neither exists in isolation. The typical system can exist in a variety of states, some ordered, some chaotic. Instead of two opposed polarities, there is a continuous spectrum.
>
> (Stewart 1989: 22)

This 'continuous spectrum' and the fractal difficulties it poses for the identification of boundaries is magnificently encompassed in a simple question: when waves break on a beach, can one separate water from sand, or model this ever-shifting boundary, structurally or mathematically?[11] Anthropology's unresolved conceptual problems in bounding 'communities' (Cohen 1985) and networks (Mitchell 1969), now demand urgent theoretical and methodological attention. A more general implication of any approach using chaos theory is that anthropology will have to abandon its past predilection for binary schemas and look more seriously to what Barth (1967, 1978) has called 'generative models' and (at least temporarily) to network theory (which has so far underpinned the new information technologies, but may not do so for much longer as these technologies develop further).

Chaos theory has replaced Newton's world of mechanistic order with the unified and ever-more-disturbing ramifications of non-linear dynamics, of the topological retention of structural relations under infinite deformation, of phase-locked oscillation, with periodic and quasi-periodic time as built-in causal dimensions of chaotic behaviour. By the late 1980s, chaos theory had yielded two major insights. First, 'a chaotic trajectory, from a given initial condition, is a non-repeatable experiment. . . . Experimental methods must be redesigned to study chaotic systems' (Stewart 1989: 289). Second, 'the identical program run on two different makes of computer can produce different results' (Stewart 1989: 21). Naturally, therefore, as Stewart (p. 138) notes, '[w]hen everyone has a computer, the *fact* of chaos is impossible to miss'! Which brings us back to the computer-linked real global world as a chaotic system.

What chaotic processes define our globalised system? Certainly *not* 'modernisation', inherited from Newtonian cosmology and conceptualised within the metaphor of the calculus, an incremental method of calculating the relationship between velocity and distance. Radcliffe-Brown (1952: 203) explained modernising change as evolutionary differentiation, based on increasing diversity and the growth of more complex from simple forms. Many sociologists (e.g. Bellah 1964; Nisbet 1969) ventured into the second half of the calculus, in their postulate of the systemic integration of the newly differentiated complex social institutions. Differentiation and integration thus appear to comprise modernisation, both as social theory and as real-life process. But if, as Giddens (1990: 63) has argued, 'modernity is inherently globalising', why did the term 'globalisation', which made its debut as early as 1962 (King 1991: 4, fn. 8), at the height of the influence of modernisation theory, become an important concept in the social sciences only twenty-five years later?

One might suggest numerous possibilities for this odd time lag, including *inter alia* relations of power within the academy and the publishing industry, and the political experiences of post-colonialism. Many would relate to how we define globalisation as one of our latest neologisms. I wish to start with Radcliffe-Brown's (1952: 190ff.) understanding of structure as a 'network of social relations' at least potentially global in scope. Giddens' (1990: 64) definition of globalisation – 'the intensification of world-wide social relations which link distinct localities in a such a way that local happenings are shaped by events occurring many miles away and vice versa' – then makes complete anthropological sense. Such intensification, fuelled by the new information technologies which by my previous definitions intensify 'knowledge' or 'intelligence', is more likely to be chaotic than to result incrementally in 'cultural entropy' (de Almeida 1992). It is therefore unsurprising that globalisation should have emerged as a major concept in the social sciences at the same time that chaos theory achieved prominence in mathematics.

Globalising processes affecting anthropology include those links (shrinking distance and speeding up communications and decisions) which, in Stewart's (1989: 145; *passim*) 'stretch and fold' or 'mix and expand' metaphors, make intensified 'world-wide social relations' not only possible and viable, but routine as part of everyday life. In 1993, ignoring all other forms of transport and up from 400 million in 1989 (Urry 1992: 1), 1.2 billion air passengers departed their countries on scheduled international flights (*High Life* 1994: 46): one for every five people on earth. 'At the expected rate of growth this figure will double by the year 2000 and quadruple a few years later' (ibid.). Clearly, humanity is moving between countries at a rate much faster than it is reproducing. Such mobility will fuel the rapid stretching, across the globe, of existing social relations (for example, in ethnic diasporas), and the establishment of new relationships (such as those between tourists and their 'hosts') which we may – or may not – wish to define as 'social relations', within 'extended' networks of the kind examined by Epstein (1969).

We should expect these individualised social relations of communication and mobility to differ in important respects from those stable social relations we have traditionally investigated: to be fleeting and irregular even when recurrent; spatially removed from patterns of permanent residence; based on specific interests even when the relations themselves are multiplex. And while we are busy trying to analyse these chaotic processes, we should, as Benson (1981: 51) cautions, resist the temptation 'to elicit regularities from the confusion of the experience, to impose an order upon events which may, in fact, best be seen as a series of accidents'. We must accept that the generation of *new* social relations involves instability, volatility, especially where contacts link *itinerant* strangers to *individual* locals, in limited and temporary interactions where one or both parties (in the context of local in-group expectations and values) may regard 'normal' constraints on their social behaviour as irrelevant.

Fundamentally, then, we are talking of migration of various kinds, including brain drains, labour migrancy, commuting, vacationing and refugee flight. The results of such movement encompass the denationalised 'corporate culture' of transnational firms, globalised 'terrorism', international professional associations, diaspora ethnicity, various kinds of cosmopolitan networks based on occupation (Barth 1978; Hannerz 1990), as well as the experiences of refugees, tourists, and members of new religious cults. Tourism, of course, is the world's fastest-growing 'industry', with an immense potential for affecting future global relations, socio-political as well as financial and ecological (Urry 1992). Tourist encounters in particular may be constructed by both tourists and hosts as unreal, hyperreal, or dreamlike. For the moment, bureaucracy may be a representational template for contemporary organisational forms, local as well as global, which make these encounters possible. However, if Toffler (1990) is correct that globalisation is dehomogenising, such templates are doomed and even 'networking' may be ephemeral, despite its current significance in explaining the 'stretch and fold' compression of space and time in globalised relations of mobility, of information as well as people.

The autonomous mobility of information is critically important in the new world communications structure. Self-fulfilling prophecies of the past, such as the Wall Street crash of 1929 and its consequent banking failures, were leisurely affairs, developing over days, weeks, months, even years as individual human minds contributed their own personal decisions to an aggregate financial disaster. In contrast, 'Black Monday' (19 October 1987) was a brief, telescoped affair following the previous year's computerisation of the London Stock Exchange. This computerised trading permitted the volume of foreign exchange transactions to exceed by several times the value of the gross world product (Rheingold 1991: 369). Today that factor has almost certainly multiplied exponentially, but the international economy has technically been bankrupt for nearly a decade. In 1987, as share prices dropped, networked computers decided on the basis of pre-programmed 'information' to offload ever-increasing volumes of scrip into a tumbling price void, in markets connected by satellite telecommunications and separated only by the delays of existing time-zoning in respect of trading hours. Ironically, therefore, because its markets close before those in London and New York open, the crisis occurred in New Zealand – at the leading edge of existing time zones – on Black Tuesday 20 October! Neither slowdown nor iterative divergence (both characteristic, as we all know, of the chaos represented by any overloaded university computer taking on new tasks) interrupted the crash. Ordinary people the world over suffered massively from a crisis created by dehumanised decisions triggered by instant information fed into 'interactive markets' reflected on computer screens. Human or social agency was conspicuously distanced from this global crisis, which exemplified perfectly what Beck (1992a, b) has called the new 'risk society', globally vulnerable to risks over which individual, popular or even state control seems, at present, minimal (see also Douglas 1992).

The new globalised information technology is capable of rocking not only the international economic order. During the Gulf crisis, this technology personalised viewers' perceptions of participating in violent conflict and war. The telewar was followed by televised Ayodhya returning not merely to haunt yet another Indian government, but also – like the Yugoslav tele-conflicts – to wreck places of worship and fragile relationships in far-flung diaspora networks, among different categories of immigrants, and between immigrant and host categories, in cities from North America to Australasia. Instant, visual, personalised 'knowledge': stochastic social results, important to anthropology, important as data, but even more important in respect of our future viability as a profession. It is precisely in our diffident representations of situations which conform to the mathematical definition of 'chaotic' (the Middle East, the former Yugoslavia), that our professional credibility in the eyes of the globalised 'western' public is most at risk (Ahmed 1992; see also Peterson 1991), now and in the future.

Perhaps part of the explanation of our professional shortcomings in dealing with the chaotic is that our anthropological modes of generating 'intelligence' are already obsolete in cosmopolitan systems. Prokhorov *et al.* (1990: 97) argue that, in the so-called advanced societies, a 'screen culture' (cognate with the 'information society' of western conceptualisations) has already developed from the new information technology. This screen culture, they allege, is quite distinct from what they call the 'two traditional types of culture' based on personal contact and writing. 'Screenies' have grown up on two-dimensional digitalised 'video-logic' with its range of pre-programmed but apparently individualising personal choices (Toffler 1990: 359–60), for which the structuring decision parameters are hidden by a complex technology rather than by mystified relations of power, as in traditional ideologies. (In the technocracy of the future, therefore, the equivalent of a bloody revolution to change the power structure will be hacking into comprehensive international databases to alter basic commands, which will have chaotic results in more than the mathematical sense.) Screenies, our profes- sional heirs and successors, understand the world differently from ourselves. But the information technology on which *their* understanding is based is already changing. 'Virtual reality', rapidly expanding out of the domain of training simulators in creating artificial worlds of sensory experience, may well (as Huxley (1932; 1959) anticipated) render past experiences of physical reality obsolete. Anthropology must confront, in these technologies of producing, transmitting, storing and retrieving *visual* mega-information, an increasing proportion of which will become the illusory ephemera of virtuality, their implications for our own professional collective memory and our future representations of representations of others' perceived realities, as well as the ways in which those other realities are differently structured by different technologies. Visual anthropology has yet to address such issues.

To conclude such a chaotic foray is – even stochastically – improbable. I shall therefore attempt merely to summarise the major lineaments of my argument in relation to the global–local interface. Firstly, conceptualising global processes and their social results as chaotic involves concentrating on individualised irregularity, in preference to older assumptions that, by definition, some form of social collectivity must be involved. For the chaotic option, our past theorising of relationships linking individuals to social collectivities is inadequate. At the global level, we are no longer dealing with territorially bounded, interactive groups; nor even with manipulative migrants who have no difficulty in selecting appropriate identities in clearly different rural and urban contexts. Instead, anthropologists must come to terms with global networks that are not, in any sense, 'groups', although their members – who may or may not actually know one another – may share specific categorical interests; and with networks of networks (cf. Hannerz 1992: 51). In these networks, multiple identifies are normal, some possibly desocialised or fictional and many involving conflicting identities operating simultaneously in the same individuals. Resulting from the personal resolutions of these multiple identities is the future possibility of small, customised, geographically dispersed 'designer societies' communicating via the new infor- mation technologies, in which new ways of defining identity and membership will diverge from past normative rules for the construction and maintenance of social boundaries and relationships. And many of these observations may well apply not only to the global level, but also to localities on the spatial interfaces affected by the globalising processes of mobility.

Second, our past modelling of individual and corporate agency has ignored decisions and processes which have no 'agency', but which are regular, patterned parts of a probabilistic information system which, as 'intelligence', materially and causally affect globalised social relations. We have also had difficulty handling those conflict-generating irregularities of human agency which impact, in the stretch and fold phenomenon, far beyond the local context(s) in which they originate. The simultaneity of individual agency and the stochastic non-agency of dehumanised processes, at both global and local levels, is a critically important aspect of globalisation. Somehow, therefore, the global and/or local anthropologies of the globalised future must find concepts to analyse the new 'knowledges' that emerge from these existing realities.

NOTES

1 It is perhaps not coincidental that the incidence of multiple personality disorder has apparently increased over the past two decades of rapid globalisation (Hacking 1992)!
2 Such as the Cambridge Videodisc (Macfarlane 1990) and Harvard Perseus Projects (Crane 1991), as well as CD–ROM facilities in Library Science.
3 In 1990 some five million computer-users exchanged twelve megabytes of infor- mation daily (Rheingold 1991: 198). These figures have risen exponentially ever since, requiring upgraded processing facilities on university computing networks merely to handle this new traffic. By early 1994, the Internet alone linked some fifteen

million users worldwide (*Guardian Weekly*, vol. 150, no. 7 (13 February 1994), p. 5). And, as a peripheral colleague recently grumbled (against new forms of electronic power), the USA is the 'default address' for e-mail, alone in the world having no country identification in its address codes.

4 Electronic publication requires new citation conventions, as suggested by Crane and Li (1993).

5 In an era where university libraries are finding it increasingly difficult to afford hardcopy journal subscriptions, these networks permit access to almost any article published, at the very nominal charge of a royalty fee and instantaneous supply by File Transfer Protocol, from databases such as Uncover. At the end of 1993, Uncover listed 14,000 journal issues containing over four million articles published since 1989, and was adding another 4,000 references each day.

6 Martin Walker, 'When seeing is no longer believing', *Guardian Weekly*, vol. 149, no. 18 (31 October 1993), p. 6.

7 In 1993 in the UK alone, some seven billion pounds sterling was invested in home cabling by major communications corporations (ITN World News, 16 November 1993).

8 *Guardian Weekly*, 5–11 September 1993, p. 8: 'Police crack CD porn ring'.

9 See *Campus Review: Higher Education News*, vol. 3, no. 37 (30 September–6 October 1993), p. 1; no. 38 (7–13 October 1993), p. 3.

10 And its arguments for a monopolistic interface protocol for computers and telecommunications equipment are disputed, at least in Australia (*Campus Review: Higher Education News*, 1993, various issues).

11 See Ralph Abraham (n.d.).

REFERENCES

Abraham, R. (n.d.) 'Human fractals: the arabesque in our mind', unpublished manuscript [1993].

Abrahams, R. (1990) 'Chaos and Kachin', *Anthropology Today*, 6 (3): 15–17.

Ahmed, A.S. (1991) 'Anthropology "comes out"?', *Anthropology Today*, 7 (3): 1–2.

Appadurai, A. (1990) 'Disjuncture and difference in the global cultural economy', in M. Featherstone (ed.), *Global Culture*, London: Sage Publications.

Barth, F. (1967) 'On the study of social change', *American Anthropologist*, 69 (6): 661–9.

—— (1978) 'Scale and network in urban western society', in F. Barth (ed.), *Scale and Social Organisation*, Oslo: Universitetsforlaget.

Bateson, G. (1979) *Mind and Nature*, Glasgow: Fontana/Collins.

Beck, U. (1992a) 'From industrial society to risk society: questions of survival, social structure and ecological enlightenment', *Theory, Culture and Society*, 9 (1): 97–123.

—— (1992b) *Risk Society: Towards a New Modernity*, London: Sage Publications.

Bellah, R. (1964) 'Religious evolution', *American Sociological Review*, 39: 358–74.

Benson, S. (1981) *Ambiguous Ethnicity*, Cambridge: Cambridge University Press.

Bridgeman, B. (1993) 'Separate visual representations for perception and for visually guided behaviour', in S.R. Ellis, M. Kaiser and A.J. Grunwald (eds), *Pictorial Communication in Virtual and Real Environments*, London and Washington: Taylor and Francis.

Bronowski, J. (1973) *The Ascent of Man*, London: BBC Publications.

Brown, D.J.J. (1992) 'Spiralling connubia in the Highlands of New Guinea', *Man* (n.s.), 27 (4): 821–42.

Cohen, A.P. (1985) *The Symbolic Construction of Community*, Chichester: Ellis Horwood / London: Tavistock.

Crane, G. (1991) 'Composing culture: the authority of an electronic text', *Current Anthropology*, 32 (3): 293–311.

Crane, N. and Li, X. (1993) *Electronic Style: A Guide to Citing Electronic Information*, Westport, CT: Meckler Publishing.

de Almeida, M.W.B. (1992) 'On Turner on Lévi-Strauss', *Current Anthropology*, 33 (1): 60–3.

Douglas, M. (1992) *Risk and Blame: Essays in Cultural Theory*, London: Routledge.

Epstein, A.L. (1969) 'The network and urban social organization', in J.C. Mitchell (ed.), *Social Networks in Urban Situations*, Manchester: Manchester University Press.

Featherstone, M. (ed.) (1990) *Global Culture: Nationalism, Globalisation and Modernity*, London: Sage Publications.

Friedson, E. (1986) *Professional Powers: A Study of the Institutionalisation of Formal Knowledge*, Chicago/London: University of Chicago Press.

Gellner, E. (1987) *Culture, Identity and Politics*, Cambridge: Cambridge University Press.

Giddens, A. (1990) *The Consequences of Modernity*, Stanford: Stanford University Press.

Gudeman, S. and Penn, M. (1982) 'Models, meaning and reflexivity', in D. Parkin (ed.), *Semantic Anthropology* (ASA 22), London: Academic Press.

Gudeman, S. and Rivera, A. (1989) 'Columbian conversations', *Current Anthropology*, 30 (3): 267–76.

Hacking, I. (1992) 'Multiple personality disorder and its hosts', *History of the Human Sciences*, 5 (2): 3–31.

Hannerz, U. (1990) 'Cosmopolitans and locals in world culture', in M. Featherstone (ed.), *Global Culture: Nationalism, Globalisation and Modernity*, London: Sage Publications.

—— (1992) 'The global ecumene as a network of networks', in A. Kuper (ed.), *Conceptualizing Society*, London: Routledge.

High Life (1994) Global Service (London: British Airways, January: 44–8).

Huxley, A. (1932) *Brave New World*, London: Chatto and Windus.

—— (1959) *Brave New World Revisited*, London: Chatto and Windus.

King, A.D. (1991) 'Introduction', *Culture, Globalization and the World-System*, Binghamton, NY: SUNY Dept of Art and Art History, in association with Macmillan.

Kuhn, T.S. (1970) *The Structure of Scientific Revolution* (rev. edn), Chicago: University of Chicago Press.

Long, N. (1992) 'From paradigm lost to paradigm regained?' in N. and A. Long (eds), *Battlefields of Knowledge*, London: Routledge.

Long, N. and Long, A. (eds) (1992) *Battlefields of Knowledge*, London: Routledge.

Lyman, P. (1993) 'Learning to use knowledge freed from the bonds of print format', *Campus Review: Higher Education News* (Australia) 3 (14): 10, 17 (April 22–28).

Macfarlane, A. (1990) 'The Cambridge experimental videodisc project', *Anthropology Today*, 6 (1): 9–12.

Mitchell, J.C. (ed.) (1969) *Social Networks in Urban Situations*, Manchester: Manchester University Press.

Nisbet, R.A. (1969) *Social Change and History*, New York: Oxford University Press.

Oxford English Dictionary (1989) (2nd edn): Information (vol. 7, pp. 944–6); Intelligence (vol. 7, p. 1069); Knowledge (vol. 8, pp. 517–8), Oxford: Clarendon Press.

Paine, R. (1992) 'The Marabar Caves, 1920–2020', in S. Wallman (ed.), *Contemporary Futures* (ASA monograph 30), London: Routledge.

Peterson, M.A. (1991) 'Aliens, ape men and whacky savages: the anthropologists in the tabloids', *Anthropology Today*, 7 (5): 4–7.

Prokhorov, A., Ragolov, K. and Ruin, V. (1990) 'A coming millennium culture', *Social Sciences* (USSR Academy of Sciences), 21 (3): 95–110.

Radcliffe-Brown, A.R. (1952) *Structure and Function in Primitive Society*, London: Cohen & West.

Rheingold, H. (1991) *Virtual Reality*, London: Secker & Warburg.

Robertson, R. (1992) 'Globality and modernity', *Theory, Culture and Society*, 9 (2): 153–61

Stewart, I. (1989) *Does God Play Dice?*, Harmondsworth: Penguin Books.

Strathern, M. (1994) 'Displacing knowledge: technology and the consequences for kinship', in I. Robinson (ed.), *Life and Death under High Technology Medicine*, Manchester: Manchester University Press / Fulbright Commission.

—— (in press) 'Surrogates and substitutes: new knowledge for old?', in I. Velody and J.M.M. Good (eds), *The Paradox of Postmodernity: Politics and Theory*, Cambridge: Cambridge University Press.

Toffler, A. (1990) *Powershift*, New York, etc.: Bantam Books.

Tong, T. (1989) 'On the intelligence revolution: the social impact of high-tech development', *Social Sciences in China*, 10 (4): 66–84.

Urry, J. (1992) 'The tourist gaze and the "environment"', *Theory, Culture and Society*, 9 (3): 1–26.

van der Ploeg, J.D. (1989) 'Knowledge systems, metaphor and interface: the case of potatoes in the Peruvian Highlands', in N. Long (ed.), *Encounters at the Interface*, Wageningen: WAU.

7 Cultures in collision

The emergence of a new localism in academic research[1]

Stephen Hill and Tim Turpin

At the far end of one university campus in Australia they have built a new, multimillion-dollar, high-technology building. It is protected by sophisticated alarm systems, embodies inner 'high security' limited access areas, and has an entrance that exudes such an image of privacy that the public would not step over the threshold at the last University Open Day – no matter how entreating were the signs inviting them in.

The building houses the separate corporate arm of the university's commercial activities. University researchers who work there are able to suspend the traditional salary levels and entitlements of academic work in favour of earning an unlimited income based on percentage of income generated. There is a thick layer of upper-level managers, largely drawn from corporate and administrative backgrounds, on incomes higher than professors, and all subject to immediate dismissal if performance falls. Company cars, car phones and other corporate status symbols steer corporate values and expectations. Senior management operates on a philosophy that commercialisation of university research will only work if academic research activity with commercial potential is managed strictly according to commercial principles and full costs, and sees the mission as 'identifying what industry wants, and then giving it to them'; not 'excellence', not adding value from new knowledge, but responding to what the market place defines as a question worth paying money for.

In the context of 1990s recession, the corporation is faltering as internal overhead costs soar above outside commercial levels and projected products and contracts falter. The cries of anger and anguish from the faculty sector are increasingly trenchant. Partly justified, partly projected, they see university moneys crossing the organisational divide from faculty to commercial sector of the institution and being soaked up into an enterprise that some identify as the total antithesis of academic values. From across the other side of the divide – within the building – there are rumblings of antagonism against 'these two-dollar shareholders' who live in ivory towers of irrelevance.

The 'building' is important in this context. Its high-technology modernism and secretiveness gather the values and discourses of the marketplace into an expensive and *separate symbol* of power that lies geographically within the academic domain, but organisationally and symbolically outside it. In line with Clifford Geertz's observations on the cultural constitution of power, that is, 'power must first be imagined before it can be used or responded to' (Geertz 1991), the 'building' therefore inscribes the symbols of commercial marketplace power deeply into the consciousness of every academic who must drive past it just *after* the entrance gate on his or her way to the cloisters; a much more insidious reminder of power than any shopping mall or industrial complex that could lie just metres *outside* the spatial boundary.

Meanwhile, *within* the faculty sector another debate started, concerning academic salary remuneration. In the interests of attracting better quality staff out of the labour marketplace, salaries for academic staff in accountancy had, for two years, been supplemented generally by 10 per cent, and salaries of computer science staff by 15 per cent. Now, however, the concern to attract and retain quality staff using salary increments had deepened and split. Following a report by external consultants, it was planned that 'general' salary increments would be phased out; in replacement, however, a system of specific rewards was being explored for individuals who could demonstrate their marketplace value.

The response of the academic union was to seek to eliminate *any* over-award payment, and therefore the intrusion of commercial marketplace values into rewards for either performance or scarcity. The twin premises for their position were 'knowledge-value' and 'equity'; that is, that academics were attracted to academia not by promises of money, but by the life and values academic life represented, and that over-award payments to some would mean a loss in general employment conditions for others, for example, in erosion in quality of libraries, space and research time.

The response by other academics mirrored conflicts in interest: computer scientists pointed fervently to marketplace salaries, and their opponents to the erosion in student numbers within that computer science faculty. Salary rewards for individual 'research excellence', no matter how such rewards might be defined, did not rate a mention.

The response by university administration was to argue strongly for individual attraction and retention rewards on the grounds that other universities were now setting such systems in place, and the local university would be increasingly disadvantaged in holding quality staff and therefore in holding on to an external competitive advantage. In keeping with the devolution of financial responsibilities that the administration had set in place over recent years, they also argued, however, that there would be no new money and that each faculty would need to re-allocate its current resources to support such market-based salary increments. Faculties were therefore thrown right back into the marketplace again; if they could raise additional moneys through commercial activity or attraction of full fee-paying foreign students, then they would have more money to attract better staff.

The social conditions for the production of academic knowledge had therefore entered a contested domain. Within academic discourse inside the institution, private interests confronted collegiality as the rules of the economic marketplace were breaching the institution's walls and setting themselves in place inside the halls of academic knowledge production.

In a third case, this time within the only commercially operated private university in Australia, Bond University in Queensland, the result has been a direct threat to traditional academic independence of the institution as a whole.

Under severe financial pressure, the original private funder of the university, Allan Bond, was forced to sell his share of the university to Japanese interests (shortly before being declared bankrupt and being imprisoned for fraudulent activity). The result was a direct contest between academic and corporate values within the university's governing body, its Council. The Chancellor and the two other 'independent' members of the University Council resigned on the grounds of the threat being posed to university independence by the university's corporate funders, the Japanese corporation, EIE International. These corporate funders sought to dominate the Council with EIE-nominated or controlled personnel as a condition of guaranteed funding of the university (*Australian* 1992: 1, 13). Meanwhile, at the same time as the voice of control issued from one side of the mouth of EIE, the other side of the corporate mouth was speaking a message that assured the university of autonomy. The managing director of the corporation, Mr Jiro Yagama, claimed, 'EIE is completely committed to the academic independence of Bond University'. It was just that 'EIE needed to have confidence in the Council in order to continue the funding of Bond.'

GLOBALISATION OF MARKET–KNOWLEDGE TENSIONS

The 'market–knowledge' interactions that these stories represent are not unusual. In varying forms, knowledge production and the commercial market[2] have been engaged with each other throughout the history of universities, as what many identify as the freedom to engage in pure research has confronted an obligation to the state to which the researchers belong (Baldridge 1971; Meek 1981; Newson and Buchbinder 1988; Huppauf 1989: 2–27; Davies and Morgan 1982; Wasser 1990; Ziman 1991). The pressure on academia from the commercial marketplace has, however, strengthened in the last few years.

This is not only the case in established market economies. The force of commercialisation has also recently crossed state ideological boundaries and struck deeply into universities in previous centrally controlled economies. To take China as an example (because it is a subject of our research at the Centre for Research Policy), in response to 'lack of vitality and entrenched isolation from the needs of industry', a recent report in the *China Daily* newspaper observed, 'the competition mechanism is spurring university teachers to become busier and richer' (1992); the Chinese Vice-Premier, Zhu Rongji, strongly advocated the community of interest between research and production units (Pin 1992); the President of the Chinese Academy of Sciences is calling for the brave introduction of the market system and the break-up of departmental and professional restrictions (Jie 1992); and a senior Chinese policy analyst and adviser recently told us that China, like the west, was seeking to produce 'a new kind of scientist – an entrepreneurial scientist'. Government policy has been to introduce knowledge into the marketplace by encouraging scientists to move from the university domain into new enterprise zones where they can 'seek out one another on a regular sustained basis' (Simon 1991). Government is also introducing the market system back inside the university institutions as well. In 1991, the Beijing Administration introduced what they called 'internal personnel management reform' into higher education institutions, involving a new wage distribution system, a new contract appointments system and a new quality control system, to provide universities with more localised control over the quality and quantity of research and teaching work carried out in their name (*China Daily* 1992). As Wasser observes, universities world-wide are experiencing 'qualitative change' that 'is so radical that the very identity of the university and the justification for even using the term itself may be called into question' (Wasser 1990: 122).

The conflicts reflected in the opening stories of the present chapter are therefore not likely to be only parochial. Universities globally are confronting an identity crisis. As with any identity crisis – in this case from the manner in which commercial marketplace values are sweeping into the university system – a serious level of questioning is emerging, also world-wide. In response to what Davies and Morgan (1982) observe within the North American experience as an environment of 'contraction and uncertainty', the President of Harvard University, Derek Bok, observes that there is a 'persistent tendency to emphasise too heavily . . . the importance of relationships between universities and industry as a means of getting ahead competitively' (Bok 1991: 15). In Britain, Shirley Williams, former Labour Party MP and Secretary of State for Education and Science, laments: 'Those who want to harness the universities to commercial objectives may destroy the very qualities they admire in them – intellectual excellence, free inquiry, scientific imagination' (Williams 1991).

Within Australia, as elsewhere, the level of concern about the erosion of university strength by commercial marketplace values is orders of magnitude higher than ever before. Strident voices have appeared in the national press, academics describing the pattern of change within universities as 'away from the road to free and fundamental discovery towards applied research . . . that is increasingly governed by market principles'; as a 'move from distinguished standards of excellence towards uniformity'; as 'creating academic slums'; or as 'rolling out the corporate carpet' (*Australian* 1991: 13). Bernie Neville, writing from within the field of education, observes: 'It seems apparent that we have been monotheistically worshipping the god of the marketplace for some time. We have seen an infatuation with the magic hand of the marketplace, enthusiastically supported by political leaders' (Neville 1992: 347).

The protests are deeply felt. Protesters mourn a paradise lost under pressure to participate in private secular advantage. And the process of *linking* scientific knowledge to commercial market value – a historical progression that parallels the history of industrialism – appears, as Shirley Williams observes, as a 'pendulum that has swung too far' (1991). The pragmatists, central policy makers and economic rationalists, standing at the pivotal end of the pendulum, do not yet see the promised commercial fruit, however. Their view is likely to be that the pendulum has not swung far enough.

Both sides are, however, transfixed on the surface of the phenomenon, assuming that whilst the balance has varied, the *form* of the relationship between commercialisation values and research has remained the same at least for the last half century. Indeed, throughout the whole period since World War II, global scientific knowledge production has been continuously and closely connected with the commercial marketplace, in the commercial laboratories that rose to prominence in the 1960s and in defence and government-run applied research enterprises that collectively contributed the lion's share of support to scientific endeavour throughout the whole period. However, whilst this is the case, and the pendulum of overall balance of effort may have swung differently under varying external attractors, there has also been a change in form. Commercial market values have penetrated across institutional boundaries into public sector science and, in particular, into universities. In the 1960s, the core 'academic research system' constituted its own 'economy' and linked scientific training to its system. The academic domain could therefore negotiate two-way exchanges of scientific knowledge for money and/or power across boundaries to the other (commercial, government and market) systems (Crook 1991: 10). And the academic domain could remain culturally separate, able to reflect on and critique the immediate and pragmatic with some level of distance. This is no longer the case.

Consequently, it is not merely a pendulum of knowledge–market linkage that has swung too far. Instead, the commercial marketplace is sitting *inside* the processes that forge the global constitution of society's knowledge, rather than standing alongside and drawing from society's knowledge capital. What the academics are responding to is a deep new penetration of commercial marketplace values into the *cultures* that have been traditionally associated with the constitution of academic knowledge.

The issue, however, is much broader historically and globally than an immediate conflict of values might suggest. Invitation of the commercial marketplace into the knowledge domain is historically situated in a fundamental shift in the wider culture that surrounds science. This is a shift from the modernist culture that reified the liberating power of science to a culture of so-called postmodernism – a post-1960s culture that has shrugged off the emancipatory certainties of science and erected commercial marketplace values and pluralistic images in its stead. The implications are profound, not only for universities but for the construction of the very knowledge base that will shape our collective future, as well as for the paths of access to this knowledge. For it is this shift in wider culture that has pressed into the halls of academic inquiry and is currently transforming it.

THE PRESSURE TO COMPETE

The pressures on academic systems to move seriously on to the commercial marketplace had been building up through the 1980s. Many of the government policy changes through the decade that followed represented a continuation of an increasingly strong movement within most countries to put science to work for the state.

Over the last four years, in particular, the pressure for relevance was applied to the Australian university system, which absorbs 55 per cent of the government research budget (Australian Bureau of Statistics 1990). There were two research-funding 'markets' to which the institutions were forced to respond: the grant-oriented funding of research activity, and the commercially oriented funds that could be gained from commercial productivity. The force of both of these 'markets', together with government policy initiatives that more specifically directed universities towards concentration and competition in their knowledge activities, all worked together to produce a university system that is undergoing considerable change.

Research funds that had previously been allocated relatively uncompetitively through university operating grants were clawed back into the Australian Research Council's (ARC) finances to be distributed to individuals and institutions on a competitive basis. Universities are further rewarded, according to a rather complex formula, through the provision of additional research infrastructure funding that approximately matches the institution's success on the open competitive market of the ARC and other Commonwealth competitive grants (Turpin and Hill 1991). However, because the pool of potential active researchers has increased faster than the capacity of government to fund research, the success rate of university researchers in gaining ARC research funds is now below 20 per cent of total grant applications. The competition is intense.

Universities and individual researchers have been increasingly forced to look beyond their traditional boundaries with the commercial world, and, therefore, the commercial 'marketplace'. Many universities have attempted to strengthen their commercial activities by establishing various forms of commercial agencies. In Australia there are many – more than twice the number of Australian universities – and their corporate structures are varied. In general, however, the commercial agencies provide commercial liaison, consultancy and patenting services to re- searchers in their host organisations. These commercial agencies have been constructed according to the organising principles of 'sound and rational economic management'. Yet, embedded in the relationship between commercial agency and university knowledge production, there is contested terrain. In 1992, as many as sixty-eight of the university companies have been served with a log of claims on behalf of academic researchers employed in universities around Australia. These claims have been principally concerned with a steady stream of complaints about the management of intellectual property. Paradoxically, the overlaying of an 'organising' managerial principle on to the commercialisation of university knowledge has yielded a 'disorganising' product.

From our own research, we have found staff and institutions increasingly moving out into a range of funding and commercial marketplaces, being required 'to compete with each other with increasing intensity to obtain funding for their research' – the essential activity of their 'knowledge domain' (Centre for Research Policy 1992) – until the very symbols of the marketplace *replace* the symbols of knowledge production that gave meaning to the knowledge domain in the first place.

It is not surprising, then, that 'organising' policy initiatives to foster commercial market-oriented competition consistently conjure up 'disorganising' consequences. This reflects less a poor choice or management of strategy than the fact that, ranged against the encroaching commercial market-oriented domain, is a domain of action (knowledge) that cannot simply be vanquished and absorbed: it must fundamentally transform. Pierre Bourdieu observes the separateness of the two domains in their steering mechanisms; the 'knowledge' side being steered largely by the authority of 'cultural' or 'intellectual' capital, and the 'market' side being steered by 'academic' and 'social' capital (Bourdieu 1988: 98).[3] The conflict between domains is producing a colonisation of the knowledge domain by the commercial market domain. But it is a colonisation that follows from a kind of fifth-column influence, as the steering mechanisms of the commercial market domain start to command the steering mechanisms of the knowledge domain.

Indeed, the colonisation does come from within. Change is most deeply occurring in the structures of power and relationship that surround knowledge production – in the social relations of production, and therefore in the culture that is produced as a consequence. Policy initiatives to encourage organised concentration, commercialisation and market competition for research funds, with all the 'disorganising' effects that have followed, have all implied *structural* change that has opened the door for managerialism to step into the *culture* of the laboratory and its institutional environment.

ENTER MANAGERIALISM: THE NEW ENTERPRISE CULTURE

A 'new breed' of research managers has entered the administrative structure of Australian universities. Called (generally) 'Pro Vice-Chancellors (Research)', and meeting regularly as a newly defined national group, their basic objective is to manage the process of gaining research funds from the research-funding marketplace for all disciplines – not to manage or lead the research itself. Many of the universities have added an administrative support system to these positions with highly paid research managers and research management offices. Their existence inserts a managerialist layer between the researcher and his or her funding. In Australia there is a government requirement of Pro Vice-Chancellors to produce Research Management Plans within short-time horizons. This has tended to centralise the institutional considerations that produce the universities' collective direction. Grass-roots involvement and faculty debate have become increasingly marginalised in favour of managerial efficiency. Within the near future, the Research Management Plan requirement by government could possibly be removed. But it has already done its job. The research management system is now in place.

While taking a particular form in Australia, the structural changes mirror a global trend. Arie Rip observes the emergence of an 'intermediary layer' (as with Australia's Pro Vice-Chancellors (Research)), at a more general level, 'of actors and institutions – like funding agencies and programme bureaus – between research practices on the one hand, and state and societal institutions on the other hand' (Rip 1991: 401). A recent OECD study of university financing trends in eleven OECD countries observes that the political climate of the 1980s stimulated a move from unconditional public funding toward conditional grants and market demands (Organisation for Economic Co-operation and Development 1990). As also observed by Maureen Woodhall, for twenty-four British universities and colleges, university management has changed dramatically to increase control over finances, to generate more income, and to reduce the numbers of tenured staff. Meanwhile:

> The decision to give greater priority to income generation has led many institutions to appoint new staff with marketing skills and to develop institutional strategies designed for local, national or even international markets.
>
> (Woodhall 1991: 49)

What we find in the 'new managerialism' that Maureen Woodhall's observation suggests is a radical shift in philosophy, not simply a move to make university financing more direct and accountable. Woodhall's observation demonstrates a shift in attitudes that aligns with a shift in the structure of decision-making and in the social relations of production of knowledge within the university system. This shift, however, is not only in attitudes as such, but more deeply in the very culture of knowledge production itself.

Why this should occur is quite clear if we are to take a single leaf out of anthropological understandings of cultures. Social groupings, whether at the level of societies or organisations, construct the meaning of their actions – in other words, their cultures – within the social relations that are formed in communicating and producing together. Change the social relations and cultures change (Hill 1988; 1991: 92–113).

Evidence of the extent of *cultural* shift that is occurring beneath the feet of those mourning the loss of academic purity is therefore visible in the shift in structures of power and of production of academic outputs that surround academic work such as we described earlier. The 'new managerialism' that is identified with this shift in the organisation of academic affairs is subject to some considerable resistance from the traditional academic establishment. A press release from the Australian Academy of Science issued in 1991 expresses this concern. Quoting a criticism by a Fellow of the Academy, Professor Derek Robinson, the press release highlights the shift in institutional control that is associated with the 'new managerialism' as a blind application of inappropriate generic methods of management theory to scientific research. The new managerialism of science is an artificial account-ancy reform which leaves little room for rational planning of long term scientific projects and, as the control of research passes from scientists to managers, its aims are changed from long term productivity to short term activity.

(Robinson 1991)

But the cultural shift is coming to ground not simply in increasing pressure to plan and 'relate' the production of scientific knowledge, but in shaping, and perhaps constraining, the production process itself according to managerialist 'best practice' rules. As one of the Australian university administrators we interviewed recently told us, when identifying his institution's vision of the future:

Our task is to homogenise the expectations of the different faculties, schools and individuals into a generally shared view about teaching and research; we need to bring disparate philosophies, ideas and expectations together into a unified set of directions and objectives.

Research in this context is a unifiable commodity, its funding linked through managerial processes to a competitive research-funding marketplace. What is entering the cloisters of university discourse is therefore not only a pressure towards application and relevance, but a culture that supports market orientation – an *enterprise culture*.

Derived originally from the Conservative political philosophies that under-lined Margaret Thatcher's influence during the 1980s in Britain, 'enterprise culture' has come to mean the managerialist culture that emerged as public institutions were constrained to reorganise to abide by market conditions. At a structural level, this has meant de-differentiation of previously distinct modes of organisation, introduction of more 'corporate' management structures, flexible employment contracts, new forms of financial control, strategic planning, and so on. At the cultural level, structural change comes to align with an emergent set of meanings that replace the specific institution user (students, in the case of universities), with references to the value of the 'consumer' (of a generalised service). These orient action through reference to 'market niches', 'product differentiation', and so forth, and place value on individual and collective 'enter-prise': initiative, energy, independence, boldness, self-reliance, a willingness to take risks and to accept responsibility for one's actions (Keat 1991a: 2–3; Burrows 1991).

The new managerialism in universities is therefore but one face of a global organisational trend which implants market values *within* the culture of public organisation. The consequence is with universities, as with public organisation elsewhere, that the meaning of 'outputs' and of work are calculated according to 'efficiency and effectiveness', according to abstract commodity value, rather than substantive significance of any other sort. Applying the 'enterprise culture' concept to the meaning of work within universities, Russell Keat observes:

> academics complain that the pressure to compete for students undermines their own conception of what is educationally worthwhile, and that the value of their research is now being judged by intellectually facile considerations of 'marketability'.

(Keat 1991b: 216)

This observation aligns with John Ziman's analysis of academic science as a system of markets. Ziman (1990) argues that the introduction of *commercial* 'market forces' into the traditional academic marketplace where research results are exchanged for varying rewards of, for example, prestige, introduces a damaging conflict between institutional and individual interests – replacing quality by price as a principle of competition.

The salience therefore of 'customer' rights orients performance towards value for money, rather than value for knowledge; privilege and authority based on knowledge are displaced, as is authority of the teacher *per se*. The relative salaries, status symbols and authority of 'executives' that are creeping into Australian universities directly mirror this shift in values, as does the symbolic power of the commercial university institution observed at the start of this chapter. The role of Vice-Chancellors, previously the symbolic and titular heads of institutions, has changed and, along with it, their symbolic value. Frank Hambly, Executive Director of the Australian Vice-Chancellors' Committee, observed:

> [Universities have] now become big business. He [the Vice-Chancellor] has to act as a chief executive, a managing director . . . they were paid peanuts. Now, they get a couple of hundred thousand in salary, superannuation and perks: house, car and whatever goes with it.

(Boag 1991: 27–8)

THE WIDER PERSPECTIVE OF ENTERPRISE CULTURE

The intrusion of enterprise culture into university affairs directly confronts cultures that are predicated on the valuing of knowledge rather than its marketability. In Jürgen Habermas's terms, 'the system has colonised the [university] lifeworld'. In other words, 'organised and abstract technique' has entered into the framework of tacit assumptions within which university research people act, live and construct the meaning of their work activity (Habermas 1984, 1987).[4]

According to Habermas's position, what is presently happening to universities is simply the extension of a broad-ranging cultural progression that has been going on in parallel with industrialism itself. Along with industrialisation and the rise of capitalism, society, he argues, has increasingly become more complex and systematised; elements of the activities that people formerly constructed within their lifeworlds – bringing up children, producing food, solving health, emotional and family problems and so on – were turned over to 'systems', systems of education, industrial systems, health systems, counselling systems, administrative, power, and, most important of all, market systems.[5] The process of reproducing society was confronted by a problem of complexity, however. The level of structural differentiation that was associated with new technological means and organisational innovations in applying systems-rationality enforced such heavy demands on the interpretive capacities of actors that whole areas of action 'dropped out of language'. 'Steering media' increasingly stepped in to provide relief mechanisms that either *condense* or *replace* the need to interpret and negotiate the meaning of action. Primary amongst the steering media is money, that reduces all knowledge values to bottom line finance, and administrative power, that indentures knowledge values to the interest of management.

The main significance of Habermas's position for the present argument is that it implies not so much that symbols of money and power step in to excise previous 'pure' values of knowledge as, more importantly, that knowledge production itself is already part of a wider system (of progressive application of rational knowledge). Its meanings are negotiated within 'abstract' discourses that individual researchers can enter, but not command. However, with the entry of the commercial marketplace directly into this knowledge system, the symbols that steer knowledge production – 'first discovery prestige', reputational status and attributed authority, and so on – become not 'condensed' into a summary version of wider meanings, but *replaced* by symbols of the commercial market place. Seen as 'ideal types', or poles of interaction, the two values systems are in direct opposition.[6]

For the scientific knowledge system:

- The 'steering medium' involves power and prestige predicated on contribution to the stock of human knowledge.
- The normative goal involves the achievement of shared understanding through persuasion and mastery of discourse.
- Communicative practices normatively tend towards public accountability, transparent and communicative discourse and an expectation of 'what would be revealed' subject to rational, criticisable validity claims.
- Core values concern rigour of validity claim, and openness of performance.

For the commercial market system:

- The 'steering medium' involves power and prestige predicated on money or administrative symbols.
- The normative goal involves the achievement of money and power through egoistic calculation of success, strategic action (implying hidden intentions), and mastery of factor inputs to competitive market advantage.
- Communicative practices normatively tend towards administrative accountability, private or bounded discourse, and an expectation of 'first mover advantage' on the marketplace through what is presently hidden.

- Core values concern measurement by output, rather than process integrity, and strategic manipulation of performance, rather than openness.

One can have no illusions about the normative 'purity' of scientists participating in the science knowledge production system. This is attested to both by the cases of direct fraud that come to the attention of the public and by the post-Mertonian literature on elites and deviance of scientists.[7] Equally, however, within a culture that values knowledge claims over monetary reward, allegiance of scientists cannot be denied to the normative quality of knowledge-based statuses, rewards, expectations and personal identity. It is into this system that these scientists dip to receive their rewards, or exchange research results on the 'knowledge' market for prestige. It is these normative guidelines that shape the socialised ability of scientists to enter into discourse with other actors within the system in order to receive these rewards which are ultimately of personal significance (Hill *et al.* 1974).

It is therefore not surprising that there has been such a depth of protest as enterprise culture has invaded the world of academic knowledge production in Australia. Nor is it surprising that the symbolic divisions appeared between the corporate arm and the faculty of the university that we described at the start of this chapter, or that conflicts appeared between varying interest groups in arguing about salary structures, or that Bond University's autonomy was threatened directly by corporate control. The 'crisis'

> is, in part, a boundary struggle between two very different domains of research activities each dominated by different sets of reward criteria, different sets of objectives, different ways of measuring success, different modes of communication and different forms of symbolic capital supported by different forms of legitimating authority. In short, they [knowledge and market] are culturally distinct.
>
> (Marsh and Turpin 1991)

But, along with the world-wide movement of enterprise culture into the organisation of public enterprise, and with the force of structural change that confronts everyday academic experience by this culture, the culture and steering media of the commercial market are deeply entering, homogenising and replacing each of the elements of the university's pre-existing and varied knowledge cultures. The resulting values are independent of the content or meaning of knowledge, but unified by the abstract symbol of dollar value – in Habermas's terms the academic lifeworld is colonised by system.

POSTMODERNIST CONTRADICTIONS: TOWARDS THE 'NEW LOCALISM'

The opening case studies of the present chapter therefore form three sides of a prism of wider cultural colonisation of public organisation that is progressing at a global level. However, progress towards global enterprise culture itself mirrors even broader moves in world culture. These moves are embedded in contradictions, with the cultural power of scientific knowledge lying at the heart of these contradictions.

The first of these contradictions was observed in the 'prism' of Australian university changes over the last five years, that is, in the 'disorganising' consequences in Australian academia of attempts to 'organise' academic knowledge production according to postmodernist market rules.

At a more general and historical level, the same contradiction – organising strategies producing disorganising consequences – can be seen in the post-World War II trend to put science to work for the state through increased *planning* of science. However the world-views within which planning philosophies were cast were continuously shifting, being impacted on by the successes and failures of scientific knowledge production itself. The consequence is that the relationship between science and the marketplace has been hidden behind other things as it emerged over the last forty years. In the 1960s the public vision of science admitted planning science for international prestige, whilst the traditional fundamental research promise of serendipitous economic benefit was a luxury that could be readily accepted within the decade's euphoria. Political leaders, at least in the case of Australia, relied on other sources of prestige and wealth and were not interested; they tolerated science as an undirected 'discretionary expenditure' that reflected Australia's image of emergent internationalism. In the 1970s, visions of science (for Australia) implied *division* – between bureaucratic planning and scientists' traditional autonomy – in the context of a nation seeking a new path in an increasingly encroaching technology-led international economy. In the 1980s, the view of science as a cultural enterprise disappeared behind technology policy, and where it neared the surface of administration and debate meant *direction* – towards economic and pragmatic utility. Behind the scenes for the whole post-war period was the vision that science could be nationally and economically useful if it was organised (Hill 1989: 67–72).

Throughout this whole post-war period the marketplace remained linked with knowledge production. However, what changed over time was the autonomy of the academic domain from what was previously a largely external marketplace domain. The culture of the marketplace had therefore crept up on the autonomy of academia, hidden as it was, behind the moves in worldview surrounding science. What was delivered by the end of the 1980s was a culture of production of scientific knowledge that was deeply penetrated by values of the marketplace towards which the planning process was oriented – both inside and outside the academic world and at the interface between academic and wider domains.

Under the impact of increasingly technology-led economic competition, science policy from the 1970s on started to assume the air of 'panic production', 'a simulation of organisation in a rapidly disorganising world', having come to prominence just when the assumed stabilities of organised science were beginning to erode. Thus, within the world-views of the 1980s, the measurement of legitimacy of scientific knowledge *generally* became attached to 'practical', 'relevant', 'market-oriented' principles. These principles promised the 'new' liberation, produced through market competitiveness rather than emancipationist and modernist ideals of the 1960s. These principles smoothed the way for the legitimised entry of planning and enterprise cultures inside the previously separate academic domain, producing the *disorganising* effects that were observed earlier as market values *replaced* knowledge values as the steering media of scientific knowledge production.

The second contradiction arises from scientific research having provided the means for wider cultural change that has in turn levelled the values of the marketplace directly at the heart of the scientific production process itself. At least this is the view of Jean-François Lyotard who seeks to depict the sources of 'postmodernist society' – the view of contemporary society that identifies present-day consciousness as arising from the shock of the late 1960s anti-war and anti-state protests from Chicago to Paris. The confrontation was in the streets and in the corridors of power. At its heart was the conflict between science and technique in the service of the state (planning of science) and the public visibility of science's inability to deliver universal good (the televised use of science-based technique to wage war). Arising from these roots, postmodernism, as a cultural movement, represented a shift in faith in the state and in public science, a movement in public consciousness that shrugged off the certainties of emancipation that modern scientific thought previously appeared to offer, and instead looked for private (and national) advantage in values of the marketplace. Lyotard (1984) argues that this transformation is an inevitable consequence of the information revolution that was coming of age at the time of the events of the late 1960s (and indeed allowed the events to reach their global impact), and which has since been the vehicle of the social relations of communication and production.

According to Lyotard, the transmission of information is of far greater significance than the content of the information itself. But the dynamics of information transmission are the dynamics of the marketplace – the form of social relations of communication embodies the values of the market. Consequently, whilst Lyotard's observation of the dominance of information exchange over contemporary global society is accurate at a structural level, the shift in society is a deeper one – in cultural consciousness, where there has been a move from a vision of knowledge as the liberating builder of futures to one of knowledge as an ephemeral market commodity. The very premises of validity and value within academic knowledge production are therefore refashioned within the wider 'information-market' domain of cultural production. And enterprise culture is able to steer scientific knowledge at its heart according to 'steering media' that replace rather than condense the traditional values of academic scientific knowledge production.

This leads us to the third contradiction. This concerns the role of actor within the discourses of scientific knowledge production. As the market enters a knowledge culture, market design parameters increasingly become built into the processes by which knowledge is produced and used. Discourse intrinsically becomes bounded and 'strategic' in Habermas's terms, and therefore secretive rather than driven by the discipline-based dynamics of display in an open 'knowledge' domain. Knowledge outputs become concerned with immediacy and workability rather than with rigour and disciplinary significance. And the general knowledge stock, rather than being valued for explanatory significance, is valued according to its depth of embeddedness within the field of organisational and economic factors that allow the knowledge to be translated into productive advantage.

Therefore, while information technologies may offer rapid access to globally generated information, what is communicated within global or cosmopolitan fields is likely to be of only limited use within scientific work. Instead, it appears to be increasingly clear that the social relations of new knowledge production within the market domain are increasingly 'local', or bounded by institutional boundaries and mediated through actor-to-actor exchanges rather than actor-discourse relationships. It follows from such an observation that the traditional understandings within the sociology of science about local and cosmopolitan domains of discourse may need to be radically revised.

Ziman has already pointed to one aspect of this revision, demonstrating that cosmopolitancy itself has been under deep threat for two decades. The 'idea' of cosmopolitancy is that it refers to a *discourse* that rises, through the contributions of 'localised' actors, to a status of abstraction and reference for continuing scientific enterprise. But, with the entry of market, the leading edge of science is increasingly secret – guided in Habermas's terms by strategic action rather than open communicative discourse – because within the contemporary industrial structure you can make money out of 'first mover' scientific ideas. According to Ziman (1991) the frontier of ideas therefore appears internationally, but through the ciphers of international organisation and their interests, translated across national boundaries but within private interest discourses. This is not 'cosmopolitan' in the traditional sense of the discourse.

In the fast-moving innovative world of computers and electronics, patenting is used to lock out all actors except the leading-edge companies, and to allow strategic access to the developments of other leading-edge companies by those who are the market leaders. University-based actors simply cannot gain access to the inter-firm discourse that is leading world innovation. John Armstrong, Vice-President for Science and Technology of IBM, observes: 'Most large companies in the world are extensively cross-licensed with each other. Exclusive licences are almost nonexistent. The key is not ownership, it is access' (1991: 21). Meanwhile, private firms gain access to the latest of university thinking through providing funding for research on which no restriction is placed on open access and publication: first-mover advantage is enjoyed by the funding firm because they are joined to the research by both money and people flows and can more rapidly capitalise on the idea before any outsider can (National Academy of Sciences 1986).

The work of Michael Porter (1990) demonstrates even more strongly that the leading edge of technological innovation is guided by 'local' processes – or inter-institutional relationships – and the traditional 'cosmopolitan' discourse of science is simply (to use Habermas's terms) 'dropping out of innovation language'. Porter demonstrates that global competitive advantage derives from competitive conditions within the local economy: innovation is particularly associated with 'clusters' of supplier, customer, producer and technological organisations, where demand for increasing quality and innovation is the requirement of competitive success. 'Local' forces – though between global corporations – and 'local' (organisationally specific) design requirements drive frontier innovation. Jacques Attali (1991) demonstrates further that there are two groups of specific actors that mediate the global innovation process between corporations and within nation states. These are the 'product specifiers' (within powerful global corporations) that lay down the criteria for marketable commodities under the auspices of global brand names; and the 'activity brokers' (similarly situated) who mediate the finance, location, technology nexus in global production, and who manipulate the global value chain across the interests of nation states as if conducting an orchestra of inputs and linkages from raw materials to sales. *Actors* mediate knowledge creation and transfer. The traditional cosmopolitan role of science provides little more than a backdrop – an essential backdrop as our own industrial interviewees observe – not to power leading-edge industrial research, but to provide the generation and testing of background concepts that are necessary in the support of applied research.

The social relations of successful innovation therefore appear to be largely 'local', even though, as Disco, Rip and van der Meulen point out, the quality and scope criteria introduced into design may well be widely accepted and 'cosmopolitan' (1991: 23). The social relations are to do with actors who retain their actor visibility within discourse, rather than with discourses that remain independent of their constitutive actors. As Sørensen and Levold observed of a Norwegian research-based company, Subtronics, 'the flow of knowledge has to be accompanied by a flow of people' (1992: 30). It is also important to realise, however, in the overall innovation cycle, that the discourses that are developed in successful use of scientific knowledge enjoin boundaries of *varying* cultures rather than seek to absorb and transform them towards uniformity.

Our own industrial research respondents in Australia say much the same thing. Researchers in private industry maintain contact with the latest and best ideas in the field by strategically attending conferences, identifying the most promising researchers, and taking them off for a drink to chat informally, meanwhile aware that others may be doing precisely the same thing to them – again in Habermas's terms, engaging in strategic action rather than in communicative action and open discourse. Most successful university–industry research relationships that we have identified so far have been established because of prior personal knowledge of the individual academic, his or her work, and, *in particular*, his or her subjective style (again, an actor rather than discourse characteristic) (National Board of Employment, Education and Training 1993).

Furthermore, from our research on the development of research cultures in the smaller and newer universities, we find that they too are fundamentally linked into subjective networks, primarily related back to their alma mater graduating institutions. In other words, there is a series of local shadows cast by the leading-edge *local* academic institutions rather than by the evolution of research groups that rely for their stock of knowledge on cosmopolitan discourse. Cosmopolitancy is mediated by localism. Irwin Feller (1990) refers to this same phenomenon – though at an institutional level – in the United States as 'mimetic isomorphism', where actions and policies of universities such as Harvard put pressure on like institutions to establish comparable policies in order to retain otherwise mobile faculties. Cosmopolitancy is therefore mediated by nests of local and actor-based networks and modelling. Reliance by academics on the 'discourse' of knowledge – contributions to the literature, as in promotions applications – is, it would seem, more a sign of marking one's territory, or of the province of those whose thinking and contributions are far from the centre of what is currently shaping the field and its questions and who count publications to gain local promotion.

The 'new localism' is widespread, deeply penetrating the production and application of scientific knowledge. As an idea, it suggests the dissolution of local–cosmopolitan as categories, for actor–actor relations that are essentially 'local' in character may cross institutional and even national boundaries.

The phenomenon represents the third contradiction of postmodernism and science. That is, it would appear that the further market penetrates knowledge constitution, the more *actors* drop *into* discourse. Meaning, as application, lies within actor–actor relationships for which discourse structures and sediments act as backdrop. This is occurring increasingly as information technology capabilities allow information exchange to be more instantaneous and comprehensive, but also as the sheer overload of information made available by new means of transmission impacts on the actors' ability to interpret what is *most* important, what is *most* able to be connected to market success, and what *other* tacit knowledge outside the immediate field must be taken into account in order for the information provided to assume meaning or application. Meanwhile, guided by actor–actor exchange within relatively closed cross-owned knowledge domains, the frontiers of marketable knowledge lead the scientific knowledge fields as a whole – leaving those outside to watch for the latest product to tell them what new laws of the universe may now be able to be tapped. And in an evocative observation on coherence and change in scientific fields, Anthony van Raan suggests that new scientific fields or new fields of technology development no longer follow the rules of dominant paradigms. Instead, as van Raan argues, the rules of field development follow more closely the rules of chaos theory: self-organising systems emerge and are continuously being replaced or marginalised by other self-organising systems; there is no hierarchical organisation of fields as would be expected under the rule of either paradigms or dominant designs (van Raan *et al.* 1992).

Actor–actor discourse in this context involves strategic action, the mode of action that aligns with the institutional contexts that increasingly bind actor relationships (including within universities) as market cultural values enter into the structures within which knowledge cultures are formed. Colonisation by market, therefore, instead of dropping actor meanings *out* of discourse, relocates the actor within them – an apparent contradiction to the culture of postmodernism. However, the colonisation is deeper, and the contradiction resolved, for actors themselves are increasingly constructing meanings (in actor–actor relations) according to the 'abstract' values of the marketplace, acting 'strategically', and being 'steered' by symbols of marketplace status and power. The knowledge lifeworld has been penetrated to the core of individual action.

BEYOND THE NEW LOCALISM

Returning once more to the stories at the introduction of this chapter, we can see in their three-sided prism a late twentieth-century moment in the global progress of postmodernist culture. What we also see, as in postmodernist society itself, is a vision of action and expectations that is ruled by the commercial marketplace, that is, short-term interest, abstract values and egoistic power.

We should also realise of course that academics are a creative lot. Many may well be adopting the outside guise and language of entrepreneurial science whilst continuing to produce what they always have been doing. Absorption, conversion and disguise may well continue to function in maintaining boundaries around a valued knowledge-oriented culture within academia. Equally, it must be recognised that cultures, all cultures, are in continuous change. The culture of scientific knowledge production of the nineteenth century – dominated by a 'gentle*man's* science' – was replaced, for example, by 'professional' science as the sheer numbers of participants and consequent modes of communication changed through the twentieth century. What we see in the 1990s – where commercial market values are penetrating deeply and in a new way into knowledge production – is therefore a *moment* in a continuous process of cultural change, not a sudden new wave of invasion into centuries-old tradition.

However, the strength and import of this moment of cultural change within the academic system must also be recognised. What is happening within the university system, at least in Australia, and apparently more generally, is not just adoption of a new set of 'spots' that can perhaps later be removed. Instead, the very social relations of production of knowledge are changing, and, along with these, the kind of knowledge that is valued, and symbols of its meaning – in other words the very base of existing university knowledge culture. And this cultural invasion is surrounded by wider social, economic and political values that are embedded in the global movements of postmodernism. So there is nowhere to return to.

In this context, one cannot contemplate return to a romantic past. However, once the present nature of change becomes transparent, it is possible at least to contemplate that something may be being lost. In the context of Australian experience, it has become increasingly clear from our own research in the Centre for Research Policy that the encroachment of enterprise culture into the crevices of science production (and vision) within academia is, like a Venezuelan cane toad in a Queensland rain forest, wiping out whole species of research culture, and perhaps transforming the very nature of the organisation and development of scientific enterprise as a whole. As with ecological taxonomies of endangered species, we need to know a great deal more about what is being lost as the colonising managerialist species is being introduced. For it is a new force that is encroaching on academic discourse through *replacing* the steering media and values that traditionally have guided the development of contemporary society's knowledge base and paradigms. The driving force of actors over traditional discourse constraints – the removal of the value of communicative action and accountability, the significance of the immediacy of knowledge – all herald an immediacy of vision.

If such a phenomenon is developing, it deserves careful scrutiny. With the entry of the postmodernist commercial marketplace into global society's knowledge base, a serious crisis may well arise where society's values and vision are so close to immediate advantage and interest that they occlude comprehension of the societal precipice we rush towards.

NOTES

1 An earlier version of this chapter appeared as 'Academic research cultures in collision' in *Science as Culture*, 20 (1994) to which acknowledgement is gratefully made. This chapter extends the theoretical perspective in the earlier article to focus more on the role of actor-networks in local and global process of cultural change.

2 We use the term 'market' throughout this chapter specifically to refer to commercial market – and thus to the rules of market-system meaning to which Habermas refers. The idea of academic knowledge and other statuses being embedded in *other* markets – as John Ziman (1990) argues – involves for us a concept of exchange systems, an issue we will not take up in the present context.

3 Bourdieu makes the distinction between what he calls two poles of the university field. These poles are represented by those who seek the 'accumulation and management of academic capital' and those who seek 'symbolic capital' or 'capital of renown' (Bourdieu 1988: 98).

4 This argument is extracted from Habermas's two-volume work on communicative action, particularly his volume 2 (Habermas 1984, 1987).

5 For a detailed analysis of the entry of technological 'systems' into the culture of industrial society, see Hill 1988.

6 Research within the Centre for Research Policy demonstrates the products of the tensions between these knowledge and commercial market dimensions in research cultures of Australian universities. See Turpin and Hill 1991; Marsh and Turpin 1991.

7 There was a particular attention to 'deviance' from Mertonian norms in the early 1970s when revision of Merton and his replacement by Kuhnian 'paradigm' thinking was a strong influence within the sociology of science. See Greenberg 1969; Barnes and Dolby 1970: 3–25; Whitley 1972, 1974; Hill 1973: 25–8; Mitroff 1974.

150 *Shifting contexts*

REFERENCES

Armstrong, J.A. (1991) 'An industry perspective on the changing university', in D. Zinberg (ed.), *The Changing University*, Dordrecht, Netherlands: Kluwer Academic Publishers.

Attali, J. (1991) *The Millennium: The Winners and Losers in the Coming World Order*, New York: Random House.

Australian , (1991) 'Experts accused of public sell-out', 6 March.

– (1992) 'Bond shocked as councillors resign', 12 February.

Australian Bureau of Statistics (1990) *1988-89 Research and Experimental Development All-Sector Summary Australia, Catalogue No. 81109.0*, Canberra: Australian Government Publishing Service.

Baldridge, J.V. (1971) *Power and Conflict in the University*, New York: J. Wiley & Sons.

Barnes, S.B. and Dolby, R.G.A. (1970) 'The scientific ethos: a deviant viewpoint', *Archiv. Europ. Sociol.*, 11: 3–25.

Boag, C. (1991) 'The fat cats of academe', *The Bulletin*, 29 October.

Bok, D. (1991) 'Reconciling conflicts – the challenge for the university', in D. Zinberg (ed.), *The Changing University*, Dordrecht, Netherlands: Kluwer Academic Publishers.

Bourdieu, P. (1988) *Homo Academicus*, Cambridge: Polity Press.

Burrows, R. (ed.) (1991) *Deciphering the Enterprise Culture: Entrepreneurship, Petty Capitalism, and the Restructuring of Britain*, London: Routledge.

Centre for Research Policy (1992) *Learning to Compete, Centre for Research Policy Report No. 7*, Wollongong, Australia: Centre for Research Policy.

China Daily (1992) 'Colleges usher in competition', 1 April.

Crook, S. (1991) 'Decomposition of the grand design: the postmodernization of science and technology', Paper presented to the TASA 1991 Sociology Conference, Murdoch University, Western Australia.

Davies, J.L. and Morgan, A. (1982) 'The politics of institutional change', in L. Wagner (ed.), *Agenda for Institutional Change in Higher Education*, Surrey: Society for Research into Higher Education.

Disco, C., Rip, A. and van der Meulen, B. (1991) 'Technical innovation and the universities: divisions of labor in cosmopolitan technical regimes', School of Philosophy and Social Sciences, Center for Studies of Science, Technology and Society, University of Twente, The Netherlands.

Feller, I. (1990) 'Universities as engines of R&D-based economic growth: they think they can', *Research Policy*, 19 (4): 335–48.

Geertz, C. (1991) 'Deep play – notes on the Balinese cockfight', in C. Mukerji and M. Schudson (eds), *Rethinking Popular Culture: Contemporary Perspectives in Cultural Studies*, Berkeley: University of California Press.

Greenberg, D. (1969) *The Politics of American Science*, Harmondsworth: Penguin.

Habermas, J. (1984) *The Theory of Communicative Action, Volume 1: Reason and the Rationalization of Society*, trans. T. McCarthy, Boston: Beacon Press.

– (1987) *The Theory of Communicative Action, Volume 2: Lifeworld and System: A Critique of Functionalist Reason*, trans. T. McCarthy, Boston: Beacon Press.

Hill, S. (1973) 'Engineers and environmental action', *Journal of the Institution of Engineers, Australia*, 45(9): 25–8.

– (1988) *The Tragedy of Technology – Human Liberation vs. Domination in the Late 20th Century*, London: Pluto Press.

– (1989) 'Promoting science policy: crossing the cultural bridge to progress', *Media Information Australia*, 54 (Nov.): 67–72.

– (1991) 'Technological change and the systematisation of organisational culture', in S. Aungles (ed.), *Information Technology in Australia*, Kensington: New South Wales University Press.

Hill, S., Fensham, P. and Howden, I. (1974) *The Making of Scientists*, Academy of Science – Science and Industry Forum, Monograph No. 7, Canberra: Academy of Science.

Huppauf, B. (1989) 'Reforming research and higher education – the example of the Federal Republic of Germany', *Universities Review*, 32 (2): 27.

Jie, Z. (1992) Quoting Zhou Guanzhao in 'Property rights will challenge scientists', *China Daily*, 21 April.

Keat, R. (1991a) 'Introduction – Starship Britain or universal enterprise', in R. Keat and N. Abercrombie (eds), *Enterprise Culture*, London: Routledge.

– (1991b) 'Consumer sovereignty and the integrity of practices', in R. Keat and N. Abercrombie (eds), *Enterprise Culture*, London: Routledge.

Lyotard, J.-F. (1984) *The Postmodern Condition*, Manchester: Manchester University Press.

Marsh, A. and Turpin, T. (1991) 'The 'Big Man' and the 'Chief': towards a model for the analysis of research cultures in Australia's new universities', Paper presented to the TASA Sociology Conference on Empowerment, Regulation and Social Change, Perth: Murdoch University.

Meek, L. (1981) *A Theoretical Model for Examining the Structure and Function of the University as an Organisation or Community*, Melbourne: Centre for the Study of Higher Education.

Mitroff, I.I. (1974) *The Subjective Side of Science: A Philosophical Inquiry into the Psychology of the Apollo Moon Scientists*, Amsterdam: Elsevier.

National Academy of Sciences (1986) 'Government–University–Industry Roundtable', *New Alliances and Partnerships in American Science and Engineering*, Washington, DC: National Academy of Sciences.

National Board of Employment, Education and Training (1993) *Crossing Innovation Boundaries: The Formation and Maintenance of Research Links Between Industry and Universities in Australia*, Volumes I and II, Report No. 26. A Commissioned Report of the Board prepared by the Centre for Research Policy and Sultech, Canberra: Australian Government Publishing Service.

Neville, B. (1992) 'The charm of Hermes: Hillman, Lyotard, and the postmodern condition', *Journal of Analytical Psychology*, 37: 337–53.

Newson, J. and Buchbinder, H. (1988) *The University Means Business*, Ontario: Garamond Press.

Organisation for Economic Co-operation and Development (1990) *Financing Higher Education: Changing Patterns*, Paris: OECD.

Pin, C. (1992) 'Industry's No. 1 driving force', *China Daily*, 7 April.

Porter, M. (1990) *Competitive Advantage of Nations*, New York: The Free Press.

Rip, A. (1991) 'The R&D system in transition: an exercise in foresight' in S.E. Cozzens, P. Healey, A. Rip and J. Ziman (eds), *The Research System in Transition – to What?*, Dordrecht, Netherlands: Kluwer Academic Publishers.

Robinson, D. (1991) 'Australian science research management: hit or miss?', Discussion Paper presented to the Council of the Australian Academy of Sciences. Quoted in the Australian Academy of Science, 'Mismanagement of Australian science', *News Release*, 24 October.

Simon, D. (1991) Quoting Hu Ziexun in 'China's acquisition and assimilation of foreign technology: Beijing's Search for Excellence', Paper of the Center for Technology and International Affairs, Fletcher School of Law and Diplomacy, Tufts University, USA.

Sørensen, K.H. and Levold, N. (1992) 'Tacit networks, heterogeneous engineers and embodied technology', *Science, Technology and Human Values*, 17 (1), Winter.

Turpin, T. and Hill, S. (1991) 'Boundaries of creation – observations on the impact of the National Unified System on higher education research cultures', *Newsletter of the Higher Education and Research and Development Society of Australia*, Queensland.

van Raan, A.F.J., Noyons, E.C.M. and Englesman, E.C. (1992) 'Mapping the science and technology interface – an exploration of bibliometric cartography', Paper delivered at the Third International Conference on Science and Technology Policy Research on New Perspectives on Global Science and Technology Policy, Oiso, Tokyo: National Institute for Science and Technology Policy.

Wasser, H. (1990) 'Changes in the European university: from traditional to entrepreneurial', in 'Higher Education in the late Twentieth Century: Reflections on a Changing System', *Higher Education Quarterly,* 44 (2).

Whitley, R.D. (1972) 'Black boxism and the sociology of science', in P. Halmos (ed.), *The Sociology of Science: Sociological Review Monograph,* 18.

– (ed.) (1974) *Social Processes of Scientific Development,* London: Routledge & Kegan Paul.

Williams, S. (1991) 'The swing of the pendulum: financing of British universities from the 1960s through the 1980s', in D. Zinberg (ed.), *The Changing University,* Dordrecht, Netherlands: Kluwer Academic Publishers.

Woodhall, M. (1991) 'Changing patterns of finance for higher education: implications for the education of scientists and engineers', in D. Zinberg (ed.), *The Changing University,* Dordrecht, Netherlands: Kluwer Academic Publishers.

Ziman, J. (1990) *'Academic Science as a System of Markets',* London: Report of the Science Policy Support Group.

– (1991) *Does the Collectivisation of Science Mean that Academic Research Ought to be Organised Internationally?,* London: Report of the Science Policy Support Group.

8 The nice thing about culture is that everyone has it

Marilyn Strathern

When Kirsten Hastrup (1978: 136) compared the 'world structure' which Edwin Ardener introduced to the 1973 Decennial conference with Jonathan Friedman's 'global structure', she was comparing two analytical models. The one addressed the totality of awareness and knowledge found within a system; the other a totality identified by the anthropologist as the conditions under which a system works. As she put it, the one attended to culture, the other to society. The world was the phenomenal world, and the global a matter of the comprehensiveness of social determinants. Today, it is sometimes difficult to use these terms without evoking instead an understanding of phenomena spread literally across 'the world'. Global culture, a new concept for what is perceived as new circumstances, turns such spreading into a phenomenon in itself.

The fate of the anthropological concept of culture in these circumstances epitomises one of the recontextualisations of knowledge outlined in the Foreword and running through this book. Contextualisation was never a neutral activity, is not without consequences. So what is implied by the invitation to focus on the relations between global and local, which was the conference's invitation to its participants? As many at the conference found, the concepts are alarmingly inadequate for much of what anthropology seeks to do. At the same time, the invocation of local and global makes explicit what everyone also acknowledges: that there are incommensurables in everyday life which cannot be systematised through constructs such as levels and domains and other conventional demarcation devices, and that on the face of it the two terms seem to capture something of the conceptual relocations required to make sense of the late twentieth-century world. At the same time they bring in losses and gains for anthropology of a specifically heuristic kind, that is, for procedures in the organisation of knowledge

The chapters in this book move from Douglas's opening remarks on knowledge loss to the horizons that Cheater, as well as Hill and Turpin, open up in commenting on the pressures of information technology with the different worlds of knowing it holds out, the new perspectives gained. To a certain extent, the dislocation and relocation of concepts that appear as losses and gains are inherent to the practice of making knowledge. In so far as knowledge consists in the process of (constant) recontextualisation – making information anew – then one effect of becoming aware of this process is to imagine knowledge as though it were itself a substantial entity that could be gained or lost, appropriated or displaced.[1]

In the case of appropriation, anthropologists' reflections cannot be only inward-turning even if they wished. It is immaterial whether or not any specific utterance has carried influence (but see note 2). Just as earlier insights were offered to / taken by evangelical missions or colonial administrations, so in late twentieth-century descriptions of society, anthropologists encounter appropriations by 'others' which they may or may not welcome. New barriers (repossessing old usages) would, of course, be as pointless as they would be objectionable; anthropologists never had exclusive claims on using ('controlling') constructs, especially ones they in any case adapted from popular parlance. But the present reappropriations do not mean that anthropology has instead extended its frontiers or that its practitioners are necessarily sharing their insights with the rest of the world. Quite apart from the fact that the discipline is based on internal contest and debate, it would be naïve to imagine that along with the borrowing of constructs goes the borrowing of the understandings that produced them. It is important to know the way such borrowings recontextualise the conceptual intent with which the constructs were once used.

Anthropology turned the concept of culture into an analytical aid to the gathering and collating of information, and created, as I shall argue, particular kinds of knowledge. The concept thus worked in the first place as a heuristic device. This was the context of its usage; and it is context which is displaced. When the salient contrast appears to be between 'the local' and 'the global', it is not culture but the difference between global and local manifestations that becomes the interesting problematic. Culture acquires a taken-for-granted status. So how useful are these terms (local and global) instead? Suppose a contrast between local and global were indeed our new heuristic, what might be the consequences of organising knowledge this way?

GLOBALISED CULTURE

The art and culture quarterly *Third Text* publishes anthropologists as well as some of the critics whom they read, although it is not an anthropological journal as such. The Spring 1992 issue was devoted to the topic of 'cultural identity'. As has become common parlance, local and global appear as substantives: the editorial takes it for granted that 'the local' and 'the global' are on everyone's agenda.

> Since its inception in 1987 *Third Text* has always argued that the issue of 'cultural identity' is not the exclusive domain of the so-called 'ethnic minorities' in Britain or Europe. In modern times the taken-for-granted signs of cultural identity are perpetually being juxtaposed with other signs. *The constant negotiation between the local and the global, the foreign and the*

familiar has become a basic condition of the modernity. If the question of foreignness has become a 'problem' it is a consequence of the way European culture perceives or constructs its own identity in relation to other people in the context of post-war immigration, and to the status of the 16 million non-European people now living in Europe.

(*Third Text* 1992: 3, my emphasis)

In discussing what it identifies as the conservative and sentimentally realist characteristics of multiculturism in the art world, the editorial then asks how we might reach new forms of understanding 'based on the genuine recognition of difference': 'How are we now to differentiate between the ethnographic, popular and high cultural object?' (1992: 5). Here is one of the problems of ubiquity. If all knowledge leads to cultural diversity, what difference is there in techniques of understanding? What use ethnography?

The text provides a small example of how anthropological constructs (here ethnography) may be appropriated in 'other' understandings of the world. This almost requires the inverse of the efforts that spurred the 1983 ASA Decennial. The concern then was how to make anthropology relevant to – *how* to be appropriated by – others. In the area of development that the 1983 conference addressed, the concern remains, and practical claims on anthropological skills are as urgent as ever. The unexpected turn is to find other ways in which anthropological knowledge has been applied. Ralph Grillo's remarks (1985: 31) at the end of his introduction to that conference volume could equally well be addressing the sense of 'having been' applied. 'Applied anthropologists need an especially high degree of consciousness of what is and is not possible, of what has historically been possible and what has not; optimism – yes – but also realism, and a stronger sense of scepticism, too.'

The question about the relevance of anthropological knowledge to issues beyond the discipline becomes ironic in the appropriation of what were once considered distinctive anthropological concepts. The way 'ethnography' has been borrowed by other social science disciplines is a case in point (Atkinson 1990).[2] The concept of 'culture' seems less straightforward since anthropology borrowed it in the first place from general usage. But what is interesting about much present-day usage is its currency in a received anthropological sense: culture as evidence for diversity in human forms of thought and practice and, increasingly salient in late twentieth-century usage, at the root of people's sense of identity.[3] At the same time, the very concept that once served to scale certain phenomena from an anthropologist's point of view (the possibility of recognising common patterns and configurations as 'cultures') now applies across all scales imaginable. It is probably not fortuitous that the concept of culture starts behaving in a 'global' way – ubiquitous, encompassing, all-explanatory – at the same time as a new and specific phenomenon is designated: global culture. The designation is already established, for instance, in a minor mushrooming of texts that appeared in the early 1990s.[4] The texts have not appeared out of nothing: cultural studies and other forms of critical practice have carved new fields out of old ones, including anthropology (Robertson 1992), and many anthropologists have welcomed this cross-disciplinary interest.[5] The interest is part of the Euro-American academic response to what seems a world phenomenon. That is, the interest is fuelled not only by the apparent scale of global culture but by the transcendent (taken-for-granted) status of any people's, everyone's, conceptualisation of culture.

Global culture seizes the imagination twice over. It offers an encompassing reference to the world through a concept that has acquired unprecedented salience in Euro-American descriptions of social life. One of the present characteristics of this concept is its ubiquitous application.

Culture seemingly crops up everywhere as a model or mode of presentation through which anyone (everyone) can describe similarities and differences between peoples and at any 'level' of epoch, organisation or self-identity. And one effect of this ubiquitous descriptive is to think that it in turn comprises a world historical phenomenon. It is as though those who talk about 'cultures' were witnessing cultures talking about themselves![6] Certainly any people, sect, company, band and/or maker of brands may draw on culture in one pervasive Euro-American sense. They know, as Marshall Sahlins adumbrated several years ago, that 'rather than serving the differentiation of society by a differentiation of objects, every conceivable distinction of society [can be] put to the service of another declension of objects' (1976: 215; cf. Connerton 1989: 64). He was comparing the opening up of consumer markets to the opening up of a symbolic set by permutation of its logic. Both create (more of) (new declensions of) culture.

Such declension is not in the late twentieth century confined to consumer markets. Culture may be uncovered wherever people differentiate people. And if their representational strategies are understood as mobilising culture, culture is then in turn understood as representation. Representations do not explain similarities and difference – rather, they give a descriptive purchase on the way similarities and differences are made apparent. Hence the synthetic quality of culture. Steven Webster (1990: 270) observes that anthropologists had long since used the concept to synthesise 'the most diverse social theories'. It is as though the synthesisers are now being confronted by people everywhere acting out just such synthesis, literally and explicitly. One Euro-American enactment is what I call the ethnicisation of identity that emerged in the 1970s.[7]

Relating a facet of this to anti-immigrant sentiment in Europe, Verena Stolcke (1995) coins the phrase 'cultural fundamentalism'. The sentiment is bound up with modern ideas about race and national identity. But she suggests that something other than a nationalist version of racism is at issue. Cultural difference provides a new platform for an essentialist sense of identity without the confrontations (relationships) implied in an overtly racist agenda. Stolcke quotes a British observation from the early 1980s to the effect that social tensions were being attributed to the very presence of immigrants on account of their alien cultural values. Equally, culture can conceal tension, presenting ethnicity in a kind of 'cleansed' state.[8] Either way, questions about similarity and difference appear to refer to self-evident manifestations of lifestyle and community. Such a context, in turn, re-creates an essentialist interpretation of cultural uniqueness.

Anthropologists cannot disclaim responsibility, and the nature of the responsibility deserves exploration. Cultural fundamentalism echoes specific ways in which they have organised their knowledge. The mid-century conceptualisation of culture, long removed from the idea of culture as the refinement of humankind, combined into a single object of analysis both 'way of life' and 'source of identity'. At the same time illumination came from putting things into a cultural context as a means of making local sense of social data. And the nature of *that* contextualisation (social data) was significant. But if 'society' has not kept up with the travelling power of 'culture', anthropologists cannot go on using the latter concept without confronting its new locations. Being parochial in this regard is simply not an option. Over-use has in any case rendered it less than useful for the discerning ethnographer. Postmodernity has generally been described (for example Bauman 1988: 798) as a post-cultural, that is, non-discerning, condition. For the discipline, there are some new and particular problems here.

Its ubiquity becomes a problem *when culture ceases to work as a relational term*. Traditionally, culture worked alongside other concepts in the analytical repertoire – gender, kinship, ritual, structure, domain, above all society – all of which problematised the relationship between different kinds of knowledge. For as long as culture was understood as referring to local forms or expressions, it was thus contextualised by other descriptions of (social) relations between people. What is likely to disappear nowadays is that relational contextualisation. What does it mean to be told that we are 'in a period of globewide cultural politics . . . [and] need to develop images of the global whole' (Robertson 1992: 5, emphasis omitted)? Appeals to globalism conceal the relational dimensions of social life on two accounts – first, when the concept of culture is globalised on the presumption that cultures manifest a universal form of self-consciousness about identity; second, when global culture appears to constitute its own context.[9]

References to global culture are found above all in the writings of commentators, critics and social scientists who have to encompass within their texts seemingly incommensurate orders of data. It is frequently imagined as the world-wide spread of otherwise localised artifacts, and is recognised above all in the spread either of Euro-American (western) products or else of 'indigenous' products facilitated by Euro-American (western) technology. If I have emphasised a problem here for anthropological knowledge, it is because of what global culture literalises. 'The world' can be taken as a source of identity for social phenomena, and culture can be taken as applicable to any order of society.

PREDISPOSITIONS

If culture ceases to work as a relational term, in British social anthropology it was always a much weaker exemplification of relationality than its partner 'society'. Indeed one might say with hindsight that in the way anthropologists deployed the concept it was already predisposed to globalisation. But then anthropologists may already have been predisposed to regard globalism in particular ways. The substance of this section was written before the conference.

Characteristic of past ways of organising knowledge was a certain congruence between the anthropologists' subject and their means of study. They described social relationships between persons by showing the relations that existed between different parts of their data (Thornton 1988). Thus relationships between affines established in bridewealth negotiation could be explained with reference to 'relations' between economic organisation (say) and kinship, between forms of wealth and property inheritance. What was meant by a relation? A relation was a microcosm of social organisation: parties interacted, had influence on one another, got into feedback loops through their communications. It was from this perspective that social relations were analogous to the kinds of explanatory relations anthropologists created in their models. This was partly because the overarching construction of 'society' (like 'model') encouraged them to perceive at the same time both the multiplicity of phenomena and the connections between them. One might say the same of culture, yet its encompassing effect was traditionally very different from that of society. I pursue aspects of the difference in relation to certain of the Decennial conference themes; references are to the other volumes in this series.

Both concepts (culture, society) encouraged anthropologists to see in specific details evidence of a general state of affairs. Thus any event could be grasped as redistributing people's relations (simultaneously revealing personal circumstances and social structure) or as endorsing specific values (revealing individual advantage and cultural norm). The more encompassing the term ('social structure', 'cultural norm'), the more it gathered other levels of detail to itself. In addition, in mid-century anthropological usage, society was understood as encompassing both manifestations of itself and features understood to be contrary to it. So while every relationship also exemplified society, individual persons could appear prior to or apart from such formations. As a consequence, much modernist anthro- pology was concerned with the relationship between individual and society. Culture behaved rather differently: it encompassed everything as part of a pattern or configuration, and apparently contradictory elements were reconciled in an enfolded, self-referential manner by the idea of 'cultural context'. A point to which I shall return is that this is similar to the self-referentiality of the global, at least in its use as a substantive.

Such enfolding would seem to apply to the idea of there being a relationship between global and local. In so far as the concepts are grounded in one another, each is also grounded in the contrast between them. However, Fardon (see *Counterworks*, ASA Decennial conference series, Routledge 1995) observes that rather than taking sides in the global/local polarity, anthropologists might want instead to take into account the broader circumstances of which polarity is assumption. Polarity implies some kind of commensurability between the terms.

Yet, unlike the understanding that comes from taking relationships to signify society or values to signify culture, 'the local' is not in itself either sign or symbol for 'the global'. Certainly the global is not understood as an entity that encompasses lower-level versions of itself. Global influences may be locally expressed, but the force that drives whatever appears as global is assumed to have its own origins.[10] Now while society was never commensurate with the individual,[11] it was commensurate with everything that individuals did as persons in relation to one another. Globalism does not afford that kind of descriptive partitioning. Whether one takes world networks (Hannerz 1992b) or the production of cultural diversity (Featherstone 1990), what is to count as global seems describable only in its own terms. To see global forms as manifestations of strictly local circumstances or to see global products locally distributed is to force a paradox so expectable it works as a truism. The one (e.g. global) is not meant to exemplify the other (e.g. local), though these most territorial of terms may – the paradox becomes banal – inhabit the same place. So what role does the polarisation between the terms play?

An initial answer lies in one of the concrete models of globalisation on which commentators draw, that of commerce and specifically the commerce of organisations socially constituted as world-wide. Multinational companies that seek out market niches may well be marketing goods on the basis of their local character. For brands are nothing if they are not identifiable, and they are often identified by geographical origin (place of first manufacture, place of conspicuous consumption). Moreover, such commerce requires that products are at once universally available in every locale and locally desirable. So globalism might refer to a communications technology (the capacity to distribute products) and localism to the points of production and consumption.

We might surmise that the anthropological notion of cultural context has already made such conjunctions familiar to the discipline. In Clifford Geertz's (1973: 14) definition, culture *is* context, the frame within which, as he says, social life can be intelligibly described. So what sustains product distinctiveness? Not just the immediate use the consumers make of it; symbolic labour is the work of (re)signification, the construction of cultural milieux according to Miller's (1987) formulation. He argues that consumption is such symbolic labour; the consumer recontextualises the product and remakes him or herself thereby. Consumption becomes 'local' in so far as product distinctiveness is endorsed by a renewal of context – everything else summoned in association. Here the media supplies access to cultural milieux beyond the consumer's experience. In this sense, the media is the locale of localities: it creates context as an object of knowledge. No one could mistake the specificity of soap opera settings, even if they get the place, time or class wrong. Yet the dramas are not only made for an audience that shares those characteristics; they can be consumed by anyone or everyone. The consumer is thus de-localised (taking in products from elsewhere) while localising the act of consumption (having his or her own desire for them). Indeed Miller has argued that local cultures may transform global forms into new elements of an almost incommensurable specificity (see *Worlds Apart*, ASA Decennial conference series, Routledge 1995). I suggest that it is the double-sided nature of this process that seems familiar: anthropology's traditional procedures of putting things into context (Strathern 1987) also made context one of its objects of knowledge.

Cultural context worked both as a self-referential device, pointing to its own significance, and created itself as a locale, that is, it localised other phenomena within its purview. Anthropologists usually had to resort to the further idea of social context if they were to describe the relationships between such locales.

Analytical constructs that identified 'domains' of action generally presented the ethnographer's knowledge as socially contextualised. The analysis of political and domestic domains, for instance, presupposed that the distinctive value of an action (food distribution, say) depended largely on the kinds of social relations it mobilised (political value at a public display or domestic at the family hearth). Such domains localised, that is, embodied one act within the locale of other acts. Now when domains were constructs drawn from social life, it was possible to transpose their character: one could ask about the political dimension of domestic relations or the domestic aspect of political action. So while contexts shaped the knowledge which the ethnographer derived from seeing something as 'belonging' to this or that social domain, the phenomena in question were not themselves completely encompassed – they always had other dimensions to them.[12] Indeed, anthropological models that carved out major domains of knowledge, such as ritual, economics or kinship, demonstrated the 'relation' between them by seeing in any one phenomenon manifestations of them all.

As a heuristic construct, then, context imagined as a domain of social action had a localising effect: definitive but not exhaustive, it gathered phenomena to itself and imparted to phenomena their distinctive part in social process. Transposing characteristics (intersecting domains) revealed connections between components of the analytical model. Transposition does not work in the same way between locales as such; when locales are imagined as localities, cross-over leads instead to the compression effects to which Paine refers (1992; cf. Robertson 1992: 155). Localities do not have dimensions: their contextualising referent is a unitary sense of place, and in much Euro-American parlance an intersection of localities is conventionally held to be fragmenting. But does not 'the global' gather localities to itself? I have already suggested not: it can only do so as another context that gives selective value to particular (specific) phenomena. If it is a mark of cosmopolitanism to be able to sample the world's products with some knowledge of their original and thus other and diverse contexts (one is at home in each, as Hannerz (1990) strikingly observes), certain items come to serve as signs of cosmopolitanism where others do not.

'Knowledge' can also have its own signs, as though not everything one knew counted. Thus Euro-Americans frequently present knowledge to themselves as though a condition were its reflexivity: one knows things because one can reflect on why and how one knows. People are especially likely to claim this kind of knowledge when they bring elements into relationship as a visibly organising or totalising act. Indeed the market's appetite for the local consumer seems equalled only by the need for institutions (including nation-states, Foster 1991) to know about the populations they encompass and about the relationships between variables.

Here it is society – in its manifestation as bureaucracy and other institutions – that may be seen to set about collecting knowledge on how it is composed and thus internally differentiated (see *What is Social Knowledge for?*, ASA Decennial conference series, Routledge 1995). From the early days of statistics collection to opinion polls and mass surveys to the computerisation of records, it would seem that Euro-Americans imagine society as though it had an obligation to know about itself. Society's knowledge about its own condition can be like the self-knowledge that a person acquires, a modelling that is indubitably localised. Giddens (1991: 32, 33, emphasis omitted) ascribes such knowledge to (Euro-American) modernity: 'in the context of a post-traditional order, the self becomes a reflexive project' to be explored in the 'process of connecting social and personal change'.[13] Self-knowledge is instrumental – supposedly conducive to responsible action, good citizenry, moral outlook – a version of the 'institutional reflexivity' to which Giddens points (1991: 20), 'the regularised use of knowledge about circumstances of social life as a constitutive element in its organisation and transformation'. So what kind of knowledge do societies acquire about 'themselves'? One condition becomes apparent. 'Society' will not appear out of information alone. Information only reveals its systemic nature if it is organised systematically; to yield a sense of society, information must be organised with the concept of society in mind. This information must be already heterogeneous. For example, we may say that knowledge is the result of organisation through the minds of, and thus through the views of, particular human agents / agencies (cf. Long and Long 1992), or point to the social divide between government agencies, inevitably endorsing modernist institutions, and the articulations of people who lay claim to what anthropologists have called indigenous knowledge. Society projects a view of itself, in other words, that presupposes the (social) divisions it organises.

'Culture' by contrast cannot precipitate the same kind of analysis. Rather it shows itself as inevitably inclusive (in the extent to which certain values are shared), or as exclusive (in the extent to which they are not).[14] There are layerings, conjunctions and juxtapositions; texts work off one another, ideas reproduce; there are hegemonic cosmologies and voices barely heard, and there are meanings simultaneously open and closed to any customer or consumer of them determining what is on the shelf. But culture ultimately projects a view of itself as a world-view.

The anthropological concept of world-view echoes, but is not to be elided with, conventional understandings of religion. Religion was regarded as totalising in so far as its practice included 'everyone', however restricted the criteria, in the community (congregation) it created; it also created as its object a vision of society as a vision of the world. Even if, as for the Uduk (James 1988), no divinities were set against the human estate, such a vision was potentially encompassing. Anthropologists assumed, then, that the encompassing character of religion belonged to the people (congregation, adherents, members of society) who endorsed it. Encompassment was sustained by their commitment (belief, worship, acceptance): the vision of the cosmos that gave these people identity derived its identity from the way they lived it. This world was the world of social action as well as the world that had power to regenerate, bless or curse, or turn the mundane sacred, bring about extraordinary times or create the liminal conditions from which people saw other versions of themselves. For such anthropological understandings of religion traditionally grounded it in society.

If religion were society worshipping itself, then world-view could be culture being expressive about itself. Now whereas the first formula is an evident heuristic – inviting anthropologists to look at religion if they wanted to 'see' society – the second begs being taken literally. Describe a world-view and you describe culture. While a world-view is always the view held by someone, global as in 'global culture' refers not to the view but to the world. So to speak of the global is less to describe a world-view than hold one oneself.

In this sense, perhaps, the new literalism is tantamount to the kind of vision that James (see *The Pursuit of Certainty*, ASA Decennial conference series, Routledge 1995) describes when she speaks of the crusading certainties of liberal rationality, national sovereignty and utilitarian progress that have been replaced by locally based but increasingly world-oriented ideologies which claim some kind of universal truth, usually couched in religious or moral terms, and which compete with one another in offering identity through personal commitment. Certainly 'the world' nowadays appears with qualities of its own. Here one would pay attention to particular icons, the planet long known as a geographical or astronomical globe, the single earth now photographable by satellite. The instruments (of detecting and recording) which summon it thus imagine a view from afar. A far view makes ants of us all, as a Nuer sage once said in reference to God. In fact, the community of persons that this world creates encompasses anyone who can view it 'as a whole'. Its congregation is those able to take advantage of whatever the planet – as a whole – offers. This could be insight into environmental change or markets created by the ability to distribute goods. The entire population of the earth could join. However, those who have a vision of the entire population do not constitute that entire population, and not all global enterprises of the late twentieth-century kind have to endorse holism. Environmentalism is necessarily holistic (Milton 1993); commerce need not be. Global environmentalism imagines the world as the relational (social) connections between everything that happens; global commerce understands the world through its own (cultural) success in operating wherever it wishes.

One important aspect of concepts such as religion or indigenous knowledge in anthropology was that they made visible the division between the discipline's own claims and the claims of those whose ideas it studied. Such divisions were modelled on social divisions. One generated others: 'our' knowledge contained a difference between 'theirs' and 'ours'; 'their' knowledge contained a difference between (say) men's and women's, and so forth. The two idioms of sociability that Fardon (1985) has identified running through Chamba kinship, gender and political relations offer an instance. If sociability were a framework of knowledge about the way in which people impinge upon one another, then it made relationships visible. Contrasting idioms of knowing could thus stand for the multiple character of knowledge itself. But that depended on reading 'ourselves' as agents in socially multiple ways.[15] Who are the ourselves to whom I refer? I mean very simply anthropologist divided from informant, informant from informant and anthropologist from anthropologist. Such differences at least created the possibility for perceiving relationships. I would recover the division that anthropology always created with 'others'[16] as self-knowledge of a kind: that the world is socially divided, and we had better pay attention to the contestability of universal claims. Moore (1988: 188) brings the point home. Anthropology's own globalism, she argues, comprised the unitary discourse it concealed beneath contested positions and competing theories. As long as it remained unitary, its questions remained locked into its own assumptions; as long as it remained Euro-American, it remained unitary. She poses her own question: what of other anthropologies? For a start, other anthropologies may not look anything like anthropology.

This is why to make not one's own position but the world a platform is not the cosmic gesture it seems (and see Barth 1989). Appeals to a world-view may not at all have the effect of making us aware of alternative views. On the contrary, a world made to Euro-American specifications will already be connected up in determined ways. If environmental change, disease or urbanisation appear worldwide, they will do so through the way that pieces of local information have been encompassed by the very idea of a world.

Attempts at comprehensive knowledge production may create a global object through just such specifications and interconnections. Think of the human genome project, which involves transnational competition and collaboration between different centres. Here we have an object (the genome) that is global not just because 'genes' belong to humanity as a whole nor only because each local endeavour is drawn into a cross-nation network, but because it exists through practitioners acting out a totalising systemisation of knowledge. Their aim is a complete map. The interesting issue is not so much that natural science creates universal objects of knowledge out of local instances; rather, it is that incommensurability disappears. An organisation of knowledge whose aim is totality generates instances of its own descriptive process (mappable places). In the same way, the anthropological truism that all human beings live social lives appears to connect up the world. Yet this connecting of social data never required that the world be mapped as a single social system.[17] It was only the knowledge that was systemic. Truisms about cultural identity, on the other hand, offer an image of endlessly replicated configurations;[18] at any one time culture yields a particular pattern but, like the genome map, as instances of its own process.

What will happen to knowledges that cannot be gathered up in a global pattern? Will they, as kinship systems must seem in relation to the Human Genome Organisation, become seemingly peripheral to the 'real world'? And if it is out of local situations that anthropologists continue to construct their concepts of relationships and sociality, will current global discourse make social relations appear parochial? What then of the totalising impetus (the study of social life) with which anthropology originally created its object? These would be displacements of some interest for its practice. Perhaps only certain ways of organising knowledge will be understood as organising a totalising view. Other people's totalising efforts may not look global at all. This is especially likely to be the case where they turn out to be premised on merely making social relationships visible. Take an instance of the kind that used to be called culture contact.

When for the first time Papua New Guinean Highlanders encountered Australian examples of Euro-Americans, they did not realise they (the Highlanders) were actors in a universal historical defeat, part of colonial expansion or entering the world market for gold. Rather, they saw versions of familiar beings, first in spirit and then in human form. This interpretation was totalising. The knowledge that these strangers were persons synthesised diverse possibilities for interaction. Highlanders' knowledge practices led them to demonstrate a potential for relationship which the strangers did not know they were presenting; for themselves, in turn, understanding had to work off and thus was the outcome of the quality of engagement.[19] An anthropologist might focus here on the incompatibilities. Both sides were ignorant of what the other knew. Highlanders did not perceive the social/historical context of the event; Australians did not perceive the relational consequences of interaction. What do we do to either kind of knowledge to summon a global–local framework?

Given their grasp of a so-called world history, one might cast the Australian view as global, in which case the Highlanders' would be prototypically local. Yet one could cast the Highlanders' strategy as global (totalising the strangers as versions of themselves) and the Australians as local (dreadfully conscious of the place they had come from and the place they were in now) to similar asymmetric effect. The trouble with making this new knowledge out of the interchange is that the global becomes as specific a descriptive as the local, and the local as general as the global. At least in that context, whatever else the global–local heuristic brought to light, it would not be much use for understanding the interchange itself. This is not because it does not enable anything new to be said, but because an anthropologist's prior understanding of the interaction *as a social matter* rests on a whole other mode of analysis.

The study of social relations pre-empts any illusion of first contact: no one encounters anyone 'for the first time', for no one has ever lived in the absence of relationships. Interaction is made possible on the minimalist premise that persons (like concepts) are inevitably lived and perceived as versions of other persons – they are always in that sense already in a relationship (cf. Weiner 1993). Indeed, I have argued that anthropology's practices of recontextualisation join a concrete perception of human relationships to the abstract formulation of relations that exist between components of knowledge: 'social relations' works as a heuristic for understanding the way different parts of social life implicate one another.

Many of the points at which the concept of culture has discriminatory and thus relational power for the anthropologist are, then, points at which reference is made back in some form or other to social relations. Divested of that social dimension, culture appears instead self-referential and totalising. In this it is predisposed, in the way 'society' is not, to a view that takes in its stride the possibility of conceptualising phenomena as global. Needless to say, I would not wish to endorse any particular nostalgia for the substantive society; the question remains as to what end anthropology will put its relational premises. One answer is that anthropologists can practise a certain kind of relationship to their data. Here the chapter shifts focus: the following section was written largely after the conference was over.

POSTDISPOSITIONS

As it emerged from the conference, 'the world' is not an inevitable source for what anthropologists might wish to call global, any more than 'locality' exhausts what they might wish to call local. There is more to say about the interplay between the terms than the spatial imagery supposes. Global and local are at once tropes and metaphors *and* capture irreducible realities in human circumstances. This double knowledge suggests a way of turning globalism to anthropological ends. In doing so I capitalise on the predisposition of the anthropological concept of culture to behave in a global way.

The rubrics for the Decennial conference ('The Uses of Knowledge: Global and Local Relations') were incommensurable from the outset.[20] Whatever relationship lies between the two parts, it divides as much as links them, renders them as much disjunct as connected. Indeed, the term relation serves both ends: one can use it either as comprising disjunction and connection together or else as a synonym of connection alone. Note that the disjunction/connection between the two phrases, 'The uses of knowledge' and 'global and local relations', borrows its connecting concept ('relation') from within one of them. Relationship thus appears to overcome incompatibility. The same effect comes from thinking of these terms as new combinations. It looks as though one can cyborg anything – mix and juxtapose elements that are thereby made compatible in so far as their combination creates a workable circuit of ideas. But perhaps one should not dissolve incommensurability so quickly.

'The uses of knowledge' could be a question appended to anything anthropologists think they know. The phrase is self-referential, presupposing that knowledge has uses or can be put to use. Yet what is self-evident can also be less than illuminating, for the rubric summons no particular information, stands for nothing other, exists as intractable a phrase as (say) 'a Bambara mask' or 'Aboriginal women'.[21] It delimits a substantive field, but not how that field will be specified or encompassed. 'Global and local relations', on the other hand, seems an altogether more enticing phrase. It invites one to imagine a relationship – how the two will contextualise each other. There is both specification and encompassment there, the promise of a dialectic. However, it tells us nothing about the field to which the terms might apply. So while the phrase already creates one of the conditions under which the epithets global and local will be significant (namely the relations between them), it yields no substantive. What the possibilities contained in the two phrases do make obvious is an incommensurability fundamental to Euro-American knowledge practices, and to anthropology.

That incommensurability lies in certain signifying disjunctions / connections which the discipline creates. These, we may say, are its instruments of measurement (Latour 1991: 113). On the one hand, it is an intractable fact that human beings live in the world and live nowhere else, and from that condition of existence anthropology extrapolates the further fact that the relations which engage them do not stand for anything else either, because for human beings there is no life outside them. On the other hand, if people forever diversify that life, and make counterfactuals out of it (Hawthorn 1991), so do anthropologists. They introduce orders of internal complexity, compose it as sets of relationships between elements, see everything as indicating something else; that is what trying to describe things does. So we may take knowledge as a totalising dimension of human activity – refashioning the awareness with which people act – or we can divide knowing actions into numerous kinds, not all of which need be marked 'knowledge' as such.

An incommensurability to the way in which Euro-American anthropologists know things rests, then, in the intractability of social life in relation to its manifold manifestations. For this particular given (social life) has its consequence: knowing how social lives are lived through relationships encourages anthropologists to diversify their approaches and specify parameters, to see everything as a problem and solutions as further problems. In focusing on relations, anthropologists tell themselves the elements they need in order to solve the problems they create; they only have to ask what relationships are at issue. Every type of knowledge that offers up a problem can thus be solved by bringing in some other type of knowledge. You want to know about sexual antagonism – well, let's look at the relationship between domestic and political domains or at the economics of montane horticulture, or at the exercise of power or the psychology of sexual identity. Anthropologists are adept at dividing the world in order to create fresh explanatory contexts for relationships.

If what is peculiar to anthropological knowledge is the explicitness of its relational premises, then it would seem that the intractable can always be encompassed and specified by other contexts. Not quite. For *what is perceived as intractable must lie 'outside' this relational practice* precisely in order to be precipitated and produced by it.[22] The same intellectual activity that connects disparate things also establishes their disparateness. Thus the comparative method does not just create the divisions it overcomes; it also produces the anthropologists' very perception of social relations as a given. There is a sense, then, in which relationality lies beyond the explicitly relational practice of anthropological inquiry. To avoid the paradox it might be preferable to follow James Weiner's (1993: 293) use of 'sociality' here. I shall return to the argument in which this usage is located. For the moment, I suggest that anthropology might see some purpose in conserving its given (relationships, sociality) as an intractable one. And this is where we might usefully appropriate for our ends the epithet 'global'.

The rubric of global and local relations provides co-ordinates. We could take the phrase as a microcosm for any relational proposition. As I said, it could even describe the relation between the rubrics themselves. By itself, on the other hand, global can be pressed into use as an epithet for whatever we imagine as intractable. On this definition, a global phenomenon summons no further exemplification: it is a macrocosm, a complete image, and requires no theoretical underpinning. It does not matter how small or large the phenomenon appears to be; the point is that it is irreducible. Thus the rubric 'The uses of knowledge', taking up its own space, expanding to its own limits, is global in this sense.

Local affords a different use. This is a relational epithet, for it points to specificities and thus to differences between types of itself – you cannot imagine something local alone: it summons a field of other 'locals' of which any one must be only a part. In this regard 'global–local relations' functions as a localising rubric in so far as it points to co-ordinates which in specifying limits thus define (confine) a field. However the terms global and local are played off against each other, each is also part of a further entity (the relationship between them). In a relationship lies possibilities for and thus a necessity for theoretical exposition. Thus to imagine that the intractable is precipitated by such relational practices itself requires theoretical underpinnings of some sort. The immediate theory on which I have drawn here concerns conceptualisation; it supposes that human subjects construct nothing without moving between macrocosm, an entity in non-reducible, self-referential form, and microcosm, a specifying and thus reducing or limiting system of references (after Roy Wagner).[23] That theoretical exposition becomes of course an exercise in microcosmic formulation: providing the co-ordinates by which to bring elements together by dividing the elements in ways that make the co-ordinates useful.

Here we might wish to deviate from those exemplifications of globalism which stress its encompassing function; insofar as 'encompassment' presupposes a microcosmic division, it is likely to lead to questions about the relations between the encompassed terms. A totalising moment re-perceived as encompassment is reduced by the components it reveals. By the same token, to bring entities into relationship presupposes a field of which they are but part. If we wish to use the epithet global for moments that are totalising[24] in a non-reducible sense, it can only apply to the point at which the elucidation of relations stops. An example is the way concern with different types of knowledge precipitates 'knowledge' as an irreducible object. If anthropologists see a (local) relational possibility in making this process intellectually explicit, there is also the irreducible (global) fact that they go on producing exactly such intractable residues in the very way they set about bringing things together.

Patently, the world that is the subject of 'global' production strategies can be reduced (as microcosm is a reduction) to a thoroughly parochial construct. After all, the simple notion of globalisation as a matter of items spreading across the earth is very much fuelled by Euro-American concepts of scale: the farther things travel, the more distance they have covered, the more global they seem to be. The spread of consumer goods or armaments is both an example of and points to this process. Yet frequently the spread of those things is accompanied by loss of cultural complexity, so that they invite re-complexification at the point of local consumption. To keep with a Papua New Guinea example, export lager is nothing if it is not locally apprehended as 'export' lager. So increase in one dimension (the number of places on earth where one can buy lager) is not necessarily accompanied by increase in other dimensions (all the local connotations do not add up together); on the contrary, it may be that the greater the spread the less interesting a commodity may become. In the same way, anything we might specifically say about the global human condition is likely to be a thoroughly impoverished version of the complexities of existence.

But while it is easy to render local anything that passes for globalspeak, anthropologists cannot close their ears to it either. If the evidence on which one can mount such a critique rests on what people say and the worlds they imagine, so too does this literal identification of the global with 'the world' comprise an imagined one. We are left with the irreducible fact that what anthropologists have been doing, among other things, is listening.[25] There is no particular virtue in listening – it says nothing about what will be communicated, misunderstood or not heard at all. But having to listen makes evident the difference between the anthropologist's localising attempts to bring things together and the global condition that this rests on, being able to pay attention to people who themselves have other things on their mind. Anthropology's imitative and microcosmic practices of analysis and description must remain incommensurate with theirs. It is both despite that incommensurability and out of it that the presence of persons is made apparent. Perhaps the anthropologist's macrocosm is this: co-presence.[26] At least the presence of persons is not, thankfully, reducible to the anthropologist's relationships with them. In this realisation, anthropology might find a purpose for the displacement of knowledge.

What also became clear from the conference is the need to investigate just how certain specific types of knowledge that people attribute to anthropology are worked out in nationalist and other political agendas. The most uncomfortable is the dogma of cultural difference ('cultural fundamentalism'), whose demonstration is nowadays laid at the discipline's door. Such an investigation would confront us with the kinds of claims the discipline has made in the past, and with the way that knowledge in the form of claims can always be claimed by others.

Perhaps it is easy to be suspicious of claims, but the same may also be true of models and theories. Anthropology exists in a world of constantly superseding generalities, of paradigm slippage, of postmodernisms already in the past tense and greedy to be at the point after next, so that the speed[27] with which models turn over reveal how little sticking power each has. This is why I would emphasise something altogether other: how to use the knowledge we already have. And if anthropology has communicated some of its knowledge to 'the world' – as in the dogma of cultural difference – then that accomplishment has given it a new task. The task is how to make already existing knowledge work for, not against, humanity.

Pressed constantly into service, 'humanity' is a term that has been used and abused by Euro-Americans since modernity began. But its deeply compromised connotations should only force us to turn it to better use. By humanity I mean something very close to the anthropologist's 'sociality'. I thus take it to refer neither to citizen subjects nor to non-animal beings, but to the amalgam of desire, capability, artifact and embodiment by which persons live. The idea of it cannot be produced either by generalisation or by the purification of other ideas: rather it is brought into existence as an awareness of what I have called the co-presence of persons. If this is an awareness anthropologists might wish to conserve as intractable, then they have cultural skills available to them. It is here that they can use their knowledge of how different orders of knowledge can be worked against one another.

I like to think that anthropologists could assert the potentials there are in being human *against* everything they know about people, individually or collectively, and against how they form particular social relationships. As Alfred Gell observed at the conference, it is no good searching for identity since it is never to be found – searching presumes one has not got it. In the same way, I suspect we do not really want our descriptions of ourselves to become true; we hope they are partial enough to hold out promise of better things. No particular description is in any case adequate to the possibilities human beings are capable of, any more than any particular set of relations encompasses people's capacity for social life. So anything we might use in claiming common humanity is just that: a claim. Rather than redescribe the world in order to find humanity within it, one might wish to conserve the concept beyond and outside descriptions of it, and even *despite* them.

How might one mobilise previous knowledges to this end? A piece of knowledge that was rediscovered in the course of the conference is that the work we do with concepts transforms them, and sometimes to the point of displacement. Identifying local and global phenomena is a prime exemplar: if one focuses on the local it vanishes in the realisation that one person's local forms are another's global ones, and vice versa. This is a cultural practice we might wish to make explicit.

The thought derives from a trenchant critique that Weiner makes apropos the anthropological search for relationality.[28] Either, he argues, relationality is the premise upon which persons act, in which case it cannot be shown, or else one may indeed show it but in doing so will take away its a priori status. Keeping 'relationality' to refer to what can be shown, and using 'sociality' for its premise, Weiner then says that for his own part: 'I am proposing a search for a form of sociality that is not mediated, that is not directly articulated, that is only made visible when one's attention is directed elsewhere' (1991: 294). Consider the vanishing effect I have just referred to. It would be too quick to draw from the displacement of local and global the conclusion that we are not making the terms work properly, with the temptation to focus harder; this would exacerbate the problem. Vanishing is a side-effect of focus – focusing always reduces in the sense that it locates the act of perception. If human beings have to work with a premise of humanity despite their attempts at describing the world, and despite their engagement in social relations, this is not because humanity is a self-evident reality. Rather, it is because they have to make it lie outside their relational efforts in order for it to be an effect of them.[29] It must appear incommensurable with such effort. As for anthropologists, I see no other place in their endeavours for the epithet global than the corresponding premise of sociality.

So if anthropologists are committed to a kind of humanism, they will not necessarily endorse it by focusing their descriptive efforts on it – the problem is that that is also the route to racism, terrorism and ethnic violence, to purifying populations into greater and lesser exemplars of it, to including some and excluding others. This is Stolcke's (1995) point about cultural fundamentalism. It claims to be about humanity at large, to be making generalisations about behaviour everywhere, in this case that people 'by nature' prefer to live among 'their own kind', in ways that are frankly discriminatory.[30] To bring to awareness the idea of humanity or sociality as co-presence, it may well indeed be necessary to focus elsewhere.

If anthropologists have to focus 'elsewhere', they know where that elsewhere will be: on social relations. Stolcke herself focuses specifically on social divisions and differences within Europe. As was said more than once at the conference, all social relations are local. They are partial instruments, and this is their virtue, for they are visibly less than the awareness with which they are used, less than the sociality that brings them into existence.

Attention to the detail of social relations has always been one of the discipline's strengths. A reason for taking anthropology's focus on local circumstance with a new seriousness is, then, because we know that is what focus does, and that includes taking as particular and local those bureaucratic structures, nationalist and internationalist ideologies and claims about universal human characteristics that appear everywhere. If we think we have something to share we shall share nothing by claiming to have produced universal insight; each and every one has his or her own vision of what is of universal importance. Acknowledging the presence of persons is a premise of another order. Those moments when we render knowledge local and people co-eval conserve the global possibilities of that premise.

ACKNOWLEDGEMENTS

I am grateful to Marian Kempny for his critical observations on an earlier draft, as I am to Annelise Riles for an unpublished commentary on global-local relations and Ilana Gershon for reminding me to be explicit. Andrew Holding will recognise several parts of this.

NOTES

1 I use 'displacement' warily: to echo a condition that has continued to affect whole populations in the 1990s – the displacement of people(s) from land and livelihood. Tasteless as it may seem, what would it mean if anthropological consciousness about the fate of certain types of knowledge were *not* also turned towards imagining displacements of grosser kinds?

2 Jean and John Comaroff reflect on anthropology having lost control (their term) 'over its two most basic terms, *culture* and *ethnography*' (1992: ix, original emphasis). For a commentary on the free-floating character of 'ethnography', see Fabian 1990. For specific borrowings of the concept of culture by management and organisation studies, see Case 1994; his paper comes from a workshop convened by Case and Chapman at the ASA Decennial conference ('On the profit margin'), and Case includes a review of traceable anthropological influences on management studies.

3 Scott (1992) discusses the contemporary anthropological 'inflation of culture', after Friedman 1987. I would comment that what is popular about 'culture' outside anthropology and outside academia are senses that have been notably prevalent in twentieth-century anthropological and ethnographically derived writing. Susan Wright reminds me that Raymond Williams (1961: 229) long ago laid the idea of culture as a way of life at the door of social anthropology. Beyond anthropology, journals founded in the 1980s include *Science as Culture* (see Chapter 7), *Theory, Culture and Society, Differences: Journal of Feminist Cultural Studies*, and *Cultural Studies*.

4 Bringing together global and local is explicit in works such as Featherstone 1990; Giddens 1991; King 1991; Robertson 1992. Hannerz (e.g. 1992a: 262) refers to 'world culture'.

5 As in the journals *History and Culture, Public Culture, Cultural Anthropology*, which began publishing in the 1980s. Appropriation has also taken the form of criticism (e.g. Desan 1989: 64). Scott (1992) makes a nice distinction between Theory's 'culture' and Relativism's 'culture'.

6 Conventionally, 'culture' was an educative abstraction (see Miller, Worlds Apart, ASA Decennial conference series, Routledge 1995). In anthropological usage, it served to condense and summarise a range of understandings about aspects of social life; it was not commensurate with these understandings but an abstraction from them, and thus a figure to the ground of anthropological endeavour. Anthropologists thereby inverted what they took as the indigenous relationship between the implicit cultural ground of people's lives and the particular understandings (figures) which people explicitly foregrounded. Where culture becomes explicit in people's understandings of themselves, a condition that Gellner (e.g. 1982) would locate in the nationalism of industrial societies, this particular relation between figure and ground (and 'anthropologist' and 'people') collapses.

7 Hall observes this process as it appeared in Jamaica in the 1970s (1991: 54). Ethnicisation does not just refer to ethnicity (cf. Strathern 1988: 32, apropos gender and sexual identities), but to the perceptions of primordial categorisation whose visibility and enactment take after ethnic identity.

8 Ethnicity in turn becomes a kind of cleansed racism, even as gender studies may work as a cleansed study of sexism (Moore 1988). (I say cleansing in the context of the current exterminations in the former Yugoslavia and Rwanda.) The political critique of 'multiculturalism' is well taken (Hall 1991: 55). But note that Stolcke (1995) lays out several important differences between racism and the new cultural fundamentalism of the last fifteen years or so.

9 An example would be the idea of a global culture based on a universal communication system that depends on a specific technology (e.g. electronics) (cf. Smith 1990) where translocal communications were both cultural means and cultural content.

10 *Pace* Lupondo and Zimbabwean concerns about human failings (see Chapter 5).

11 The model of the person as a 'socialised' individual (socialised by virtue of consuming social values) is a homely Euro-American way for thinking about the local consumption of goods that makes a person a 'globalised' local.

12 The connections here were merographic (Strathern 1992: 72f.). Annelise Riles (personal communication) adds the important qualification that in this regard local societies, cultures, situations are not in themselves specific. Whether they are general or specific, universal or particular, will depend on the perspective one takes on them.

13 'The idea of collective responsibility for knowledge and human government, and of the "innateness" of the individual and the incidental, is characteristic largely of the rationalist movements that sponsor and emulate the culture of science' (Wagner 1978: 23). Rose (1990: 213f.) observes that governing society today means governing (persons') subjectivity; this has come not through the growth of an omnipotent state but through 'a complex and heterogeneous assemblage of technologies', including psychoanalysis. 1995 sees the publication of a new journal, *Culture and Psychology*.

14 A powerful rendition of this is given in Sahlins' 'Goodbye to tristes tropes', where he points to the extent to which commentators underestimate the scope and systematicity of cultures, 'always universal in compass and thereby able to subsume alien objects and persons in logically coherent relationships'. He continues: 'Every society known to history is a global society, every culture a cosmological order' (1993: 15, 16 – note how he plays culture off against social relationships). Whatever cultural differences there are between the voices of different persons, they belong to the same social universe of discourse. The notion of culture as permeable and less than bounded, he argues, mistakes culture's powers of inclusion for the inability to maintain a boundary. The difference here to some extent plays on that long established in the anthropological repertoire between societas and communitas.

15 As a constructed (interpreted) difference, the relational effect of division and the divisive effect of relationships play off against each other.

16 While registering Béteille's (1990: 9) reservation about other cultures, I use 'other' as a deliberate metaphor for the objectified status of what is under study. ('Object' as in Hegelian externalisation and sublation (see the discussion in Miller 1987); or as the moment of meaning in deconstructive practice, viz. that 'stops' interpretation; or as in dialectal objectivity, one of Meghill's (1991) four types (following Fabian).) Self-knowledge instantiates this as a relation, minimally of knowledge 'to' the self.

17 Except in an extended historical sense (e.g. Wolf 1982), the 'world system', was not world 'society'. 'The world' understood as the most general term for the holistic totality of cultural meaning given in the notion of context (Rabinow and Sullivan 1987: 14) existed as an object of interpretation. Harvey (1990: 252–3) cites de Certeau's critique of the map as a totalising device – it eliminates the heterogeneous practices that produced it in favour of a homogeneous reduction to certain coordinates. My argument has been that, in anthropology, 'culture' is a much more amenable instrument for such reductionism than 'society'. The latter concept conserves incommensurables (*vis-à-vis* individuals) and the heterogeneity of internal divisions, not to speak of contradictions, while also gathering all of these to itself.

18 We may understand this repeated image holographically or fractally.

19 With respect to relational possibilities, the Australian interpretations of the High-landers were, by contrast, partial. Interaction was envisaged – the explorers certainly wanted to 'make contact' with these primitive peoples / human beings – but they imagined it would always be limited by cultural difference.

20 Incommensurability after Feyerabend and Kuhn; Fischer (in Clifford and Marcus, 1986) refers to Lyotard's dictum that postmodern sensibility reinforces the ability to tolerate incommensurables. Fardon (see *Counterworks*, ASA Decennial conference series, Routledge 1995) comments nicely on the inevitability of the 1993 conference making its rubrics 'work'.

21 Bambara mask: Clifford 1988; Aboriginal women: Kaberry 1939.

22 The intractable is not a base on which the knowledge builds, nor is it what I think Hastrup (1993) means by the 'hardness of facts' except in so far as she argues that the difference between 'hard' and 'soft' facts is established by a community of agreement. I use the concept to refer neither to what is reached after variables have been accounted for, nor (as I think Braidotti (1991) does for the irreducible) to entities that remain in a stable state. Rather it is the residue of relational thinking produced by the focus on interconnection. Anything may be, situationally, intractable / irreducible. In Derridean terms (cf. Fitzpatrick 1993), what is suppressed or marginalised in the constitution of an entity is, on recovery, always subject to further deconstruction; hence the incompleteness of 'representation', for entities are only completed by further elements that then themselves are revealed as representationally incomplete. In other words, referential coding constantly evokes intractable elements that are reduced by further coding. Wagner's (1986, and see 1977) obviation sequence offers an exemplification of such tropic restriction and expansion. When obviation takes the cultural form of a recontextualisation that sees parts of one entity as also belonging to parts of another, as it does in many Euro-American knowledge practices, I call the exercise 'merographic' (Strathern 1992).

23 Wagner 1978; 1986 *passim*. 'The invention of a microcosm by abstraction from a perceptual macrocosm is half of a highly charged dialectical interaction, establishing a sensory continuum within which the ordering and refiguring of meaning is accomplished. The other half of this charged interaction is an equally significant expansion, or concretisation, of microcosm into macrocosm that occurs in the formation of analogy' (Wagner 1986: 19).

24 On de-totalisation as the embodiment of discursive signification, and thus a spatial and temporal ('localising') process, see Weiner (1991: 183).

25 'Listening' was picked out by the *THES* report on the RAI's press reception and seminar in the context of the 150th anniversary celebrations of the London Ethnological Society (Claire Sanders, *THES*, 4 June 1993).

26 Co-presence echoes Fabian's (1983) appeal of a decade ago to cotemporality or coevalness in the anthropological apprehension of 'others'. Hastrup's (1993) 'solidarity' carries more positive overtones than I would give to co-presence.

27 Brennan (1993) devotes a chapter of *History after Lacan* to the significance of speed in the way capital maintains its profits. The sense of things speeding up, as one encounters in paradigm shifts or reflexive criticism, is consonant with an economic system which seeks to enhance reproductive capacity rather than allowing raw materials to reproduce at their own rate.

28 Work of mine was one of the objects of Weiner's criticism; I acknowledge the stimulus of his intervention.

29 Although I draw these points from recent positions in symbolic analysis, they will resonate with what effect–producers have long known, whether the effects are produced through sorcery, sermonising or shamanistic trance.

30 Thus Stolcke argues that cultural fundamentalism furnishes reasons for the exclusion

of immigrants on the grounds that *cultural* difference is a powerful source of identity for all human beings. Both Enoch Powell's earlier racism – 'An instinct to preserve identity and defend a territory is one of the deepest and strongest implanted in mankind' – and Cohn Bendit's latterday description of xenophobia – 'Much indicates that the reserve *vis-à-vis* the foreigner constitutes an anthropological constant of the species' – make appeals to universals.

REFERENCES

Atkinson, P. (1990) *The Ethnographic Imagination*, London: Routledge.

Barth, F. (1989) 'The analysis of culture in complex societies', *Ethnos*, 54: 120–42.

Bauman, Z. (1988) 'Sociology and postmodernity', *Sociological Review*, 36: 790–813.

Béteille, A. (1990) 'Some observations on the comparative method', Wertheim Lecture, Amsterdam: Centre for Asian Studies.

Braidotti, R. (1991) *Patterns of Dissonance: A Study of Women in Contemporary Philosophy*, Oxford: Polity Press.

Brennan, T. (1993) *History after Lacan*, London: Routledge.

Case, P. (1994) 'Tracing the organisational culture debate', *Anthropology in Action*, 1: 9–11.

Clifford, J. (1988) *The Predicament of Culture: Twentieth-century Ethnography, Literature, and Art*, Cambridge, Mass.: Harvard University Press.

Clifford, J. and Marcus, G. (eds) (1986) *Writing Culture: The Poetics and Politics of Ethnography*, Berkeley and Los Angeles: University of California Press.

Comaroff, J. and Comaroff, J. (1992) *Ethnography and the Historical Imagination*, Boulder: Westview Press.

Connerton, P. (1989) *How Societies Remember*, Cambridge: Cambridge University Press.

Desan, S. (1989) 'Crowds, community, and ritual in the work of E.P. Thompson and Natalie Davis', in L. Hunt (ed.), *The New Cultural History*, Berkeley and Los Angeles: University of California Press.

Fabian, J. (1983) *Time and the Other: How Anthropology Makes its Object*, New York: Columbia University Press.

—— (1990) 'Presence and representation: the other and anthropological writing', *Critical Inquiry*, 15: 753–72.

Fardon, R (1985) 'Sociability and secrecy: two problems of Chamba knowledge', in R. Fardon (ed.), *Power and Knowledge: Anthropological Approaches*, Edinburgh: Scottish Academic Press.

Featherstone, M. (ed.) (1990) *Global Culture: Nationalism, Globalisation and Modernity*, London: Sage Publications.

—— (1991) *Consumer Culture and Postmodernism*, London: Sage Publications.

Fitzpatrick, P. (1993) 'Relational power and the limits of law', in K. Turri, Z. Bankowski and J. Ussitalo (eds), *Law and Power: Critical and Socio-Legal Essays*, Liverpool: Deborah Charles Publications.

Foster, R. (1991) 'Making national cultures in the global ecumene', *Annual Review of Anthropology*, 120: 235–60.

Friedman, J. (1987) 'Beyond otherness or: The spectacularisation of anthropology', *Telos*, 71: 161–70.

Geertz, C. (1973) *On the Interpretation of Cultures*, New York: Basic Books.

Gellner, E. (1982) 'Nationalism and the two forms of cohesion in complex societies', *Proc. British Academy*, LXVIII: 165–87.

Giddens, A. (1991) *Modernity and Self-Identity: Self and Society in the Late Modern Age*, Oxford: Polity Press.

Grillo, R. (1985) 'Applied anthropology in the 1980s: retrospect and prospect', in R.

Grillo and A. Rew (eds), *Social Anthropology and Development Policy*, ASA Monograph 23, London: Tavistock.

Hall, S. (1991) 'Old and new identities, old and new ethnicities', in A.D. King (ed.), *Culture, Globalization and the World-System*, London: Macmillan Education Ltd.

Hannerz, U. (1990) 'Cosmopolitans and locals in world culture', *Theory, Culture and Society*, 7: 211–25.

—— (1992a) *Cultural Complexity: Studies in the Social Organisation of Meaning*, New York: Columbia University Press.

—— (1992b) 'The global ecumene as a network of networks', in A. Kuper (ed.), *Conceptualizing Society*, London: Routledge.

Harvey, D. (1990) *The Condition of Postmodernity*, Oxford: Blackwell.

Hastrup, K. (1978) 'The post-structuralist position of social anthropology', in E. Schwimmer (ed.), *The Yearbook of Symbolic Anthropology*, London: Hurst.

—— (1993) 'Hunger and the hardness of facts', *Man*, 28: 727–39.

Hawthorn, G. (1991) *Plausible Worlds: Possibility and Understanding in History and the Social Sciences*, Cambridge: Cambridge University Press.

James, W. (1988) *The Listening Ebony: Moral Knowledge, Religion and Power among the Uduk of Sudan*, Oxford: Clarendon Press.

Kaberry, P. (1939) *Aboriginal Woman, Sacred and Profane*, London: Geo. Routledge & Sons Ltd.

King, A.D. (ed.) (1991) *Culture, Globalization and the World-System*, London: Macmillan Education Ltd.

Latour, B. (1991) *We Have Never Been Modern*, trans. C. Porter, London: Harvester Wheatsheaf.

Long, N. and Long, A. (eds) (1992) *Battlefields of Knowledge: The Interlocking of Theory and Practice in Social Research Development*, London: Routledge.

Meghill, A. (1991) 'Four senses of objectivity', *Annals of Scholarship* (spec. issue, *Rethinking Objectivity*), 8: 301–20.

Miller, D. (1987) *Material Culture and Mass Consumption*, Oxford: Basil Blackwell.

Milton, K. (ed.) (1993) *Environmentalism: The View from Anthropology*, ASA Monograph 32, London: Routledge.

Moore, H. (1988) *Feminism and Anthropology*, Oxford: Polity.

Paine, R. (1992) 'The Marabar Caves, 1920–2020', in S. Wallman (ed.), *Contemporary Futures: Perspectives from Social Anthropology*, ASA Monograph 30, London: Routledge.

Rabinow, P. and Sullivan, W.M. (1987) *Interpretive Social Science: A Second Look*, Berkeley and Los Angeles: University of California.

Robertson, R. (1992) *Globalization: Social Theory and Global Culture*, London: Sage Publications.

Rose, N. (1990) *Governing the Soul: The Shaping of the Private Self*, London: Routledge.

Rothfield, P. (1991) 'Alternative epistemologies, politics and feminism', *Social Analysis* (spec. issue, *Postmodern Critical Theorising*), 30: 54–67.

Sahlins, M. (1976) *Culture and Practical Reason*, Chicago: University of Chicago Press.

—— (1985) *Islands of History*, Chicago: University of Chicago Press.

—— (1993) 'Goodbye to tristes tropes: ethnography in the context of modern world history', *Journal of Modern History*, 65: 1–25.

Scott, D. (1992) 'Criticism and culture: theory and postcolonial claims on anthropological disciplinarity', *Critique of Anthropology*, 112: 371–94.

Smith, A.D. (1990) 'Towards a global culture', in M. Featherstone (ed.), *Global Culture: Nationalism, Globalisation and Modernity*, London: Sage Publications.

Stolcke, V. (1995) 'Talking culture: new boundaries, new rhetorics of exclusion in Europe', *Current Anthropology*, 36: 1–24.

Strathern, M. (1987) 'Out of context: the persuasive fictions of anthropology', *Current Anthropology*, 28: 251–81.

—— (1988) *The Gender of the Gift: Problems with Women and Problems with Society in Melanesia*, Berkeley and Los Angeles: University of California Press.

—— (1992) *After Nature: English Kinship in the Late Twentieth Century*, Cambridge: Cambridge University Press.

Thornton, R. (1988) 'The rhetoric of ethnographic holism', *Cultural Anthropology*, 3: 285–303.

Wagner, R. (1977) 'Analogic kinship: a Daribi example', *American Ethnologist*, 4: 623–42.

—— (1978) *Lethal Speech: Daribi Myth as Symbolic Obviation*, Ithaca: Cornell University Press.

—— (1986) *Symbols that Stand for Themselves*, Chicago: University of Chicago Press.

Webster, S. (1990) 'The historical materialist critique of surrealism and postmodern anthropology', in M. Manganaro (ed.), *Modernist Anthropology: From Fieldwork to Text*, Princeton: Princeton University Press.

Weiner, J.F. (1991) *The Empty Place: Poetry, Space, and Being among the Foi of Papua New Guinea*, Bloomington: Indiana University Press.

—— (1993) 'Anthropology *contra* Heidegger: Part II: The limit of relationship', *Critique of Anthropology*, 13: 285–301.

Williams, R. (1961) [1958] *Culture and Society, 1780–1950*, London: Penguin Books.

Wolf, E.R. (1982) *Europe and the People without History*, Berkeley and Los Angeles: University of California Press.

Afterword
Relocations

I was represented by another woman, and the representation denied my presence in my own story. I was extremely surprised that they had used my proper name and my own wordings in such a literal manner.

(Hastrup 1992: 334–5)

Thinking about relations between the local and the global forces a sense of paradox. It is not alone: this paradox belongs to a whole late twentieth-century field of them. I draw briefly on a recent work of Bruno Latour to bring this field into view. The epithets global and local lead to the idea that relationship might occupy only a part and not the whole of the kinds of understandings in which anthropologists might be interested, just as it seems scale might characterise a part but not the whole of the kinds of measurements that can be used. The paradoxes rest on the fact that both relationship and scale are concepts otherwise encompassing in their reach. A similar paradox has been posed with respect to actors as human beings. Together, they suggest a way of reading the contributions to this book.

When Mary Douglas cites string figures as an outmoded fieldwork technique, an instance of forgotten skills, she was not to know that Donna Haraway's contribution to the Decennial conference drew from a paper where the string figure becomes a new trope for critical practice: 'cat's cradle is both local and global, distributed and knotted together', a repertoire passed back and forth between players.[1] It locates both the subjects and objects of knowledge-making practices.

In Douglas's original citation the string figure is a device the anthropologist may well have had to learn for the occasion, on the grounds, among others, that it would be encountered almost universally among field locations. Haraway warns, however, that we should not take the universal as indicative of global any more than we might wish location to refer to the merely local. Location, she says, is not the concrete to the abstract. Like the sign that refers to both signifier and signified, it is both, and thus the fraught play of foreground and background, text and context, that constitutes critical inquiry.[2] Globalisation is found in the distribution of knowledge-making as practice(s) that can travel; the globalisation of the world is for her the travelogue of a specific technoscience. The difference is between the situated and finite nature of critical inquiry and the distributed and layered nature of the narrative fields across which such an inquiry might flow. But the interesting point of her argument is that this is also no difference, that is, Haraway is not making it work as a relationship in her account.

Perhaps some of the inadequacy of thinking in global–local terms for the kind of work that anthropologists might have asked from their constructions comes from imagining these terms as substitutes for certain (very productive) polarities. When anthropologists worked under such rubrics as concrete and abstract, particular and general, unique and universal, and so forth, they were apprehending a world where internal events were made intelligible by reference to external ones, where it seemed important to be aware of the reach of particular actions or of world history or regional systems, or of the interplay of variables. An expanded horizon could always yield an expanded inquiry; perspectives could be dovetailed to open up the constant possibility of fresh perspective; above all there was the question of sequencing, of cause and effect and of relationship and interrelationship. In Haraway's reading, by contrast, there can be no relation 'between' location and distribution, for it is location that gives us relations; relationships are both located and locating.

What is gained? That sense of interlocking domains and infinite perspectives that led Euro-Americans to imagine universal conditions and specific instances might have been part of the purificatory work that Bruno Latour (1993) attributes to the modern 'constitution'. But those polarisations seem less easy to explain away than others more readily critiqued, such as subject and object, nature and culture or human beings and their props / artifacts, although these too required the observer to specify the relationship between them. The critique is that such polarities make it difficult to see that there are no entities that are not in fact, in Latour's phrasing, simultaneously real (like nature), narrated (like discourse) and collective (like society). So how do these particular entities appear 'now'? The action in technoscience, in Haraway's words, mixes up all the actors; miscegenation between and among humans and the unhumans is the norm.

If one were setting out to assemble such entities, a simple but powerful device could be through rendering the idea of relationship paradoxical. This is exactly the role that the concepts of 'local' and global' seem to occupy in some current discussion. For the paradox is that, when they are brought together, the difference and thus the relationship between the two seems to dissolve. Latour can ask whether a railroad is local or global. Neither, he can say. 'It is local at all points, since you will always find sleepers and railroad workers, and you have stations and automatic ticket machines scattered along the way. Yet it is global, since it takes you from Madrid to Berlin', though, he adds, only when the railroads are paid for. I would not have added that in turn if in her conference address Wendy James (see *The Pursuit of Certainty*, ASA Decennial conference series, Routledge 1995) had not so poignantly drawn attention to the fact that many ordinary networks – and she refers to road, rail and water – are working less efficiently than they did three or four decades ago. At any event, the railroad is in these terms a hybrid entity. However, Latour then metaphorises his network analogy as though one could *link* local and global thereby. 'There are continuous paths that lead from the local to the global, from the circumstantial to the universal, from the contingent to the necessary' (1993: 117). The thread that 'allows us to pass with continuity from the local to the global, from the human to the non human . . . is the thread of networks of practices and instruments, of documents and translations' (ibid.: 121). What he means is that we occupy both at the same time: it is the narrative that strings us along as though there were movement between. The metaphor of network thus returns us the idea of relationship, if no more than the relational sequencing of the imaginative journeyings by which a person (by rail, by e-mail or by word of mouth) moves. But it is precisely such sequencing that ideas about the global and local render impossible to think.[3]

Let us return to Haraway's interesting insistence on location. If location is a point of relationality, a gathering together that makes visible relations between things, the field across which they are distributed must be without relations. So how is this field to be imagined? Only by analogy. Suppose we made the local more than 'merely'. Suppose we were to appropriate the epithet local for those locations where persons act, and act to make the world work. It would then be the point where they mobilise their resources, seek influence, labour, reproduce, spend energy, talk. The continuities people see between their actions – their effect on others, the reactions of colleagues, antecedents and futures, setting things in motion, in short the apprehension of a life that is larger than any of its moments – would be equally part of making the world work. The local would also be the point, then, at which both commensurables and incommensurables, including the difference between local and global, are created. In other words, if location gives us relationships, the local gives us scale. And if globalisaton is a field without relations, can we then use the global to indicate a dimension that is itself without measurement? Support might come from those situations where scale too is rendered paradoxical. Again I take an example from Latour.

How large, Latour asks, is the IBM? An actor of great size, mobilising hundreds of thousands of people, it is always encountered via a small handful, as the CVCP party (see Foreword) encountered British Petroleum via the handful of words that were its vision statement. We never in this sense leave the local. The local is not just the people you talk to at the IBM or BP but the desks, the paperwork, the conventions distributed throughout the system, that is, the instruments that create a global field. From this point of view it makes no sense to go along with the literalism, that 'global' is bigger than 'local'.[4] It is simply where one is at. Yet if one never leaves the local, where is the global? It has to be the infinitely recurring *possibility* of measurement – not the scales but the capacity to imagine them.

As part of their ability to act, pressed into operation as design or intention, people's sense of scale produces a reflexive sense of context or locale. That is, it is a capacity which prompts comparisons, whether of commensurate things (along one scale) or of things not reducible to a common scale at all. Either way, we can imagine that it enlarges the world ('deepens' it (Geertz 1983: 233)). If so, we may take such scaling as a technique for knowing onseself to be effective (have relational effects: Law 1994: 102–3) regardless of agency. Erik Schwimmer (1984: 253) observed of the pairing of male Papua New Guinea dancers from two moieties: 'each knows himself to be a man, but when he looks at his partner he can see a spirit'. Anthropologists will never understand the power of those who think the world is their market, or who have access to spirit beings, or whose dilemma in seeking places to dump toxic waste is to find a place that does not give itself local value, unless they appreciate the energising effect of such expanded horizons. The expanded horizon, like the world-view, is how things are made effective locally. Anthropologists have no need to aggrandise their own accounts;[5] in any case, to do so runs the risk of failing to see the work that aggrandisement does in human affairs.

The final paradox is to make human beings appear a part and not the whole of agency, even though it is human agents who 'make' the paradox. Latour chastises the anthropology he would otherwise endorse for never having undertaken 'the symmetrical work of bringing delegates, mediators and translators back home, into their own community', by which he means not just human persons but actants in a much wider, functional sense, including the fetishes, machines, figurines and angels that inhabit the world (1993: 129). He would thus weave a continuous narrative between Haraway's human and unhuman kinds, much as Ingold imagines for the organism and its life. In John Law's rendition, it is 'people, texts and devices' that must be analysed in common, 'props' folded 'into the person' (1986: 258; 1994: 33). There are many such actants in these chapters. Human and unhuman alike, I refer to them as locations. In 'relating' (narrating) these chapters to one another, I conclude, in local and microcosmic terms, by pointing out certain locations that recur in the writing. They pass back and forth between the different hands, held like a cat's cradle holding the hands in place.

When Mary Douglas (Chapter 1) brings back early anthropological ideas about primitiveness and the origins of culture by reference to the 'fossilised remains of early humanity', she did not know that Mary Bouquet's exhibition of *Pithecanthropus* would be the subject of the chapter that follows. Douglas's phrasing is not accidental. She locates the artifacts (fossilised remains as a sign of early humanity) that were the material through which early anthropologists discussed their relationship to their subject matter. It is exactly this relationship that is the subject of Bouquet's exhibition. *Pithecanthropus* has to be dealt with because it exists. She deals with it by juxtaposing the fossilised remains with other artifacts: she would have been putting a copy of the Bible there at some point over the period that Douglas has been devoting to its study, a book whose existence also demands attention.

But these are also different Bibles, Judaic and Christian, a difference echoed in another doubling of locations. The early anthropologist Rivers has a different place in these two chapters. Douglas draws on him for his interest in demographic and cultural survival against all the odds of population decline, forgotten traditions and memory holes, fuelled by the trauma of cultural discontinuity in people's confrontation with a colonial regime. Bouquet (Chapter 2) by contrast draws on Rivers as the origin of the genealogical method in anthropology, the artifact that both demonstrates people's sense of continuity between the generations and links exotic reckonings of time with the familiar European pedigree. There is a nice play on locale as Bouquet moves between the different rooms of the exhibit. But a central location for the exhibition is the genealogical tree. Whereas one of Douglas's locations is a missing text, the lack of continuity in interpretative tradition that requires her to put back into the past / bring forward into the present a special reading of the Bible, Bouquet's is the overdetermination of genealogy. There are too many connections. Hence her diverse trees with their diverse time scales – 'biblical, geological, historical and ethnographic'. The genealogical tree in her exhibit is a double device: she both exhibits this means of representing connection through time and deploys it to represent connections between times. Relations illustrate relations. The tree has similar possibilities whether it refers to continuities between persons, between species or between human and divine worlds.

When Bouquet was setting up her graphic trees, she did not know that Tim Ingold (Chapter 3) would be reproducing von Uexküll's drawings of the tree of life. Note how his illustrations are truncated: here the pivotal location is not the genealogical tree with its spreading branches, but the nest in the tree. On Ingold's argument of course the nest is not 'in' the tree any more than the tree is 'in' the nest: animals lodge there as human thinking does, and the tree as such is neither continuous with nor discontinuous from such an activity. And while Bouquet's trees are all specific and particular as to the connections they make, Ingold's tree is a generic, for which unhuman artifact one can as well substitute a human one, the house. As he is at pains to note, trees are of course as much made by human beings as houses are found by them. Indeed he points out the absurdity of the search for origins when the search is for the 'first artifact' (the first hut).

Bouquet's museum is a house for exhibit, designed to show the constructed nature, the building, of human artifacts, yet an exhibit which dwells within a nest of ideas about continuity and evolution and history that come from every quarter. Ingold's building is with ideas. He deliberately constructs one model to substitute for others, differentiates one perspective from another, so that the text describes its own construction step by step. But, if I may put it thus, he locates his own dwelling place at those moments which require no difference between a tree and a house or between the conscious and unconscious generation of form. Nor, perhaps Manambu would add, between a human and spirit world.

When Ingold writes that the body incorporates in its orientation sets of relations with an environment cumulatively shaped by the actions of predecessors, he had not heard quite how Simon Harrison (Chapter 4) would be describing the procedures by which Manambu men from the Sepik River in Papua

New Guinea engineer certain bodily orientations in explicit reference to their predecessors. Here the location of Harrison's exegesis is the male body in one of its forms – ready for war. From that specific and contrived artifact he derives contrasting worlds of moral and amoral behaviour, the points at which Manambu discriminate between the works of men and the work of spirits, the moments when they are aggregated with or disaggregated from their necessity to act out the behaviour of their ancestral totems. It is only because they dwell in a world where men are continuous with spirits that, to paraphrase Heidegger's remark quoted by Ingold, they can build their bodies in particular ways.

Headhunting? If the Leiden museum is the epitome of the built environment, into which Bouquet introduced Sepik as well as Asmat skulls, substituting in this case for genealogical trees the organic remains of our human ancestors, where do such remains dwell? Do we find them 'dwelling', anthropologically speaking, in their homeland? Those skulls in Leiden were made into artifacts by people just such as the Manambu and Iatmul. Yet putting them, as Chapter 4 does, into an ethnographic context – understanding why Manambu and Iatmul men collected them in the first place – does not 'naturalise' them, that is, show them up to be ordinary and taken for granted in their own setting. On the contrary, we encounter in the skulls the revelation of the extraordinary power of the spirits who accompanied the headhunters. And far from personalising these trophies, turning them back into human beings as it were, discovering them in their ethnographic setting in the Sepik uncovers them as the generalised power of a cult. The cult is an aggrandisement, more powerful than the power of any one man, while giving evidence of its power through the bodies of individuals, alternately decorated living flesh or stripped-down / over-modelled bone.

I have no idea how much account Harrison took of the abstract of Richard Werbner's paper for the conference, which is the basis for Chapter 5. In his argument Harrison makes quite a lot turn on the Manambu treatment of Australians and Japanese. They interpret these incursions from an outside world as incursions from within, thereby pinpointing for Harrison what he has already deduced from bodily orientation; in Werbner's account incursions are the location for understanding morality. That the self-doubts and questions which worried Lupondo and his family in Kalanga should be set side by side with the exhumation of unburied bones is brutal. If anyone thinks it is poor taste to make a further connection between these horrors and what otherwise might have lain as unremarked coincidences between these chapters – as with the skull in the museum exhibit; the headhunted victim – an incursion into taste is a textual device for bringing home the shocking. The trauma of the second destruction of the temple to which Douglas refers comes to us via a text, just as the Gulf war did to many Britons at home.

Violence is a location, a point of reflection and action, for Lupondo's family insofar as it arises from the same kind of loyalty and betrayal that compels family members both to defend and attack one another. Reflection shows violence to be close to hand. For how to derive accountability from apparently distant acts, how to foreground them in action, is an axis by which Lupondo's family conserves its social identity. What becomes painfully evident are the devastating implications of supposing continuity through time. The bones of the past, precisely because they were unburied, become artifacts brought into the present and across intentions; in this context Kalanga persons do not separate out parts of themselves through different bodily orientations as Manambu claim to do but must take into account actions which are diverse and contradictory. They have to force a conjunction between loyalty and betrayal, between inward and outward orientation, at least in so far as their theories of accountability take the whole person as the agent.

The agent is a figure who stalks Angela Cheater's (Chapter 6) narrative, now present, now absent. At this point one might question the working conjunction of human and unhuman. Information technology was already, as it was said in 1937, 'dehumanised', in that it appeared to bypass communication between persons; its late twentieth-century 'personalisations' are in addition customised to the point of stripping the person of social and collective character outside the nexus of technology. But Richard Werbner was not to know that I would juxtapose his account, and suggest a location between Kalangan management of moral accountability and the amoral innocence of IT artifacts. Despite the drastic effects of telecommunications, as in the stock market crash, or the wrecking of places of worship, in Cheater's world it is still by and large supposed to be what human beings do with the information that counts. So we have unhuman systems of accountability (such as measurement indices for university output) that may take some of the responsibility for refashioning the conditions of work but are not the actants who are rewarded or punished thereby. Accountability in this sense is something that the human actants continue to have to bear.

As for myself, I did not know when I first cited the CVCP document (Foreword) that I would subsequently ask Stephen Hill and Tim Turpin to include their paper as Chapter 7,[6] any more than they were knowingly echoing Cheater's comments on chaos theory. And I had forgotten, since I first read the paper, the reason for which they cite anthropology, the location they wish it to be. They do so in order to make a point about cultural change in the context of social change, the very coupling of culture and society that I suggest the changes they describe have also uncoupled (Chapter 8). The discourse on which they draw is at once inside anthropology and outside it. I was, however, drawn to their remarks on the new managerialism by Emily Martin's descriptions of lean managers and their flexible capabilities.[7] Here I would just draw attention to the fact that it is not globalism (cosmopolitanism) which emerges as Hill and Turpin's leading term but what they identify as the marketplace's new localism that identifies key actors and personal networks.

To see people passing artifacts between them, or to see the locations that hold these authors together, like casting on and off so many cats' cradles, holds promise for tracing networks. It might be with some amusement, or wariness, therefore, that the anthropologist notes the actor–network theorists' (friendly) appropriation of the concept of 'social relations', not perhaps from anthropology but possibly with some consequences for it.[8] The concept is being pressed into service to emphasise networks as the active partnership of humans as well as unhumans in one another's existence. Note that what is borrowed is not just the appeal to relations but their characterisation as social.

I have not worked this appropriation into my account, although one might wish to raise a question as to whether all passages and networks between actants are usefully designated 'social'. Anthropologists, for their part, might yield the term social in so far as it is used to refer to relations in a local and localising sense. But they might then have to appropriate from elsewhere a term to denote its global counterpart, sociality as the co-presence of persons. In all likelihood, they would need to re-invent some scales.

M. S.

NOTES

1　'Cat's cradle is . . . a mathematical game about complex, collaborative practices for making and passing on culturally interesting patterns'; the game is the practice of a critical theory ('anti-racist multicultural feminist studies of ethnoscience'). I am grateful for permission to cite from the longer version of Haraway's conference paper (n.d.); for a companion piece see Haraway 1994.

2　As she goes on to say, location (after King) is always partial in the sense of being for some worlds and not others. The point about globalisation (after Latour and Schaffer) is that science travels as scientific practice. Douglas, in recalling an earlier anthropology, might have named this diffusion – a term ('global diffusion') already given to the spread 'of themes, elements and processes which were once considered local and vernacular' (Giri 1993: 284).

3　'[T]he words "local" and "global" offer points of view on networks that are by nature neither local nor global, but are more or less long and more or less connected' (Latour 1993: 122). Mol and Law (in press) develop the concept of 'social topology' to indicate the diversity or severality (of different kinds) of space in which actions (operations) take place. Networks are just one; the others are regions and fluids

4　Featherstone (1990: 146): a global frame of reference is 'the "highest" level of possible synthesis'; Geertz (1983: 168): 'wisdom comes out of an ant heap', quoting an African proverb to underline the local character of legal and ethnographic knowledge.

5　Strathern (1988: 337); cf. Latour (1993: 125): 'Let us not add power to force.' Perhaps aggrandisement is part of what Law (1994) calls 'ordering'.

6　I am grateful to Sarah Franklin for drawing my attention to the paper in the first place; it was given to a conference in Gothenburg, Sweden, on Science, Technology and 'Development' in 1992, and then published in *Science as Culture*.

7　Martin (1992) describes how the new managers keep the simultaneous flexibility and specificity of potentially useful information flowing by training themselves for innovation. Her argument is that the shape of life under late capitalism (the regime of flexible accumulation, after Harvey) leads to new concepts of personhood, one example being a conceptualisation of the personal body as an immune system.

8　As a rhetorical device to break down the social–technical divide (elements both sides of the divide are also examples of one or other side), the usage is most effective. Actor–network theorists include Callon, Latour, Law (see Law 1994).

REFERENCES

Featherstone, M. (ed.) (1990) *Global Culture: Nationalism, Globalisation and Modernity*, London: Sage Publications.

Geertz, C. (1983) *Local Knowledge. Further Essays in Interpretive Anthropology*, New York: Basic Books Inc.

Giri, Ananta (1993) 'Critique of the comparative method and the challenges of a transnational world', *Contributions to Indian Sociology* 27: 267–89.

Haraway, D. (1994) 'A game of cat's cradle: science studies, feminist theory, cultural studies', *Configurations* 1: 59–71.

—— (n.d.) 'Modest witness @ second millennium. The FemaleMan © meets Oncomouse™ ', Paper delivered at ASA IV Decennial conference in section convened by H. Moore, 'What is social knowledge for?' (1993).

Hastrup, K. (1992) 'Out of anthropology: the anthropologist as an object of dramatic representation', *Cultural Anthropology* 7: 327–45.

Latour, B. (1993) *We Have Never Been Modern*, trans. C. Porter, London: Harvester Wheatsheaf.

Law, J. (1986) 'On the methods of long-distance control: vessels, navigation and the Portuguese routes to India', in J. Law (ed.), *Power, Action and Belief: a New Sociology of Knowledge?*, Sociological Review Monograph 32, London: Routledge.

—— (1994), *Organizing Modernity*, Oxford: Blackwell.

Martin, E. (1992) 'The end of the body?' *American Ethnologist* 19: 121–40.

Mol, A. and Law, J. (in press) 'Regions, networks and fluids: anaemia and social topology', *Social Studies of Science*.

Schwimmer, E. (1984) 'Male couples in New Guinea', in G.H. Herdt (ed.), *Ritualized Homosexuality in Melanesia*, Berkeley and Los Angeles: University of California Press.

Strathern, M. (1988) *The Gender of the Gift: Problems with Women and Problems with Society in Melanesia*, Berkeley and Los Angeles: University of California Press.

—— (1992) *After Nature: English Kinship in the Late Twentieth Century*, Cambridge: Cambridge University Press.

Name index

Subject index